The Politics of Financial and Regulation

The biggest corporate failure ever in British history occurred in 2008 with very little forewarning. The management of HBOS, a major national bank with a long history of prudence prior to the merger in 2001, were allowed to act incompetently. Auditors and regulators failed to act, ignoring a key senior whistleblower, and the 'competitive' stock market failed to spot management failure in time.

This book is the first academic study of this collapse, uncovering some surprising evidence on the power and politics of large financial institutions. It details the processes and degrees to which financial challenge and regulation are undermined by this power. The research exposes a pro-active process of regulatory risk management by these institutions; the ease with which auditors and regulators can be captured; and how politicians and investors can be all too happy to hop on the stock market and management spin ride – with other people's money. The study questions the ideology and politics which supported and encouraged the management hubris, raising profound questions about the 'politics' of the academic disciplines of banking, finance and accounting today, and the theories they underpin.

This account of management gone wrong is essential reading for students, researchers and professionals involved in banking, finance, credit infrastructure, economics and management studies.

Atul K. Shah is a Chartered Accountant and member of the Institute of Chartered Accountants in England and Wales. He has a PhD in Accounting and Finance from the London School of Economics. He is also a Professor in Accounting and Finance at Suffolk Business School, Ipswich, UK.

The Politics of Financial Risk, Audit and Regulation

A Case Study of HBOS

Atul K. Shah

Routledge
Taylor & Francis Group

LONDON AND NEW YORK

First published 2018
by Routledge
2 Park Square, Milton Park, Abingdon, Oxon OX14 4RN

and by Routledge
711 Third Avenue, New York, NY 10017

Routledge is an imprint of the Taylor & Francis Group, an informa business

British Library Cataloguing in Publication Data
A catalogue record for this book is available from the British Library

Library of Congress Cataloging in Publication Data
A catalog record for this book has been requested

ISBN: 978-1-138-71430-4 (hbk)
ISBN: 978-1-138-04235-3 (pbk)
ISBN: 978-1-315-22875-4 (ebk)

Typeset in Bembo
by Taylor & Francis Books

MIX
Paper from responsible sources
FSC
www.fsc.org   FSC™ C013985

Printed in the United Kingdom
by Henry Ling Limited

To all who seek a fairer, ethical finance and a banking and academic culture of honesty, integrity and contentment, endowed with servant leadership.

Contents

Foreword

When I interviewed James Crosby, chief executive of the newly merged Halifax Bank of Scotland back in December 2001, he insisted that HBOS represented something new, exciting and worthwhile in the world of British banking. Speaking in his corner office on The Mound, perched high above the Christmas shoppers on Edinburgh's Princes Street, the former actuary talked of reorienting his 60,000 'colleagues' so they could sell more aggressively and declared his goal was to 'open a Pandora's box' with a view to 'generating as much pain as possible for our competitors'.

What he perhaps didn't realise is that the evils he unleashed would also cause self-harm and wider economic and social destruction by bringing down the bank he led, with dire long-term consequences for many of its customers, staff and other stakeholders.

Halifax Bank of Scotland set out on a disastrous course pretty much from day one. Its leaders' inexperience, incompetence, greed and absence of ethics, combined with the unrealistic and hubristic goals they set themselves, made the bank's September 2008 collapse inevitable.

From its inauspicious birth on the eve of 9/11, the bank went hell for leather into the UK retail and corporate financial services markets, intent on boosting its market share in every sector in which it operated to 15 per cent or 20 per cent. Not long after I interviewed him, Crosby raised the stakes by increasing HBOS's return-on-equity target from an already stretching 17 per cent to 20 per cent.

As the Edinburgh headquartered bank ballooned its balance sheet from £275 billion in 2001 to £631 billion in 2008, a cavalier disregard for risk set in, coupled with an insatiable appetite for growth, inside what was a moral vacuum. The bank had no qualms about encouraging self-certified mortgage borrowers to commit mortgage fraud; about lending scores of billions of pounds to a bunch of seemingly clueless property tycoons, many of whom defaulted on their loans in 2008–9, without anything resembling proper credit checks; or about imposing a bunch of sleazy known embezzlers posing as "turnaround consultants" on between fifty and two hundred of its small and medium-sized corporate borrowers.

Over and above such activities, HBOS adopted a dangerously flawed and short-termist business model, funding the Topsy-like growth in its loan book with wholesale funding – a policy that left it with a gaping £213 billion chasm between its loans and its deposits when the wholesale funding markets froze up after August 2007. The bank had left itself with nowhere else to go other than into a state-sponsored intensive care ward or into an anti-competitive merger with a slightly less reckless rival such as Lloyds TSB.

The Parliamentary Commission on Banking Standards, chaired by the conservative MP Andrew Tyrie, interviewed many of the bank's former directors and reached the conclusion that the chimera of success in the bank's early years gave rise to an internal arrogance and self-delusion:

> The culture was brash, underpinned by a belief that the growing market share was due to a special set of skills which HBOS possessed and which its competitors lacked. The effects of the culture were all the more corrosive when coupled with a lack of corporate self-knowledge at the top of the organisation, enabling the bank's leaders to persist in the belief, in some cases to this day, that HBOS was a conservative institution when in fact it was the very opposite.

In this book, Atul Shah brings home these and many other failures that contributed to HBOS's collapse – as well as the astonishing post-crisis failure of the British authorities to hold the individuals responsible to account.

The book differs from others on HBOS in calling out the bank's auditors, KPMG. Atul assiduously covers their failures, their conflicts, their failure to communicate their concerns to the regulator, their collusion with the Board – and therefore their key role in fuelling the bank's collapse. As he says, it's jaw-dropping that, eight years after HBOS's collapse, the Financial Reporting Council has not yet properly investigated KPMG's pivotal role in the HBOS disaster, or that the audit partners responsible haven't been hauled over the coals by their professional institutes.

But the uniqueness of the book lies in its unstinting critique of financial theory and ideology. Many academics shy away from tackling this, fearing that to challenge the status quo might hamper their careers and harm their institution's ability to raise money from the private sector. Others are too steeped in their models, assumptions and calculations to see the big picture. Even the various political and regulatory probes into HBOS steered clear of examining the half-baked ideological framework that underpinned its collapse – sometimes known as the 'Greenspan doctrine' – which included a strong belief in deregulation and a blind faith in the ability of unfettered free markets to boost global prosperity. Atul, however, does not pull any punches in this regard. Indeed, in putting the bank's calamitous seven-year journey into its wider ideological context, his book will, hopefully, be a lodestar for future generations of students and scholars as they chart a course towards constructing a more sustainable, diverse, ethical and fair financial system.

If financial education – and, indeed, finance itself – is to be reformed, it is essential that politics, culture, ethics and history become a core part of the curriculum. We continue to exclude such subjects from the core finance and MBA courses at our peril. We must never forget, for example, that Andy Hornby (second HBOS CEO) derived his own financial world-view from the MBA that he did at Harvard Business School – and that this was the intellectual framework he applied as he led HBOS to disaster.

Atul's book provides us with a timely reminder that the finance curriculum must change – moving away from a monocultural, technical discipline that promotes little other than greed, avarice and, indeed, financial disaster, towards becoming a less cynical and more inter-connected subject that will enable us to build a better financial system. It is ripe for disruption. We've already paid far too high a price from the financial collapses of 2007–9. This book illustrates not just how such disasters can be averted, but also how finance can be changed for good – and, indeed, how the Pandora's box so determinedly opened by James Crosby back in 2001 might once again be slammed shut. I strongly recommend it.

Ian Fraser
Author of *Shredded: Inside RBS: The Bank that Broke Britain*
www.ianfraser.org
Twitter: @ianfraser
November 2016

Acknowledgements

Foremost, I would like to thank HBOS whistleblower Paul Moore for his full cooperation with this study. He was generous with his knowledge, interviews and documents and correspondence which he had preserved meticulously. Encouragement for the research and framework for this study came from the indomitable Professor Prem Sikka, my friend and mentor, who has a distinguished record in analysing the modern industries of finance and accounting, and is a pioneer of tax justice. Research papers which led to this book were presented in seminars at University of Leicester, University of Suffolk, Cardiff Business School, and the British Accounting and Finance Association conferences at the London School of Economics and Manchester University. All the related research papers are available on-line at www.academia.edu/atulksha h, and 5000 people have read these papers to date. I would like to thank Professor Chris Humphries, Professor Yuval Millo and Nina Sharma for commenting on and encouraging the research. I would also like to thank the team which successfully campaigned for an investigation into the KPMG audit failure over HBOS – Brian Little, Ian Fraser, Tony Shearer, Prem Sikka and Paul Moore. Harriet Agnew at the *Financial Times* helped publicise our efforts in a timely way which enabled us to have maximum impact. Bloggers Richard Murphy and Ian Fraser helped this research reach a wide audience, and Carlos Tomero also generously helped promote the campaign. Professor Simon Hallsworth at University of Suffolk was very supportive and encouraging throughout. I am grateful to Ian Fraser for his foreword. My family were very patient with this project, tolerating books and papers all over the house, and a messy office. My friends Professor Al Bhimani, Professor Pat Arnold and Professor Janette Rutterford helped me stay focused on the research, and John Christensen and Nick Shaxson at the Tax Justice Network were also very supportive. My father and role model, Mr Keshavji Rupshi Shah, passed away just before this research was born, and I felt his spirit encouraging me all the way. My brother Ritesh also helped me a lot on this academic journey. My publisher at Routledge, Kristina Abbots, stayed supportive throughout and answered all my queries promptly. I am forever grateful for my Jain upbringing and inheritance, which has given me the wisdom to question with equanimity, and the fearlessness to seek and reveal the truth, in spite of its consequences. Fortunately, the truth has also protected me.

Any weaknesses in the research, presentation and analysis belong to me – I beg your forgiveness.

Atul Keshavji Shah PhD ACA
October 2016

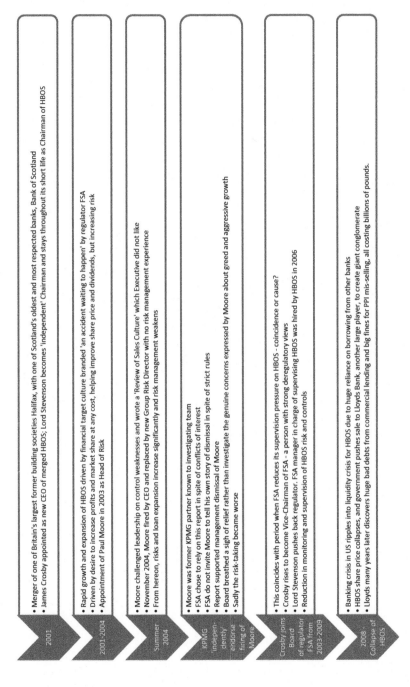

2001
- Merger of one of Britain's largest former building societies Halifax, with one of Scotland's oldest and most respected banks, Bank of Scotland
- James Crosby appointed as new CEO of merged HBOS; Lord Stevenson becomes 'independent' Chairman and stays throughout its short life as Chairman of HBOS

2001-2004
- Rapid growth and expansion of HBOS driven by financial target culture branded 'an accident waiting to happen' by regulator FSA
- Driven by desire to increase profits and market share at any cost, helping improve share price and dividends, but increasing risk
- Appointment of Paul Moore in 2003 as Head of Risk

Summer 2004
- Moore challenged leadership on control weaknesses and wrote a 'Review of Sales Culture' which Executive did not like
- November 2004, Moore fired by CEO and replaced by new Group Risk Director with no risk management experience
- From hereon, risks and loan expansion increase significantly and risk management weakens

KPMG independently endorse firing of Moore
- Moore was former KPMG partner known to investigating team
- FSA chose to rely on this report in spite of conflicts of interest
- FSA do not invite Moore to tell his own story of dismissal in spite of strict rules
- Report supported management dismissal of Moore
- Board breathed a sigh of relief rather than investigate the genuine concerns expressed by Moore about greed and aggressive growth
- Sadly the risk-taking became worse

Crosby joins Board of regulator FSA from 2003-2009
- This coincides with period when FSA reduces its supervision pressure on HBOS - coincidence or cause?
- Crosby rises to become Vice-Chairman of FSA - a person with strong deregulatory views
- Lord Stevenson pushes back regulator. FSA manager in charge of supervising HBOS was hired by HBOS in 2006
- Reduction in monitoring and supervision of HBOS risk and controls

2008 Collapse of HBOS
- Banking crisis in US ripples into liquidity crisis for HBOS due to huge reliance on borrowing from other banks
- HBOS share price collapses, and government pushes sale to Lloyds Bank, another large player, to create giant conglomerate
- Lloyds many years later discovers huge bad debts from commercial lending and big fines for PPI mis-selling, all costing billions of pounds.

Table 1 HBOS timeline and key events
Source: Parliamentary investigations of collapse of HBOS

1 Introduction

This book is primarily about the link between finance and politics, by focusing on the UK's largest bank failure in history – HBOS. Its direct and indirect damage to the UK economy, in terms of pension and investment losses, housing bubbles and crashes, government bailouts, consumer exploitation, unemployment and economic collapse cannot be easily quantified but is in the hundreds of billions. As a reality-check, we must remember that HBOS was not a Chernobyl but a man-made institution with a long history and tradition, which exploded in the space of a few hubristic years. Even though lots of people were watching it closely, or required to monitor it, the failure was indeed sudden and dramatic. It is critical we learn lessons from such failures, including what they mean for our received wisdoms and expertise in finance and accounting. For students and researchers in finance, this detailed interpretive case study should open their eyes and minds to the critical role of theory and academic knowledge in the creation of such bubbles. It exposes the 'expert' detachment from social conscience and cultural devastation, and aims to awaken students to the urgency of reconnecting finance to its basic roots and meaning. This book exposes how the academic finance world is living in a 'scientific' bubble, whilst the real world is suffering from the ravages of financialisation. Given that both business and finance are practical endeavours, this book exposes the perils of ivory tower theorisation and the 'rigorous' testing of the theories whilst the practice is experiencing huge scandals and crises. It opens up the significant possibilities and opportunities of inter-disciplinary research in finance and its potential to reform both theory and practice.

In most business schools across the world, finance is taught in an apolitical and technical way with a focus on models and methods to help shape value and efficiency in business and markets. In fact, even the science of political economy is rarely taught, despite the undisputed fact that big business is hugely powerful and many multi-nationals run bigger economies than whole countries. Furthermore, the politics that shapes the financial institutions and markets is ignored, in the process subconsciously denying its very nature and importance. There are dreams and ideologies of perfect markets where everyone behaves rationally and satisfies the desires of the scientist to create neat models and valuations. However, the reality is very far from this, and both history and recent experience has shown that the industry of finance is highly political and compromised by greed, selfishness and hubris.

Political economists have long understood the link between finance and politics and written many research papers and books on the subject (see e.g. Strange 1986; Coggan 2012; Moran 1991; Hertz 2001; Palan et al. 2010; Hancher and Moran 1989; Hutton 2010; Germain 2010). However, there is rarely an interaction between the highly technical and clinical teaching of finance and the real-world politics of finance. In actual fact, there is a denial of politics in mainstream finance teaching and research, which seems bizarre. In line with some academics (see e.g. Gendron and Smith-LaCroix 2015; McSweeney 2009; Daly and Cobb 1994; Frankfurter and McGoun 2002), I conclude from this observation that finance theory and research have a deliberate tendency to obfuscate the truth and hide behind a disciplinary boundary shaped for its own convenience and status – something which Daly and Cobb call 'disciplonatory'. There is also research emerging (see e.g. Whyte and Wiegratz 2016) which argues that the very idea of neo-liberalism is helping to shape a moral economy of fraud, where fraud becomes a norm in modern society. Thus finance research and teaching, which has a strong neo-liberal bias, is potentially complicit in this. Perhaps the denial of politics is deliberate and profoundly ideological rather than scientific (see e.g. Froud et al. 2006).

The focus on politics in this book enables us to look closely at key people, their culture and values, the networks and influence they commanded and the thinking which drove their actions. The themes of risk, accounting, auditing and regulation all have significant political undertones as they are administered and managed by people, and interpretations are often very subjective. Politics helps us focus on the decision-makers and opinion formers, be it individuals, professional firms or networks and leadership cultures. The research here is not a technical analysis of a bank failure. Fundamentally, financial risk, accounting and regulation are social phenomena, and it is often misleading to study them in pure technical terminologies.

This chapter sets the tone of this study by examining the history and politics of the finance discipline, the processes of financialisation, teaching in finance, the origins and nature of money, connecting finance to ethics and issues of power and politics and then setting the backdrop for HBOS and the research methodology of this study. The chapter explains why a personal approach has been adapted in the writing of this investigation, expressing the underlying values and motives of this study. It encourages readers to take a personal interest in finance and its academic future to help shape its reform and transformation.

Ethics, Values and Financial Power

As an academic discipline, finance is relatively young (Mackenzie 2006) – only fifty years old, yet its size and reach has grown exponentially. The curriculum of finance taught in different parts of the world is virtually imported wholesale from North America. Economics, its mother discipline, is also presently in crisis, and huge questions are being raised about its scientific credentials (PCES 2014; Chang and Aldred 2014; Kay 2011). There is no allowance for the cultural and contextual diversity of finance in different countries – it is theorised and taught in an acultural manner. Given the huge crises we have been experiencing resulting from finance, this arrogance and mischief has to come to an end. Humanity has already paid a huge price for failures in banking and financial markets, and continues to do so. As I write, the Wells Fargo frauds are in the news. There is an endemic culture of greed and disdain for honesty and fairness, in the very industry which requires and depends on trust and integrity.

It is an undisputed fact that banking and finance occupy a hugely powerful and influential role in the modern world (Froud et al. 2006; Lewis 2012; Das 2011). As evidence of this, we only need to look at the size and reach of firms which operate in this arena – Goldman Sachs, Citibank, Barclays, HSBC, RBS, Deutsche Bank, UBS, Credit Suisse – a few global conglomerates with billions of dollars in assets and capital. Theories like efficient markets, perfect competition and rational choice are demolished by the size and growth of these institutions. The evidence of monopoly, inefficiency and hubris is all around us, but somehow ignored in the discipline.

In reality, the big banks dominate and control products and markets and are growing ever bigger through acquisitions and consolidations. Many of these firms have also faced allegations of corruption, fraud, market and investor manipulation, customer exploitation, conflicts of interest and even financial meltdown, but, somehow, they have still survived and prospered. Some have even argued that their size and reach have made them very difficult to manage and police centrally (see e.g. Admati and Hellwig 2013), yet they seem to soldier on, with no decline in management rewards and bonuses. Many argue that contemporary finance is like a gravy train – you are lucky if you can hop on for the ride, but no need to fear the consequences of failure as they will be someone else's problem, with no recourse to the perpetrators (Das 2011; Kay 2015). Contradiction is rife in the science and industry of finance, although the experts would not like to admit it. It is possible that, as Beck (1992) has predicted, for the experts, it is very convenient to keep the field highly technical and sophisticated so that it is very difficult for others to probe into what is really going on, or to regulate and control it. Whilst this behaviour may not be concerted or deliberate, it has the effect of removing any powerful challenge from the academy, and instead fuelling the significant cultural and ethical problems. Also, the technical nature can be a convenient method of hiding and disguising the underlying values, ideologies and subjectivities (Tett 2010).

The sources of banking power come from certain very basic facts – the money multiplier, where the private banking system effectively have a licence to create money; their size and reach; the ease with which banks can raise loans and capital for themselves; and the state protection given to them in the event of failure. Their regulation is a chimera, continuing to fail in bigger and more devastating ways, but somehow after every crisis the response is the same – revision of regulation. What is avoided by both the science and industry is the actual culture of finance – the behaviour of the people who run and manage the teaching, research and the financial institutions that continue to breed exploitation and inequality. When anthropologist Luyendijk (2015) investigated the global finance industry in London through anonymous interviews, the findings were truly shocking. Not only is the power of the industry ruining the wider economy and society, but it is also eating into its own people and ruining their personal lives, relationships, health and happiness. There is something deeply disturbing about the modern world of extreme finance, but society seems paralysed about substantive reform of its power and accountability. A recent review of banking culture, demanded by the UK parliament, was actually quietly abandoned by the Financial Conduct Authority (Dunkley 2015). In its effort to distance theory from observed fact, it seems finance has also distanced the human being from acknowledging his or her own pain and suffering. It is therefore no surprise that there is also a mental health crisis in finance (Lewis 2016; Luyendijk 2015).

Finance Literature and Teaching

There are tomes written on the practice and science of finance, financial risk management, auditing and even banking regulation and supervision (Eales 1994; Roggi and Altman 2013; Saunders and Cornett 2014). Whole professions and bodies thrive on these 'expert sciences', giving credibility and generating income for the practitioners. Sadly here again, the politics or culture are rarely mentioned, even though the primary role in these exercises is played by people, networks and institutions. Whilst a risk management text may admit that culture is important to creating a measured risk environment, it will feign from looking at the links between culture and the ways in which risk is measured and hedged. One has to become suspicious about why this is so, and how it is that such denial has been sustained for so long. In fact, not only politics but human values and norms are also rarely discussed, and if so, in a very technocratic or legalistic manner. Given the state of modern-day financialisation, we cannot avoid conducting a microscopic analysis of big financial institutions and their behaviour and politics. Effectively, they are both the market and the financial system (see e.g. Goldman Sachs – Cohan 2011; Lehman Brothers – McDonald and Robinson 2009; RBS – Fraser 2015). These books show very clearly that politics and power are at the heart of the management of such institutions.

As an example, let us look closely at a series of international textbooks in the fields of corporate finance, accounting and risk management published by McGraw-Hill, pioneered by the original Brealey and Myers which is now in its eleventh edition (Brealey et al. 2014). All of them are into several editions, and very popular among business schools all over the world. That is correct – business education, like business, has become formulaic, like a factory and a production line. In none of these books is there any serious mention of politics or even culture and ethics. For example, Hillier et al. (2016) makes this very short and sweeping statement about ethics (p. 53):

> Given that this book concerns financial decisions and how to use these decisions to maximise firm value, it is implicitly understood that the decisions will be ethical.

It shows that the authors know little about ethics and its significance to finance. Similarly, Saunders and Cornett (2014), an international text on financial institutions management and risk management, does not have a single chapter on politics, culture or ethics. Deegan and Ward (2013) is a highly technical text on international financial accounting and reporting, where politics, culture or ethics have no place.

Such a technical approach to the teaching of finance, risk, accounting and auditing helps sustain the illusion that people, culture, networks and power do not matter. For a student sitting in these classes, it can be a very disempowering experience, as the knowledge is in denial of human norms and subjectivity. In fact, it is often the case that research and consultancy in finance is a much bigger priority than teaching, so there is an academic distaste in engaging with the ethical culture of learning and education. It forces students to detach their emotions and personal experiences of meeting bankers, risk managers or accountants and auditors. Students are also customers of banks and consumers of financial products like bank accounts, credit cards, student loans and cash and currency exchange services. Somehow none of this experience matters or is related to in the teaching of finance.

Subtly but deliberately, finance (and economics) research is putting numbers, measurements and profits above people and society (Frankfurter and McGoun 2002; Bakan 2004; Ekins et al. 1992). Instead of describing selfishness, it is shaping it. This is in stark contrast to what is reported in the business news and financial news on a daily basis. Students are drowned in technical detail, detaching them from connecting with the wider world and the real stories and methods of big business. Business schools are scared of exposing these truths, as they are businesses themselves, trying to show how firms are great and good, and how their expert science is complex and worthy of dedicated study. The technical complexity can paradoxically attract students to mastering the expertise – especially those who want to get rich quick and discover hidden formulae of doing so. A core part of public economy, taxation, is hardly taught at all, except as a cost to business. The vast benefits taxes provide to ensure smooth finance and markets is completely ignored (Murphy 2015; Tax Justice Network 2015). The impression given is that anything that is private is good, and anything that is public is bad. Above all, business schools believe that firms are right to be greedy profiteers and selfish. If such selfishness leads to the acquisition of influence and power, so be it, but here in the business school, we will repeat the mantra that the success has been achieved purely through merit and ability. Individualism and utilitarianism have become the ethic of business education, sadly.

Much more disturbing is the growing awareness that the very ideas of neo-liberalism are fraudulent (Whyte and Wiegratz 2016). There are immense and rising contradictions denied by contemporary finance research. The phrase 'efficient markets' disguises market failure. Free markets need public bailouts. Perfect competition is replaced by the reality of giant multi-nationals and monopolies or oligopolies. Individualism leads to egoism and hubris, and instead of creating happiness, often leads to cultural and social breakdown, insecurity and mental health crises. Materialism has led to emotional and cultural bankruptcy. Instead of markets being a source of fair distribution of wealth, we are cultivating an increasingly unequal world. We will see in this book that HBOS had a long history and played an active part in the communities in which it operated. All this was destroyed very quickly by a neo-liberal ethic and mind-set, with no punishment for the leaders or compensation for the sufferers. We cannot analyse this case without examining the ideology that underpinned the hubris and lack of moral, professional and regulatory restraint.

Nature of Money and Finance

At root, money is a social construct – it is created by society to facilitate exchange, saving and investment (Simmel 1978; Graeber 2013). Economists have forgotten this abstraction and virtually denied its impact on society and the environment for decades. Instead, finance scholars treat money as an objective fact. There is a 'fallacy of misplaced concreteness' which has come to prevail, with devastating consequences for society (Daly and Cobb 1994). The symbol has come to dominate the reality – what is a symbol of value has become value in itself. As the subject and practice of finance is the management of money and wealth, the discipline is a further abstraction from the reality (Kay 2011), as its focus is on the accumulation of the symbol that is money. Furthermore, instead of selfishness being a theory, it becomes reality through the teaching of finance in business schools. The silos and complexity of finance teaching are used to disguise the abstractions of money. Paradoxically, the more finance is critiqued, the more academics have dived into their theories and boundaries, digging an even deeper hole for wider society (Kay 2015; Das 2011). The power and politics of the finance academy itself are not subject to independent research scrutiny. Mackenzie (2006) has proven that the academy is an engine, not a camera – it has a direct influence on products and markets. Fundamentally, the value of money is derived from public confidence, trust and responsible economic management. By making money, prices and values the ultimate reality, and at the same time ignoring ethics like honesty, trust and content-ment, finance connives in the disruption of society. When we look at and examine HBOS in detail, we will see the hubris executives had about their power over society, and the total ignorance of the fundamental nature of money and wealth. As in the collapse of RBS (Fraser 2015), they were able to destroy thousands of jobs and billions of pounds in the space of a few years, and get away totally unpunished.

What is most surprising is that people and networks are at the heart of finance – yet there is a virtual silence about this in the mainstream literature both in finance and in accounting. People are not perfect: they can be selfish and conflicted, and they may miscalculate risk or be driven to ignore certain aspects of risk while the going is good. Their actions can be very subjective and influential. Power and status can get into people's heads, and the kick of doing a deal, or becoming the biggest, or winning a war with a competitor can drive financial decisions emotionally rather than rationally – tendencies of psychopaths (Hare 1996; Kets de Vries 2012). Where challenge is weak, finance leaders can start believing in their own Midas touch and consider themselves infallible (see the story of Lehman Brothers in McDonald and Robinson 2009). Hubris often leads to irrational decision-making, influencing whole institutions and markets. Collusions or networks of people can undermine a whole market, as happened in the case of LIBOR and FX, but no finance text discusses the dangers of these. Instead the ideology of efficient markets drives the science and the theories.

Fiction and Financialisation

Some strongly argue that the modern industry of finance is a powerful fiction – where even the objective treatment of money and measurement is fictitious. For example, 'The Keiser Report' is a popular RT (Russia Today) media-sponsored YouTube series fronted by Max Keiser and Stacy Herbert which regularly exposes the fictions using a mixture of analysis and humour. Modern money is a fiat currency, no longer backed by gold but instead by state power and manipulation, and the price and value of assets is relative with little understanding of absolutes. Markets are regularly exploited and undermined by powerful interests. Instead of spreading equality of access to finance, fairness in pricing and practices, democratic values and open competition (Hawken 1994; Kay 2015; Das 2011), the focus is on what they can get away with, and how quickly – society and the environment are far from the horizons. Instead of truth, trust and honesty, its lies, mistrust and fraud have become the norms. Even after the huge public outcry over the 2008 Global Financial Crash, bankers continued to deceive and manipulate in the foreign currency, rate fixing and stock and commodities markets. This proves that it was the culture which needed changing. The values of assets seem to be determined more by the perceptions that can be created about future potential than the risks and uncertainties behind their pricing. It is a sad fact that most of the books and studies critical of finance still come from outside the academy (examples include Lewis 2011, 2012, 2014; Das 2011; Kay 2015; C. Ferguson 2012). Even the Academy Award-winning film on the crash, *Inside Job*, was researched and directed by a non-academic (Ferguson 2010).

One of the biggest developments of the last fifty years is the financialisation of everyday life (Froud et al. 2006; van der Zwan 2014). For a long time in human history, the basic needs were food, shelter and clothing, and these were met outside the monetary economy, through shared village and communitarian lives (Finel-Honigman 2010; Graeber 2013). In fact, money and currency are a relatively modern invention. However, today, virtually nothing can be done without money. Even intangibles like family and relationships, love and romance, learning and opportunity are increasingly ruled by money. The complexity of the industry of finance is such that wide swathes of society are overwhelmed and overpowered by it, leading to a type of self-imposed debt slavery. Aspects over which individuals have no control, like interest rates, exchange rates and booms and busts, regularly disrupt their lives. It seems to be of no concern to the finance academy that one of the keys to everyday living, financial literacy, is very poor and deteriorating (Xu and Zia 2012; Engelen et al. 2012). Whilst the science and models become ever more complex, the suffering and inequality increases. Even the big dream of 'corporate social responsibility' has come to an end (Fleming and Jones 2012).

In an era of financialisation, it is imperative that we closely examine the firms which have the most influence on personal borrowings, savings and invest-ments. How they choose to practice and behave will have repercussions for wider society and their financial futures. In theory, financial institutions should be servants of society, but instead they have become masters. Some have even argued that we are living in an age of the Finance Curse (Shaxson and Christensen 2013), where societies with 'advanced' financial institutions and markets are actu-ally cursed by this hugely powerful industry which breeds unfairness, political corruption and inequality.

The themes explored in this book – risk, politics, auditing and regulation – are generally researched and studied in disciplinary silos (Tett 2015). Political economists look at the power of banks and banking institutions, without closely analysing the theories of finance. Finance scholars develop techniques and theories of financial innovation and valuation, without discussing any abuses of power or the connection between political power and firm performance or valuation. There is a virtual avoidance of looking at issues of behaviour and culture in the practice of finance, apart from the separate field of behavioural economics (Shefrin 2000; Thaler 2013) which is based on individual psychology. Sociologists and management scholars understand culture and its importance but get lost in the technicalities of finance and accounting. Business ethics is often seen as a soft discipline and marginal to the mainstream, especially in finance, where concerns about ethics are virtually ignored. If ethics were allowed to be central to finance teaching, then the whole curriculum would need to be altered radically.

Whyte and Wiegratz (2016) argue that whilst there is a lot of empirical research about corruption in the third world, white-collar crime and fraud in the first world is significantly under-researched, even though it is rampant, hugely damaging and unpunished. A rich case study can open these silos but requires the researcher to be aware of the contributions of the above disciplines and have an open mind. That is why such studies are actually very difficult to conduct and execute. Also it is often very difficult to publish and communicate such research in the contemporary world, where the primary medium of disseminating expert research is through scholarly articles in highly rated refereed journals. In the field of finance, these tend to be primarily North American, highlighting even more the huge cultural and materialistic bias in the discipline, even though this bias is rarely admitted. While an article may reveal a new intellectual insight, a case study has the potential to expose the breadth and depth of deceit which influence behaviour and practice – it is interpretive. The disadvantage of such an approach is that there may be few neat theoretical insights, and readers would have to weave through the data to understand its implications. The advantage is that the data and evidence is closer to the real world, and theories and ideas are forced to clash with one another in the desire to learn and draw inferences from the research. For someone committed to neo-liberalism, the findings of such forensic investigation can feel unnerving, and this may explain why such research is often avoided. As Feyerabend (1975) said, method should not override everything, but it is important that a scientist genuinely attempts to unlock the truth. This study has not been motivated by the desire to score intellectual points or theoretical breakthroughs. It is a humble attempt to learn from a major banking fiasco, and hope that the lessons will transform behaviour and policy. It is proudly normative in its intent.

Taking It Personally

As author, I am declaring the values underlying this research straight up front. I am concerned for the world, for fairness, equality and justice, and this study has been motivated by these values. This comes from my upbringing as a Jain (Shah and Rankin 2017; Shah 2007b), one of the oldest living cultures of the world, and a tradition very different from modern western culture. The Jains have had an enduring success in finance over thousands of years, but this has not been achieved through greed, competition or market dominance, but instead through service, humility, profit-sharing and nurturing social and eco-logical capital. Our 'servant' and silent leadership has influenced whole societies and economies, helping to bring peace, prosperity and stability in communities all over the world.

In her reflective paper on the 2008 crash, Arnold (2009) asks scholars to make their values explicit, as in the past they have been hidden, resulting in a failure to warn society of the dangers of financial excess and hubris. For a long time I have been researching the ethics and regulation of finance, with a series of papers exposing the problems of regulatory arbitrage, systemic risk and derivatives regulation. The topics I had chosen for investigation expressed my concerns for building a just and fairer society – and they continue to do so. This study has been motivated by a concern for the welfare and exploitation of society (Shah 1995, 1996a, 1997b, 1997c), and is consistent with a number of studies which predicted the financial crash as a 'normal accident', and exposed the cracks in global regulation and governance (Shah 1996b; Shah 1997a). The research showed that although the banking business had gone global very quickly, its regulation was largely local – the risk-taking and arbitrage was far ahead of its regulation and governance. Systemic and regulatory failure seemed to be in-built in banking and finance, the studies warned in the 1990s – though the warnings were unheeded. In spite of this, we are led to constantly believe that regulation can work, and one day will work. This turned out to be a fiction and an ideology which was spread from experts to politicians. In contrast to my worry about the nature and effectiveness of banking regulation, I discovered that the engine of finance research in the 1990s and 2000s was ideologically driven, where markets were assumed to be self-regulating. How wrong this proved to be.

The truth in the finance academy is that there are deep underlying values and assumptions which influence the teaching and research, but these are rarely exposed, discussed or critiqued. In fact, the modern heights of finance research are so technical that even the vocabulary of exposing and critiquing the deep cultural assumptions has disappeared. Greed is not just a practice of bankers and financiers, but deeply embedded and endorsed in the very 'science' of finance (Das 2011; Kay 2015) – leading to a moral and cultural economy of fraud (Whyte and Wiegratz 2016). It is unclear the extent to which academics steeped in finance have allowed their personal lives to be influenced by the theories they promote, though it's unlikely that scholars can separate their behaviour from their research and writing. There is plenty of evidence of the bad behaviour of bankers and finance experts in the real world (Angelides et al. 2011; McFall et al. 2009a; Reinhard and Rogoff 2011; Luyendijk 2015).

When I teach finance to my students, I make it personal. I bring my own values and ethics into the shaping of the curriculum, and encourage students to similarly share their own values and experiences (Shah 2014; Shah 2016c). I start with discussions about students' own family and personal experiences of finance, and how they influence everyday life. As a result, they begin to connect with the discipline in an intimate way, and begin to see the frauds and hoaxes early on. For example, several of my students have been affected by their personal credit scores in getting credit cards or loans. This is not even mentioned in most university finance or accounting textbooks. In reality, it is an act of spying on private lives, a kind of 24/7 monitoring of individual behaviour and financial transactions. In one student's case, there was fraud conducted by a previous tenant which went into her credit file, even though she had nothing to do with it. It was a huge struggle to remove this error from her credit score. The power and mystique of finance begins to unravel when we make it personal. Perhaps that is why the study of finance tries to keep its distance from personal experience – its fraudulent precepts do not like to be exposed. What results is that students then become either disengaged or treat finance as a vehicle for personal gain, irrespective of its consequences to society and the environment. Their innocence and vulnerability is exploited by the experts. Students often become indoctrinated by the theory and start to behave like the models and their assumptions – investment banking has been a preferred career choice of top students for several decades.

In truth, money is a symbol of a social contract where values like trust, assurance and confidence are key. Laws and regulations are meant to preserve its authenticity and reliability, and ensure public trust. Financial institutions get a public licence to operate, and are supposed to be closely regulated and monitored. Theirs is a highly privileged and responsible role, for which leaders and professionals must exercise the highest integrity and accountability. When it comes to banking, which is an industry which manufactures money, we must never forget these key denominators of money and finance. Sadly, ethics in finance are not a mainstream subject (Hendry 2013; Boatright 1999), and instead meaningless phrases like 'ethical neutrality' are used to abstract from the underlying ethical assumptions that are made. It is possible that most finance scholars have a very weak understanding of ethics, if at all. In doing their science, they have managed to detach money and value from its original roots. Like their financial instruments, the science has become a 'derivative'.

Academic Culture, Incentives and Professional Politics

I believe this change in academic culture is partly evidence of the huge pressures on academic accountability and performance evaluation, which relies on peer review processes to police quality and output (Harney and Dunne 2013). Harney and Dunne (2013) call this a phenomenon of extreme neo-liberalism, where there is extreme externalisation of costs and extreme regulation of value. Academic behaviour has become business-like, so how can they critique business, they argue. Such incentives can seriously influence and overwhelm a sense of public duty and responsibility among scholars, and instead the way research performance is measured becomes the 'truth' about an intellectual breakthrough.

This behaviour is also an abstraction from reality – we use proxies like journal rankings to decide on the quality of a scientist or their discoveries. And the proxies have become the reality. The history of the 2008 banking crash shows that the experts were keen to pursue an ideology of free markets and push through an agenda of light-touch or no regulation, resulting in global disaster (Ferguson 2012; Tett 2010; Kay 2015). They had the power and resources to influence policy. Very few warnings came from academics. I believe that as academics, we too need to be conscious of our power and responsibilities to society. So when we avoid case studies, we are also possibly avoiding the policing of academic ideologies and bubbles – by detaching ourselves from the 'messy real world'. A large number of big and well-known banks went bust in the crisis – RBS and HBOS in the UK; Kaupthing based in Iceland; Bear Stearns and Lehman Brothers in the US; Freddie Mac, Fannie Mae, New Century – all large US housing finance institutions. Whilst there have been many books on the crisis, I have yet to see a single academic investigation into a particular 2008 bank failure in the form of a rich case study. It appears that the obsession with research quality has increased the silos, distancing truth and its wholeness. Also it is unclear what the 'academic' status is of research monographs like these, which take a significant amount of skill and effort to research and write, and the learnings may not be neat and precise, and policed and refereed as academics would prefer to see them. As many have predicted, serious long-term investigative research is in decline under these pressures.

Large organisations are complex to manage and run successfully. A focus on certain techniques and numbers may create the temporary fiction that an organisation is profitable and well-managed, as markets are often fixated on measures (Froud et al. 2006). Numbers can also be manipulated with the help of qualified accountants and other professionals to manage the reported performance in a way favourable to the managers and their incentive schemes (Shah 1996a; Shah 1997b). In such an environment, technical and calculative professionals may thrive, but the numbers can lead to an obsession, driving a selfish and aggressive culture. All this has real effects on the practice of accounting and finance. Even though numbers may imply objectivity, they are often very subjective by nature and design, and therefore misleading.

In her review of the 2008 crash, Arnold (2009) calls for more studies of 'accounting in action' revealing the underlying politics and motives of institutional and regulatory failure. She explains that (p. 209):

> Accounting scholars are uniquely positioned to use our knowledge of accounting institutions, the intricacies of accounting rules, and the socially and politically contested nature of accounting practices to identify and explain how seemingly neutral accounting practices facilitated and continue to facilitate, the massive wealth transfers that mark this extraordinary financial crisis.

She also notes the huge power and influence of the Big 4 global accounting firms and the significant profits they have been making from their services to financial institutions. Their actions are worthy of critical study if we are to understand the politics of the financial crash, she argues. Hopwood (2009) echoes this. There is a call for more inter-disciplinary cooperation in research in accounting and finance, and Vollmer et al. (2009) show how this would enrich our understanding of its social impact. The study of risk management needs to integrate issues of corporate governance, management accounting and the degree to which risk is reported, measured and analysed (Bhimani 2009). Webb (2014) introduces the concept of 'people risk' which is never measured, and argues that inside banks, there are three key strands of business bureaucracy in a state of permanent antagonism:

> Upper management either blithely assumes that safe policies are being implemented or is happy to collude with risky practices that deliver short-term profits. Risk assessors are left to contend with the contradictory demands of executives who maintain that greater performance can go hand-in-hand with greater caution. Frontline staff don't understand – or don't care to understand – the implications of policies that stop them maximising their earning potential through targets and bonuses.

The boundaries of risk management do not just lie at the level of the organisation – Miller et al. (2008) emphasise the need to study hybrids in risk management – there is potential for collusion between different organisations and institutions in the enterprise of risk. We will see in this book (Chapter 4) how the audit and consulting firm KPMG endorsed excessive risk-taking at HBOS.

About HBOS

In May 2001, one of Britain's largest retail banks, Halifax, merged with the Bank of Scotland, a very prestigious 300-year-old Scottish commercial bank, to form HBOS, the fifth largest UK bank with total assets of £275 billion at the end of 2001. The chief executive of Halifax, James Crosby, became CEO of the merged Group, and the chairman of Halifax, Lord Stevenson, also became chairman of the merged Group. HBOS collapsed on 16th September 2008, two days after the Lehman Brothers bankruptcy, with a £198 billion gap between its lending and its deposits, and was rescued by Lloyds TSB at the intervention of the UK government. Significant bad debts hidden in HBOS's loan books appeared much later – amounting to 20% of the 2008 Corporate Loan Book – at least £25 billion (Tyrie et al. 2013a, para 12). Later these numbers were actually £52 billion (PRA 2015a). In 2012, the FSA investigated the causes of this serious risk management failure, and issued a Final Notice which would have involved a multi-million pound fine, were it not for the collapse of the Bank in 2008 (FSA 2012). The report details the serious failings in the Bank of Scotland's risk management and control practices.

From the outset, HBOS had a strong rhetoric of aggressive competition against the established Big Four British Banks. James Crosby gave a public target for the new Group to increase the return on equity from 17% in 2001 to 20% in 2004. According to the Parliamentary Commission on Banking Standards (Tyrie et al. 2013a, para 19):

> The strategy set by the Board from the creation of the new Group sowed the seeds of its own destruction. HBOS led a strategy for aggressive asset-led growth across divisions over a sustained period. This involved accepting more risk across all divisions of the Group. Although many of the strengths of the two brands within HBOS largely persisted at branch level, the strategy created a new culture in the higher echelons of the Bank. This culture was brash, underpinned by a belief that the growing market share was due to special skills which HBOS possessed and which its competitors lacked. The effects of the culture were all the more corrosive when coupled with a lack of corporate self-knowledge at the top of the organisation, enabling the bank's leaders to persist in the belief, in some cases to this day, that HBOS was a conservative institution when in fact it was the very opposite.

From above, risk and culture were at the very heart of the collapse. There were pro-active policies and practices of risk management and control – 150 professionals were involved in this area across HBOS Retail Bank and reported to Moore (Moore, private interview). There is a Non-Executive Board of Directors whose primary job it is to govern, by approving business strategy and overseeing culture, risk and regulatory compliance (Financial Reporting Council 2013). Spin appeared to have been applied in the management of HBOS communications led by the same person throughout – who won an award for his communications in 2008 (Fraser 2012). The auditors KPMG approved the accounts every year without qualifications. The FSA were concerned at the outset, and took some actions, but later somehow acquiesced. One major rule is that only 'approved persons' can be in senior and responsible managerial positions in the bank (Dewing and Russell 2008). Specifically, under Section 59 of the Financial Services and Markets Act 2000, no person can perform a 'controlled function' unless the FSA has given prior approval. So all Board members have to be pre-approved, and the same applies to key risk management functions. The FSA also possess powers of enforcement if such people are found guilty of misconduct – these were not applied in the case of HBOS during its heady days.

In the field of financial risk management, the literature tends to be technical and positivistic. There are many textbooks written on it (Eales 1994; Hopkin 2012; Roggi and Altman 2013), and the approach is to show students how to understand banking risks and techniques of its measurement and management. Even the fact that definitions of risks are disputed and questioned by researchers is ignored in these texts (Shah and Baker 2015). The practical need for risk measurement and management overwhelms the science. Similarly, auditing is usually taught in a technical way and practiced as such, even when the reality of auditing is very political, conflicted, commercially motivated, and influenced by the Big 4 global accounting firms. Regulation is often the outcome of political negotiation, captured by powerful private interests, and there is confusion about regulatory objectives, and conflict between regulatory institutions and blame-shifting in the event of a crisis. However, in a banking text, regulation is often presented as a set of rules or principles which need to be followed, abstracted from their political nature.

Research Methodology

The research here draws from a range of primary and secondary sources, many of which were unearthed by parliamentary and regulatory investigations into the HBOS failure. It is based on three years of work. In many cases, the analysis was very penetrating and forensic, using expert lawyers and inquisitors. This helped to unravel a range of mysteries about the operation of the firm and its management. One key aspect of this study is the revelation of evidence from whistleblower Paul Moore, who was Head of Group Regulatory Risk at HBOS and gave us full cooperation for this study. In late 2004, he foresaw the cultural and risk problems of the Group and warned the Board about it, but was fired. This is a critical point in the history of the organisation where we are able to see what happens when integrity and professionalism clash with management greed and hubris. We draw from different theories about the politics of risk, audit and regulation to analyse the evidence unearthed and identify key learnings from this episode.

One could well ask, given the two extensive multi-million pound parliamentary and regulatory investigations of the failure of HBOS, what really is new about this study, or even why do we need a separate study? The first reason is simply that this is an academic study, focusing on how this case affects our theoretical knowledge about banking and finance – none of the investigations were concerned about this feature, as they were designed to develop policy and regulatory reforms. This study effectively utilises the hard work and evidence unearthed by the two investigations, and teases out how this evidence affects the way we theorise and teach finance and accounting. Given the size of HBOS and its cost of failure, there are genuine reasons why such a study is extremely important. How else would we learn about the faults in our knowledge and theories? Secondly, there is a simpler and more practical reason which inspires this book. The real world matters. Large banking failures matter (Black 2002). Academic and expert resources need to be dedicated to such analyses in order to help control and regulate better in future, and to encourage students to see contemporary banking in its wider context. If such a book were not written, it is unlikely that students on their own accord would pick up the government reports, as there would be no easy peg as to how the HBOS failure affects the theory and knowledge of banking and finance.

I would also like to make clear from the outset that the research resources devoted to this study were very limited – due to my own limited time. There was no external funding, nor any leaves of absence to conduct the research. In contrast, millions were spent by the government on the investigations, and of course billions on the bailout. This should give readers a context for the unevenness in research support and funding, when it is critical of the mainstream. Most of the work was done after a busy teaching schedule, in evenings and weekends and vacations. The skill that was brought into the study came from two key sources – my experience as a trainee Chartered Accountant and auditor with KPMG in London, and my PhD studies at the London School of Economics in the early nineties. The years of teaching and research in finance following from my study helped in focused investigation, questioning, analysis and presentation.

The research method used to analyse HBOS is a combination of interviews and review of primary and secondary documents, including private email correspondence and internal reports and papers, not normally available to the public. In addition, the regulatory and political influences prevailing at that time have been analysed through a review of press and secondary literature. The documents examined include:

- the Tyrie Report – 'An accident waiting to happen' and other parliamentary investigations over HBOS (Tyrie et al. 2013a, 2013b, 2013c, 2016);
- the PRA Reports – PRA 2015a, 2015b, 2015c;
- annual Reports and Audited Accounts of HBOS;
- internal memoranda and correspondence between Moore and the Finance Director/Chief Risk Officer, and the HBOS leadership;
- minutes of HBOS Board and other executive and strategy meetings and business plans, revealed by the parliamentary investigations;
- the 'Retail Sales Culture and Systems Control Review' conducted by Moore which critiqued the aggressive sales culture and its impact on risk, and led to his eventual sacking;
- PWC s.166 investigation of risk management skills and systems at HBOS (Price Waterhouse Coopers 2004);
- Moore's interviews and statements to the Parliamentary Committee;
- the full report of the 'independent' KPMG investigation into Moore's dismissal, and his rebuttal of this (KPMG 2005);
- the legal defence case Moore presented through his lawyers to HBOS to protest his dismissal (Hamilton 2004);
- interview of KPMG UK Head of Quality and Risk, Mr David Matthews;
- press and blog comments on HBOS;
- Moore's personal autobiography detailing his HBOS and KPMG experience (Moore 2015);
- detailed probing interviews of HBOS Board members and non-executives, and written reports submitted by them in answer to specific questions by parliament. This was revealed in the Tyrie reports above.

Paul Moore was regarded by Tyrie et al. (2013a) as a highly critical witness to the parliamentary investigation – he was promoted to Head of Group Regulatory Risk in early 2004 which made him deputy to the Chief Risk Officer. His full cooperation in this study and meticulous record-keeping has given us substantial new insights into the politics of risk management and the audit and regulatory failure due to the seniority of his role and his twenty years of expertise in the field. The Tyrie committee rigorously probed several key risk officers in the Group including the Chief Risk Officer, the Non-Executive Chair of the Risk Committee, and also the Chairman and Chief Executive. Even the Prime Minister, Gordon Brown, acknowledged Moore's evidence in parliament and said that his claims would be investigated (Pagano 2009).

There are limitations to a case study approach – the biggest being that the evidence may not be generalisable as it is specific. The significant size of HBOS (fifth largest bank) and its reach and influence mitigates this somewhat, as it was a major institution in the British economy – it was systemically very important. Also the aim of this research is more to tease out the detail of the processes of risk management and regulatory failure. A large sample study would not be able to reveal this detail. Another potential limitation is that we are focusing on a failed bank – so we are deliberately looking at the failure of management and avoiding the possibilities of successful risk management. However, so many key institutions failed during the crisis that successful risk management was virtually non-existent at that time, and this mismanagement went largely unhindered. Hindsight has its drawbacks, as the evidence may be selective and may itself be politicised. However, hindsight can also be revelatory about the causes of risk management failure which are critical to understanding how and why institutions succeed in transferring significant risks to society. The tools for public and forensic scrutiny are much greater after a scandal than before it. Care has been taken in the method and approach of this study to focus on objective evidence and documentation prevailing in the critical period, and not seeking to blame individuals but instead draw generic lessons. It is left to the reader to decide whether or not this case study is beneficial.

Inspiration for This Book

Usually, when research is published, it appears as a finished product, with neat theories, evidence and analysis. It is very difficult to know the process by which the ideas and data emerged and which avenues were opened and which were closed and why. It also is wrong and misleading to disguise the truth and imply that all was smooth sailing and the data was just waiting to be analysed. I strongly feel that revealing this method is very helpful to students and researchers, who may want to replicate or learn from their peers and mentors. It also exposes the human and cultural dimensions of research, which are critical in the field of social sciences. There is a story behind this book and the underlying research which really helped shape what you are about to read. It goes like this.

In April 2013, a fascinating parliamentary report into the failure of HBOS came out. In all, it comprised nearly 700 pages of documents, interviews and evidence as to what went wrong. In addition, since 2009 there had been much media publicity about a key whistleblower, Paul Moore, who had given strong warnings about risk and culture long before the problems were exacerbated. I decided to contact him, and ask if he would cooperate with my research. We had never met each other, but it turned out that he had been waiting for such a call from an academic for a long time, and being a barrister by profession, had been meticulous in keeping records of his meetings and correspondence with HBOS. Yes, it turned out to be a researcher's dream. He cooperated fully in telling his story, and also started working on writing his own autobiographical book (Moore 2015) about his experiences both as a partner at KPMG and as Head of Risk at HBOS. He shared draft chapters of this with me also.

So the basic truth is that this book would not have emerged without Paul Moore's cooperation and support. Yes, he was very emotional about his betrayal by HBOS, but also what came across clearly was his huge skill as a professional, and his knowledge and vast experience of the practice of risk management as opposed to its abstract and often irrelevant theories. Moore was also passionate about doing the right thing for the bank and ensuring its safety and soundness. For him the right culture was central to creating an effective risk environment, based on twenty years of experience. He had suffered hugely from the sacking in 2004, and was not able to get a proper job thereafter. It is a sad fact that many whistleblowers have the same fate. Even when they are trying to expose the truth, they are left alone and unsupported throughout. Speaking truth to power can be draining physically and emotionally. Moore (2015) gives a detailed autobiographical journey of his experiences. At the same time, whistleblowers give us hope that not all is lost in society and that large organisations can be checked in their hubris and corruption. As academics, it is our public duty to listen to them and work with them.

Readers may wonder why, given his revelations to parliament in 2009, it took five years for an academic to contact Paul Moore. I wonder too. Ninety-five per cent of elite business school research is pro-business – so it is possible that few academics wanted to hear or side with him. Given the huge power of the finance industry, academics on lucrative research or consultancy contracts have become highly compromised in their choice of research (C. Ferguson 2010; C. Ferguson 2012). For me scandal and collapse were great opportunities to learn from mistakes and help society not repeat them in the future. What if academics are not interested in public failures or even public policy, but narrowly in pursuing their own careers and status? This would be consistent with the values and assumptions of contemporary finance theory. It would then be no surprise that academics ignore real-world crises and hide inside their theory bubbles. Also the skills for good inter-disciplinary research are lacking because of silos. It is also in truth very hard to do well, as it requires knowledge in a range of disciplines. It may also be that field research is dirty and not easily controllable – the data and evidence may not be publishable or reliable or come packaged in neat boxes which are familiar to researchers. But surely people should want to know.

In the last fifty years, there has been a growing movement towards positivist research – studies which explain what is rather than what ought to be (normative). This has had a huge influence on the study of finance, which has moved further and further away from the real world, and deeper and deeper into abstract theories and innovative schemes of wealth maximisation. The fact that in every one of those decades, there have been major financial scandals and crashes, having global repercussions, were somehow ignored by the academy, which instead of crashing, grew in size and influence. In my opinion, the boundary between positive and normative is totally spurious, as even when we study what is, we are influenced by our subjective prejudices and ideologies. What positivism does over time is to create and enhance a whole academic culture of ignorance of the real world and its concerns and crises. So even if someone heard about Paul Moore in the news, they may not be interested in calling, or if they did call, they would not know what to ask.

What was also very interesting about interviewing Paul Moore was that he was a senior partner in KPMG, the firm which audited HBOS and regularly gave it a clean bill of health. He knew the KPMG culture and conflicts of interest. In my discussions with him, I discovered the potential to also go behind this huge and influential but opaque audit firm, and its conflicts of interest and chimera of professionalism and independence. This combination of skills and experience helped me to not only look at the risk management failure of HBOS, but also the audit failure, in considerable depth and detail. Also, Moore had great experience in dealing with regulators, so this opened the window of the regulatory failure at HBOS, which was a mixed story, as in the early years, the FSA were seriously concerned about the firm and its future prospects, and Paul Moore was hired to appease them. Unfortunately, Moore was later fired, as he did not appease the CEO in his desire to grow the firm at any cultural cost. In presenting this research, I have tried to weave the multiple layers of this story, and show that there was no one reason for the failure but a series of people, networks and events which came together to prevent remedial action in a timely manner.

One of the most effective ways in which powerful and influential organisations hide the truth of their inner workings and culture is through their might and resources. Even when Moore was sacked, he was forced to sign a confidentiality agreement so that he would stay quiet after leaving. When we reflect on this through a macro lens, a publicly owned bank, regulated and licenced by central government, has the power to use its 'public' financial resources to silence challenge or dissent from the inside. This seems odd, but it actually happened in the case of HBOS, in full view of the auditors and regulators. 'Bizarre' does not even come close. The power and might of the Board explains how this was made possible.

Initially, two HBOS-related working papers were compiled to present the research at conferences and share with the wider audience – one on risk management (Shah 2015a) and one on audit failure (Shah 2015b). These were presented at workshops and conferences and shared publicly through www.academia.edu. In addition, I started to engage with bloggers and social media to disseminate the findings of this research, and also formed a group with Paul Moore to campaign for an investigation into the audit failure. To date, nearly 5000 people have read these academic papers, which is a significant result, given how few people actually read a single academic paper. Members of this group also comprised Brian Little, Prem Sikka, Ian Fraser and Tony Shearer. We wrote up an appeal letter and sent it to parliament and the Tyrie committee. We even managed to persuade Harriet Agnew of the *Financial Times* to write a newspaper article about our campaign, giving reasons for the regulatory failure of the Financial Reporting Council (Agnew 2016). *The Accountant* magazine very helpfully published an article with a timeline about our HBOS campaign (Tornero 2016). Finally in early 2016, we got the result we were aiming for – the FRC announced an investigation into the audit of HBOS by KPMG, though this was far too limited in scope for our liking, and very late for them to issue any penalties (Shah 2016a).

In the next chapter, we set the detailed scene about HBOS, explaining its history, management, successes and failures. Thereafter, we look at particular aspects of the case in detail – risk management, auditing and regulation in Chapters 2, 3 and 4. All of these three aspects are inter-connected. Good risk management inside an organisation would help ease audit concerns, as the performance would be closely monitored and guarded. Similarly, regulatory work reduces where a financial institution is soundly managed and audited, and has an internal culture which monitors, controls and regulates risky behaviour.

2 About HBOS

When we look at history, banks and scandals have not been uncommon in the British past. Even in recent history, in the 1980s and 1990s, there were major scandals like BCCI, Barings and Johnson Mathey. But the size and scandals in 2007 onwards were to surpass all. In spite of these, the teaching and research in accounting and finance by and large stayed at a technical level and in fact got more sophisticated. History and experience were removed from student memory in the training of bankers, lawyers and accountants.

In hindsight, it seems shocking that the Bank of Scotland, which was nearly 300 years old, and Halifax Building Society, which was set up as a mutual and also 160 years old, would die within seven years of their merger. History has taught us another lesson in finance – nothing is solid, and all depends on people and prudent management. The Bank of Scotland had a reputation for being one of the most prudent banks in Britain, where lending was made to secure clients, and speculation was not tolerated at all (Perman, 2012).

History

As a building society, Halifax was a 'boringly safe' mutual institution, borrowing from savers and lending only to individual property owners, who had enough earnings to cover their mortgages several times over, and where the security for the loan was title to the property. They had always been closely regulated, with restrictions on the type of business they could do and the risks they could undertake, and this close regulation worked very well – there were hardly any spectacular failures of building societies. Given the mutual ownership structure, building societies had a culture of respect towards regulations and regulators. Risks were highly measured, monitored and carefully and prudently managed. Culture takes a long time to build and maintain, but the experience of HBOS suggests that the wrong leadership can destroy it very quickly. There was other internal resistance besides whistleblower Paul Moore, given the huge upheaval that was created by the new bosses (e.g. the case of senior treasury executive Claire Bright who accused her boss of being a 'mini Hitler' and sued for unfair dismissal and victimisation; even the head of Group credit risk left unhappily soon after Moore's dismissal). However, it must have been weakened or silenced.

Perman (2012) has written a beautiful account of the history of the Bank of Scotland, its relationship culture, prudence and huge status and respectability, with a tradition of regular support to local communities. Its age and reputation had given it a rock solid image, and even though it was a FTSE 100 member, it never used its size and power greedily or arrogantly. It was proud of its personal relationships with customers, and phone calls were returned by named people. In the 1980s and 1990s it showed solid performance and sound management, attracting positive press in the media. In 2000, it made a bid for rival bank NatWest, which it lost against rival Royal Bank of Scotland, and it was its CEO Peter Burt who approached Crosby for a merger. Initially Burt stayed on as deputy chairman of HBOS, but retired soon after the transition was completed, saying it was 'like chalk and cheese' compared to the old Bank of Scotland (Fraser 2012).

The Halifax Building Society was founded in 1853, and by 1913 it was the UK's largest building society. In 1997 it demutualised and became a stock market quoted company, joining the FTSE 100, and now having the status of Bank where it could have much wider freedom over its lending operations, and raise capital and debt finance from the markets. Over 7.5 million customers of the Building Society now became shareholders of the new enterprise. This was a major shift in its motives and structure and, as with many other building societies, led to a huge increase in risk-taking and borrowing. A cooperative bank with a culture of mutuality now chose to become fully commercial, disrupting its traditional culture overnight.

Purpose and Mission

In essence, a bank does not make anything – it is an intermediary, and its management uses other peoples' money, to make a profit. In fact, the money multiplier means that anyone who has a banking licence can effectively print money legally and make profits. This licence is a truly rare privilege, and requires leaders to both understand it as a privilege and also fully respect rules and regulations and adhere to them. A bank manager has the effective licence to an open chequebook if he/she wishes to buy power and influence and undermine any supervision or regulation. It can easily be a gambling licence where profits from high stakes can be kept by the managers, and losses can be accumulated and left to the capital providers. All that is needed to prevent this is prudence and good management, and regular and careful auditing and supervision. Hence we cannot ignore the people, relationships and culture of a bank in deciding its health, vitality and viability. By the fact of its very status and position, any leadership role of a large public bank endows huge power, status and privilege. This also makes such roles very political.

Similarly, auditors and regulators need to be very watchful of this element, if they are to be effective in their work. Having a large public bank as a client can bring great kudos and privileges, including access to other large corporate businesses through the bank's networks and ancillary loan and investment projects. We will see in Chapter 4 how instead of an auditor/client relationship, the KPMG/HBOS nexus was more of a strategic partnership. It also turns out that the lead auditor for HBOS Group was the same person throughout – KPMG senior partner Guy Bainbridge. This is in spite of the fact that the Group Audit Committee regularly reviewed the independence of KPMG and monitored the rotation of the members of the audit team (see e.g. 2006 HBOS annual report). Within the staff of the FSA which supervised HBOS, there was a lot of turnover, with the manager poached by HBOS in 2006 (PRA 2015a), leading to a serious internal supervisory crisis at the FSA, at a time when close and tough supervision was most needed. At a very basic human and moral level, there should be a public conscience of safeguarding the trust endowed upon such senior and powerful people by others.

One of the critical concerns of finance theory in the context of modern corporations is the divorce between the owners of a business and its managers (Jensen and Meckling 1976; Boyer 2005; Erturk et al. 2007). This has the effect of separating responsibility and encouraging managers to be self-interested, given an American and now growing western and global culture of individualism. Jensen and Meckling (1976) proposed a theory of agency, where these problems can be overcome by incentivising managers to act in the best interests of shareholders and reduce moral hazard. Later, incentive schemes which supported the maxim of share price maximisation were developed and became common corporate practice, through the issuance of performance bonuses and share options. The finance ideology was that managers should focus on appeasing shareholders above any other stakeholders. However, in the context of a banking institution, such an approach can create significant risk, as managers can potentially maximise risk-taking to improve short-term profits and share prices but in the long term bankrupt the bank. Furthermore, given the 'too big to fail' philosophy, regulators bail out big banks irrespective of the losses, as there is a fear of systemic contagion. This increases the moral hazard problems of banking. We will see in later chapters that HBOS's management were driven to maximise their own rewards and boost share price performance at any cost.

When HBOS collapsed, Tyrie et al. (2013a) concluded that there were three key people who were central to its greed culture and mismanagement – Lord Stevenson who was chairman throughout, James Crosby the founding CEO and Andy Hornby the second CEO. It turns out that none of them had any banking experience prior to these very powerful and influential roles, and the regulator had approved their appointments in spite of this. In 2002, Crosby had joined a pressure group called the Financial Services Practitioners Panel whose main role was to exert pressure on the FSA to weaken its supervision (Fraser 2012). James Crosby had been publicly critical of the toughness of regulators and their inefficiency, and yet was appointed to the Board of the regulators in 2004, later becoming the deputy chairman of the FSA. Lord Stevenson was very well connected in the then Labour government, becoming chair of the government Honours Committee, and James Crosby was even knighted in 2006. Both Stevenson and Crosby had close links with Gordon Brown, who was Chancellor and then later Prime Minister. So HBOS leaders had amassed significant political and economic influence in a very short space of time – and they behaved very politically rather than rationally as predicted by finance theory.

Finance Theory and Practice

As is usual with contemporary business, growth and expansion comes from mergers and acquisitions. It is much harder to create and sustain organic growth – then management would need to work. Also contrary to economic theory about competition and the evils of monopoly power, much of modern business is dominated by monopolies – as these are the easiest way to earn very high returns and reduce competition. Politics and power are hard-wired into big finance, but somehow finance theory and research refuse to believe or acknowledge it. The HBOS deal brought together some of the UK's best-known financial services brands – including Bank of Scotland, Birmingham Midshires, Clerical Medical, Esure, Halifax and Intelligent Finance – covering retail and commercial banking, insurance and asset management. Other major acquisitions, like BankWest in Australia and Equitable Life and St James's Place in the UK, were made very soon after the merger, and there was later a huge expansion into Ireland. Somehow, the Board seemed unconcerned by scale or geographical distance – and a huge number of problems later stemmed from overseas and international operations. The primary activities of the new bank were also wide ranging covering retail and commercial banking, stockbroking, fund and investment management, insurance, pensions and personal financial products and investments. In hindsight, this expansion was an expression of the executives' thirst for power through growth in size and scale, in spite of the fact that management knowledge and skills were lacking.

In the language of banking, a cheap source of finance (retail savings) can now be used to profit from a lucrative source of income – commercial lending. So expectations were high from the outset. And the stock market thrives on big organisations which make fat profits, irrespective of the wider social and environmental consequences, as the nature of such investors and fund managers is that they too want easy money with the least effort and sacrifice. Excitement about the potential was such that the new Group CEO, James Crosby, announced a growth target of 20% per year over the next five years and was happy to be publicly accountable for making this promise. Such announcements are unusual, as management do not want to impose pressure on themselves – if they failed to meet the target, their jobs would be on the line. The CEO's bonuses and incentives were designed to ensure big wins if he achieved the targets. Given his role and power, he would have had a strong influence in recommending his own remuneration package, although this cannot be easily proven. In a crude way, legalised bank robbery can be said to be hard-wired into the contemporary banking system, where size can buy wealth, power and remove obstacles, including the likelihood of any personal penalties, regulatory sanctions or arrest.

Another key monitor of business is supposed to be the stock market. In finance theory, it is treated like a god to be worshipped, something that is all-knowing and competitive and fully transparent. Often the share price is treated as an objective fact, divorced from factors like market sentiment, spin and hubris. Theories of market competition and efficiency suggest that for publicly traded equities, there is a significant interest from market players in monitoring corporate performance, and penalising management hubris, fraud or incompetence. It is therefore a surprise that throughout its short life, HBOS's share price and profits continued to rise, without much wider scrutiny. One key reason it did so was the huge effort and resources management spent in managing the image of HBOS and its perception of solid performance – the annual reports detail the efforts devoted to this by the Investor Relations team, and annual surveys and regular meetings were held with large investors.

Crosby identified from the outset that his main priority was to appease the shareholders who he saw as the true owners of the business (2002 annual report) – other stakeholders such as employees, customers, regulators and suppliers were put on the sidelines. One result of this focus was a regular increase in dividends paid (between 5% and 15% jump every year), something which finance theory suggests is most unusual, as, in future, management would be bound to sustain this level of dividend at least. It is a signal to the market of great confidence in the future potential of the business. It reveals the management's interpretation of business potential by using its internal information and resources which are not accessible to external shareholders, or so it is posited. Unfortunately, the problem with such theories is that management can subvert them to give false signals to boost their own bonuses. In the context of a banking institution, such false signals can be hugely damaging, as we have seen in the case of HBOS where deep problems and risks were hidden for a long time, surfacing in a big explosion. Signalling theory in finance assumes management confidence when dividends are raised, but ignores the fact that even hubris could play a role.

Short-Termism

When CEOs have a short-termist orientation, they may not be too concerned about future pressures to sustain dividends. Shareholders love dividend increases, and they also boost share prices – giving them a dual gain in income and price. At the same time, HBOS also used its own funds to do multi-billion pound share buybacks, which have the effect of boosting share price, a form of financial engineering. Theory has encouraged this behaviour, although it seems very odd as the company is using its own money to cancel its shares (a zero sum game), but somehow it has the effect of raising share prices. In the era of financialisation, such engineering has become the norm taught by theory and encouraged by practice (van der Zwan 2014).

Empirical research in finance has consistently shown that linking pay to performance does not necessarily lead to better performance, yet the management rewards continue to be performance-related in practice (Tosi et al. 2008). There is also empirical evidence which shows that corporate size is linked with management rewards – the larger an organisation, the greater the remuneration. In HBOS, we see a very strong push to expand the size of the organisation with very large acquisitions undertaken in a very short space of time, even before the two separate organisations had been properly consolidated. These included very large groups like Equitable Life and St James's Place, in the UK, and Bank West in Australia. There was also a huge push towards international expansion into Ireland, the USA and Australia – HBOS wanted to quickly become a global bank. There was also an attempt in 2004 to acquire another very large UK bank, Abbey National, which failed. It is widely acknowledged that there are serious integration challenges with mergers and acquisitions, within one country and also internationally, which has its own unique difficulties due to cultural and institutional variations (Froud et al. 2006). However, the HBOS Board did not seem deterred by this, and went on a huge buying spree, using public money, of course. All the evidence points to a very calculated and financial focus, rather than an interest in building the right culture and values and good long-term relationships with customers and suppliers. People and culture were totally secondary to profits and short-term rewards.

Like HBOS, the people who invest in the stock market and have influence are managers of large institutional funds like pensions or investment funds. They too are investing other people's money (Kay 2015), and the personal consequences for them for poor decision-making are never clear, and often covered up by spin. Also, it is now widely accepted, even from history, that often there are speculative bubbles, when a sense of truth and accuracy in valuation disappear, and everyone gets driven by a general hype of higher and higher share prices. The truth often gets replaced by fiction, and everyone hops on the ride, either believing it will last for a long time or planning to exit just before the bubble bursts (McGoun 1997; Das 2011). There is now also growing evidence of the hype and frauds generated by financial intermediaries whose sole focus is on driving deals and volatility so as to earn large fees from transactions (Folkman et al. 2008).

One episode in the early history of HBOS shows the blasé culture that was being encouraged (Fraser 2012). Lord Stevenson met the now infamous billionaire retailer Sir Phillip Green (who is alleged to have mismanaged the sale of BHS and run down its pension fund) at an event in 2004, and suggested to him that if he were to acquire Marks & Spencer, HBOS would be happy to fund the acquisition. This is already after HBOS had earlier bankrolled his bids for Arcadia Group and BHS. The prize for Lord Stevenson was to become senior independent director of Marks & Spencer if the deal was to succeed – no conflict of interest in this was seen by HBOS. This would have been in addition to the chairmanships and other non-executive directorships he already had, which initially included another very large FTSE 100 company, Pearson plc.

Transactional Banking

When we examine the early heritage of the two financial institutions, there is slow and steady growth, stability and respectability, and prudent management (Hobson 1953; Perman 2012). The demutualisation and merger changes all that virtually overnight. Contemporary finance theory is obsessed by wealth and profit maximisation, at any cost, and therefore it has huge difficulty with concepts like trust, reputation, history, tradition and memory. Without saying so directly, it implies that these are a hindrance to success and progress, where the only thing that matters is the latest transaction and the future potential profits and value of the firm. The theory transactionalises the institution, and removes the very idea of culture and ethics, let alone valuing it. So given the nature of stock markets, and the UK political and financial climate prevailing at that time, we should be less surprised about the swift and eventual demise of HBOS – not dissimilar to the hubris at RBS (Fraser 2015). If the markets wanted quick and steady growth, and they were unwilling to take account of the wider cost of such change, such as cultural and ethical bankruptcy, then they got the outcome they deserved. However, the people who lost out and continue to lose out are ordinary savers and pensioners, through zero interest rates and smaller pension pots.

In later years, it transpired that HBOS was involved in the US housing bubble through the selling of mortgage-backed securities, Credit Default Swaps and PPI, one of the largest UK scandals in retail banking. As a result of PPI, billions of pounds in compensation had to be paid to customers because of mis-selling. In addition, there was aggressive and high-risk property lending at the peak of the property bubble, including lending to Ireland, fraudulent trading and lending in Australia, and aggressive accounting practices where loan fees were booked before they were earned. Lloyds Bank, which took over HBOS for a song at the height of its crisis, thought it had got a bargain. Little did it know that lurking under the headlines were serious bad debts, mis-selling penalties and imprudent risk-taking, which cost billions of pounds. Even this takeover by Lloyds happened overnight, without any serious due diligence done by the bank in spite of knowing that HBOS was sinking. The hubris in the finance industry at that time beggars belief. At a very simple level, the image is of bank leaders who did not have a conscience about the seriousness of running a public financial institution, and the dangers of excessive growth and risk-taking. Somehow, the very notion and concept of prudence and responsibility were not understood.

Where there is a strong financial performance culture, the numbers and targets replace people and culture, and there are many examples of how HBOS achieved this in the early years. For example, if branch employees did not hit their retail sales targets, cabbages were left on their desk to remind them of their failure (Fraser 2012). Phoney new current accounts were opened to hit sales targets. After 2005, to earn both fees and profits, HBOS went into equity investments of target businesses, lending them both share capital and loans to support their business. This was a new and high-risk area, really expanded during the difficult years after 2005 when retail profits and earnings were going down, and huge pressure was applied to the corporate bank to make up the difference.

In December 2005, one of the most senior former executives at HBOS from the old Bank of Scotland, George Mitchell who headed the corporate bank, retired at the age of 55. Peter Cummings took over the reins, and he was later blamed and fined by the FSA in 2012 for his mismanagement – something which he bitterly complained about, as he said his strategy was endorsed and fully supported by the executive. In March 2007, one of his colleagues, Colin Swanson, committed suicide by hanging himself in the bathroom of the Millennium Hotel in London. Former insiders said that Swanson was 'under massive stress because of unrealistic targets he had been given and because he had questioned the bank's business model' (Fraser 2012). In spite of all this, in May 2007, HBOS shares had climbed to a height of 1153p.

One other huge damage which HBOS inflicted onto the finance markets was to fuel the bubble in housing through cheap, low-cost mortgages, and in corporate lending through cheap loans. When a large player undercuts the competition in this way, it creates a race to the bottom, where entire products and markets are affected. As a result, general risk-taking increases and risk management becomes poorer. For example, cheap and easy mortgages fuelled a housing bubble in the UK which burst in 2008. In a similar way, the Irish property bubble which burst spectacularly was fuelled by huge amounts of cheap and easy finance, in which HBOS also became a key player. So the bankruptcy of HBOS had much wider market and economic ramifications for householders and corporates than the losses suffered by the bank alone. This is another very important reason why we need to learn from such failures, and transform finance thinking and education to try to avoid repeats in future.

Boardroom Dancing and Hubris

The Board of HBOS is in theory (and by law) responsible for governing the bank, asking challenging questions and in particular commenting on and endorsing business strategy. Their appointment is also supposed to be independent, though the parliamentary investigations revealed that the CEO was a member of all the appointments committees for non-executive directors. When HBOS was formed, Lord Stevenson was chair of two large public companies – Pearson and HBOS – and no conflict of interest was seen by either Boards even though this was against the Higgs recommendations on corporate governance. Famous names such as Sir Ron Garrick (deputy chairman for five years) and Sir Charles Dunstone (founder of Carphone Warehouse) were on the Board, but the subsequent Tyrie enquiry showed that there was little banking experience even among the entire non-executive team. More importantly, Lord Stevenson admitted that the Board rarely commented on the overall risk and growth strategy of the Group, even though this was its core duty and responsibility under the Code of Corporate Governance. The Board met once a month for two hours, and they considered this was sufficient. Tyrie et al. (2013a) were very critical of the Board and their failure to check and control management greed and hubris. Shockingly, one of the Board members (Sir Ron Garrick) admitted to Tyrie that it was the best Board he had ever sat on, and would love to continue in this role even in hindsight if given the opportunity. Somehow, the Board was made to feel very comfortable and unruffled by the breathtaking scale of problems accumulating in the bank.

The PRA report (2015a) found serious deficiencies in the process by which Board meetings were led and managed. They tended to be short, with a large agenda, and controversial matters were discussed with individual directors prior to the meeting, and if there was no consensus, the item was taken off the agenda. Here is the full finding (para 851):

> Board meetings were usually scheduled to run for two to three hours and a typical agenda had between nine and sixteen separate items, which provided little time to consider each item. All directors interviewed felt that the Chairman expected everyone to have read and digested papers before the meeting so that the time allocated for discussion and debate was optimised. However, in oral and written evidence from both executive directors and NEDs, it is clear that a number of matters were discussed among the directors before Board meetings. These discussions meant that on many matters and proposals a consensus among directors was reached before formal Board meetings, and if this could not be achieved the item was removed from the agenda to be reassessed at a business level. There was a risk that this practice stifled debate as the directors were approached on a one-to-one basis and therefore unaware of concerns raised by their colleagues.

The above suggests that either the CEO or the chairman or both in collusion had structured the Board process in such a way that challenge was undermined – so the principles established for good governance and accountability were subverted. It is rare for such revelations to come out on real-life Boards of companies, as such matters are usually impenetrable to outsiders, including shareholders and investors. The requirement for an independent chairman of a large company was imposed to ensure genuine challenge to power and authority. The above suggests that in the case of HBOS, this was cosmetic rather than real, and no official rules were broken.

HBOS Annual Reports

The annual reports of HBOS are vast documents, over 100 pages long, sometimes nearing 150, with detailed Board reports, financial statements, and the usual boiler plate audit report, which is one page long but supposed to give independent credibility to the reported performance. There are facts about management remuneration, about risk management policies and strategies, about profits, dividends, cash flows, balance sheets and detailed notes to the accounts. They comprise a very useful source of information about what happened from one year to the next, and how performance was influenced by this. As they tended to reflect past performance, and focused on actual transactions, they are not great in terms of risk measurement and risk warnings, sadly. Generally speaking, financial statements do not give easy to interpret measures of risk, a crucial area of investment evaluation and solvency. The information usefulness of annual reports is a chimera often falsely or misleadingly taught to students of accounting.

Throughout the short life of the bank, the Board reports are ebullient and optimistic, except for 2007 when things began to turn sour. In 2002, the annual report opens with a challenging interview by an external investment expert of CEO James Crosby. Fortuitously, its title is 'How do you make sure the wheels don't fall off?', and the interview was conducted by David Rough, nine pages long and published right at the front of the 2002 annual report, with pictures and graphic design. If we examine the questions he asked with the experience of hindsight, it is clear that Rough was very thorough and prescient – he gave all the important warnings in his penetrating questions, and the answers Crosby gave show his hubris. For example, Rough questioned the fast pace of growth and its impact on risks, the complexity of the business and related challenge to management, and the significant power and influence of Crosby. Here is a critical question Rough asked:

DAVID ROUGH: Often, chief executives make sure that the next level down are open to challenge but avoid effective challenge to their own position?

JAMES CROSBY: If we're judged to have been successful during my time as chief executive, my greatest ambition thereafter will be to pick up the newspapers and read about further success in the organisation. So yes, there's plenty of challenge. I've got outstanding colleagues; colleagues who can take over from me any time.

As we can see, Crosby has completely ignored or not understood the question, and does not seem to want any challenge to his decision-making. Instead, he sees challenge as a matter of transition, rather than robust operations.
Here is another question Rough asked:

DAVID ROUGH: Finally, what really turns you on? What motivates you? Is it the returns to shareholders and thus your pockets? Or destroying the competition?

JAMES CROSBY: Shareholders are our owners, ultimately we really only exist to create shareholder value.

Rough also queried Board composition and size:

DAVID ROUGH: Corporate governance. My own personal view is that boards with over ten members do have real problems. How do you make a board of 17 function in a satisfactory manner?

JAMES CROSBY: Ours is a highly regulated and complex business. Our non-executives have to devote a considerable amount of time, not just attending main board meetings but working on the various committees and getting close to the business. We have six main Audit and Risk Control Committees and all the other committees you'd expect us to have. But you are right. If 17 people got together once a month and that was all they did, it wouldn't work.

Corporate Governance

The picture all this paints is one of a Board driven by process rather than substance, and perhaps a cosmetic assurance to the markets that the Board is large enough to be challenging and comes from well-known respected names. The reality of challenge in the boardroom is much more complex – at a very practical level, it is much easier for an NED to keep nodding and collect their high remuneration and kudos than to ask tough questions (Marnet 2010), whose answers would need to be followed through with more meetings and time spent on the matter. Also, effective challenge requires cooperation from other non-executives, and where the chairman and CEO are closely connected, it is very difficult in practice to break this power base. All the indications are that this was true throughout the life of HBOS.

One issue which was very irksome for Tyrie et al. (2013a) was the level of boardroom discussion and challenge on business strategy at HBOS, and they repeatedly asked these questions to the NEDs. In their final summary of the findings they wrote (para 91–2):

> The corporate governance of HBOS at board level ... represents a model of self-delusion, of the triumph of process over purpose. ... The Board, in its own words, had abrogated and remitted to the executive management the formulation of strategy, a matter for which the Board should properly have been responsible.

Yet when we look at the chairman's report over the years, there is a statement that strategy was decided collectively by the Board (e.g. 2006 annual report, p. 69):

> The Board determines the strategic direction of the Group and reviews operating, financial and risk performance which includes: ... approval of the Group's annual Business Plan (which defines the operating and strategic objectives of the Group and the risk framework within which it operates).

On page 93, there is a statement that the 'Chairman has a key role in the joint development of strategy and oversight and implementation.' Thus it seems the Board was not even following its own proper duties and processes.

What one also sees from reading the annual reports is that throughout the life of the business, the stated focus was on revenue growth, capital discipline and cost control – in fact, the phrase often used was 'cost leadership' which means trying to bring down the cost/income ratio to the lowest in the industry. While risk management was mentioned and discussed, it seemed the overwhelming focus was on the bottom line, and the importance of risk control was relegated in spite of the spin. The risk management reports were full of processes and committees, showing the various layers of 'defence', which later turned out to be empty and conflicted – see Chapter 3. One crucial area of risk which contributed to its downfall was the liquidity trap: for a long time, HBOS funded its loans by borrowing from the markets at short-term interest rates and lending long term. Yet even in 2006, when we read the liquidity risk analysis in the annual report (pp. 86–7), there is no mention of this huge problem and instead a lot of detail about policies and committees responsible for monitoring liquidity. More generally, in the audited financial statements, there are no specific risk measures provided to help investors understand the quantity of risks undertaken by the business. Nor is there any warning from auditors of the huge build-up of liquidity risk. The reporting of a key measure for investment analysis, the riskiness of a bank's assets, is patchy at best, exposing that the rhetoric of accounts as being useful for investors is just that – empty rhetoric.

In the 2006 annual report, the chairman's report starts with the huge importance of corporate responsibility and how HBOS should respect the various stakeholders. He notes that (p. 5):

> This reflects the real understanding that our business will only prosper if we seek to serve the interests of all our key stakeholders. Shareholders, customers, suppliers, colleagues and society in general all require HBOS to be responsible, forward thinking and prepared to be measured against pre-determined standards.

However, throughout the report, the principal focus seems to be on profits and shareholder appeasement. The contradictions are in plain sight.

Challenge and Accountability

A lot of research has shown that annual reports are flawed documents, primarily based on past performance and information, and prepared using controversial and subjective accounting policies which are not always consistent or even true and fair (see e.g. McBarnet and Whelan 1999). The narrative and numbers imply accuracy and reliability, but the truth is often far from this. Business growth, acquisitions and complexity add new dimensions of confusion and chaos in the interpretation of annual reports and their usefulness in decision-making and performance evaluation. They are also very weak in the area of risk reporting. As a result, the very documents issued to provide credibility about financial stewardship and performance are deeply flawed, making them very easy to be manipulated by management with the help of expert advisors, to deceive and hide risks, losses or true underlying performance.

From the above, it seems that the executive were hell bent on removing challenge from any quarters, internal and external. They did so internally by sacking staff, or by controlling Board agenda and appointments, and externally by managing auditors and regulators through their influence and offers of consultancy fees or employment as we will see in later chapters. The entire focus was on generating good performance figures and keeping investors happy through high-quality communications and spin. The internal culture of an organisation is not easily visible, and often confidential. Also when markets are focused on short-term performance, they tend to ignore ruffles in internal culture or even management as anomalies, rather than something symptomatic of a deeper malaise. Perhaps they understand that numbers trump culture for lunch but do not care, as all they are interested is in good short-term profits and a growth trend. When hungry for growth, investors can also get carried away by the hubris, and look at the share price as a guide to what is really going on in the company, believing somehow that the markets must be right and that profits are the real proof. Everyone loses sight of truth, and gets carried away by hype and fiction when they are on the gravy train. Any critics against such growth or profits could easily be deafened by the rising share price.

The real politics of HBOS was that a few white men, three in total, commanded significant power throughout its short shelf life, both internally within the bank and its non-executive Board, and externally with government and regulators. Their behaviours were exposed to be deeply political in the Tyrie and PRA investigations. They had access to the billions of pounds of borrowing power of a branded and respected institution, and exploited this fact throughout its short shelf life. And even more paradoxically, when the ship sank, they did not suffer any fines, penalties or imprisonment. They were able to keep all their bonuses, remuneration and retirement pensions. And finance theory is generally very quiet about such behaviour, as its belief is that it should not or could not possibly happen in transparent and competitive markets. The science of finance and its academy does not and will not accept blame for inducing such behaviour, by encouraging managers to constantly appease shareholders and maximise profits and share prices. The highly politicised nature of such theory, where other stakeholders are excluded, is not admitted. This fiction needs to be exposed widely, as society continues to pay a huge price for the scientific justification of greed and hubris. Even more concerning is the fact that this theory is spreading all over the world, influencing future generations of finance practitioners to transform their behaviour and appease market greed. This is culturally naïve and very damaging to society and the planet.

Restraint of such hubris and misappropriation of scarce public resources also requires power, conscience and timely action. Inside the organisation, this can come from risk and internal audit managers and the non-executive directors. Outside the organisation, auditors and regulators have powers and a duty to challenge and prevent failure and catastrophe. Investigative journalists and sophisticated investors should also be monitoring and asking tough questions all the time. Sadly, investigative journalism has been dying for many years, and concerned investors often find it easier to sell their shareholding than to challenge and critique the management. The result is that the public do not hear of the concerns expressed – critics walk away quietly. In the next three chapters, we look in more detail as to why risk management, audit and regulation failed to warn in time and with effect. The findings reveal a murky tale of capture, conflicts of interest and poor leadership and conscience. Overwhelmingly, the rising share price kept everyone quiet and the parasites hungry for more fees and profits.

The next chapter focuses on risk management failure, one of the key reasons why HBOS collapsed. It examines the evidence to help us understand how it is that the systems and processes failed so miserably, and what contributed to such managerial and governance weaknesses. In the process, the underlying politics of risk management in large financial institutions is revealed, including the role of expert professionals and their firms in endorsing it and covering it up. Everyone seems to be seeking comfort and reward when working for such institutions. There are many thirsty people at the feeding trough that is the modern giant bank.

3   The Politics of Risk Management

A critical explanation for the 2008 global financial crash was excessive and uncontrolled risk-taking by large systemically important financial institutions. Risk is the bread and butter of banking business, and its accurate assessment and management can make all the difference between a good bank and a bad bank. Given that there existed within HBOS a combination of internal controls and external regulations in this area, and armies of professionals to oversee and monitor, it would be very revealing to understand why the controls failed so extensively. There have been a large number of books and articles about the causes of the crash – an industry of 'concern' has been unleashed. Very few scholars were able to predict the timing, depth and severity of the crash, despite economics and finance being a huge academic industry. In terms of risk, finance scholars have been primarily focused on mathematical tools of measurement and management, whose aim is to help measure and profit from risk-taking (see e.g. Roggi and Altman 2013; Hull 2012). The field is full of jargon and technical complexity, with studies showing that this very complexity has generated significant and unforeseeable systemic risks which regulators and management often fail to understand (Shah 1996g, 1996f).

Recent research is showing serious cracks in the very 'technology' of risk management. Power (2009) shows how the burgeoning of 'enterprise risk management' has fundamental intellectual flaws in the definition and specification of risk, yet it has been a very influential method of providing the *appearance* of risk control and auditability. Studying the major scientific breakthrough of the Black-Scholes Option Pricing Model, and its extensive use in risk management, Millo and MacKenzie (2009) find that its success has been more to do with its acceptance and communicability and less with its accuracy and reliability. Similar evidence was found on the use of Capital Adequacy as a principal tool of global banking regulation – it was used for its practicality rather than its effectiveness, with profound economic and political consequences (Shah (1996c, 1996f). It persisted as a regulatory tool in spite of serious problems with its effective measurement and interpretation. Mikes (2011) found evidence of different sub-cultures in banks – 'calculative' and 'holistic' with different approaches to risk management, and her research exposes the cultural and boundary tensions of risk management. Regulators, whose task it is to monitor the risk exposures of financial institutions and contain them if necessary, have a consistent record of failure. Both in the UK and the US, investigations of the crash have put significant blame on the regulators (Angelides et al. 2011; Tyrie et al. 2013c). Thus there is a wide gap in the literature in understanding the politics of financial risk.

Fundamentally, risk is a social, cultural and political construct, not a technical one (Douglas and Wildavsky 1982). In their taxonomy of risk, Douglas and Wildavsky (1982, p. 5) show that only in very specific circumstances is risk measurement a technical challenge – when knowledge about the future is certain and the consent about the most likely prospects complete. This calls into question a lot of the work in finance which is primarily calculative, and assumes knowledge certainty even where it is not there, as for example Das (2011) and Tett (2010) have shown. In reality, knowledge about the future is often uncertain and consent about the most desired prospects is contested – an area where there are no easy solutions. Finance theory is silent on the political character of risk, and through its emphasis on risk measurement and unrealistic assumptions, creates the illusion that all risks are measurable and therefore by apolitical coincidence, manageable. There is a subtle denial of the uncertainty of risk itself. Also there is a deliberate refusal to engage with the people dimension of risk management – somehow the measurements and models are seen as sufficient for the understanding and control of risk.

The theoretical work of Power (2005a; 2007) is particularly relevant to this study. He analyses the burgeoning industry of risk management, influenced by changes in the law and corporate governance, such that there is a tendency towards the 'risk management of everything', in spite of there being poor understanding and definition of risk. Often, Power sees risk management as a triumph of form over substance, with its measurability and auditability more important than its substantive understanding and management. Risk management can be a way of reducing or shifting blame, and managing reputation as opposed to containing core risks, Power argues. Changes in regulations are often driven by crises or scandals, an approach which deals with past experiences of known risks, rather than the future of new and unexpected risks. There has been an increasing shift by regulators towards delegating and 'internalising' risk regulation by asking firms to monitor and control their risk-taking. In his analysis of the burgeoning industry of 'Enterprise Risk Management' (Power 2009), he finds significant flaws in the knowledge base and dubs it the 'risk management of nothing.' Power exposes the fundamental political tension between 'risk appetite' and 'risk management', a tension which is completely ignored in the finance literature. The phrase 'risk appetite' itself suggests that risk is something that is palatable and controllable, even if it may not be fully understood, let alone managed. The industry appears to be driven by commercial motives and covers up weaknesses in its knowledge base and expertise. In the definition of 'Operational Risk', Power (2005a) exposes the political tensions of its measurement, management and regulation.

In a recent empirical study of risk culture in financial institutions, Power et al. (2013) subtly avoid the political issues by using a positivist interpretative methodology which does not challenge the evidence, concluding that organisations should become 'more aware' of the risk-return trade-offs! There is no identification of the conflicts which arise when these trade-offs are made in practice. This shows how difficult it is to gather evidence of the politics of risk management, even when one suspects it. The sad reality is that access to the detail of risk management practice and tensions is difficult to obtain, and if successful, given under conditions of anonymity (see e.g. Mikes 2011).

This chapter builds on and tests Power's extensive work empirically by revealing the politics, culture and psychology of risk management, in a significant corporate setting. Given the paucity of this type of research and analysis in the financial risk literature, the findings help us to understand the practical nuances of risk and the critical role of power and culture in determining which risks are measured and managed, which are ignored and which are manipulated and subverted. It uses subtle approaches to get the data and probe into the political conflicts to understand the realpolitik of financial risk management. Such an investigative method of getting at the nuances of risk is rarely used in the literature, but shown here to be very revealing. By focusing on a collapsed bank, some data and confidentiality problems are avoided and the political tensions exposed. In normal circumstances, it would be very hard to get evidence on the internal politics.

As we have already seen, HBOS's collapse has been explained by aggressive risk-taking by management, with very poor governance and regulatory failure. In 2012, the FSA (FSA 2012) issued a very serious and significant 'Final Notice' to the Bank of Scotland, which was a major source of the losses for HBOS. They had breached Principle 3 which states: 'A firm must take reasonable care to organise and control its affairs responsibly and effectively, with adequate risk management systems.' The treasury and parliamentary investigations have also been very revealing about the processes of risk monitoring, management and mitigation. This chapter also examines the independent risk governance architecture – non-executive directors, auditors and regulators – to analyse its methods and effectiveness. Finally, it examines the political and economic climate prevailing at that time and its influence on risk appetite and behaviour.

In their review of the collapse of HBOS, the Tyrie Parliamentary Committee interviewed key witnesses – Board members throughout the life of the Group, the FSA, the chief executives and also examined minutes and other confidential documentary evidence. They used special legal counsel to interrogate the witnesses, and employed high-quality bank analysts as staff to assess the evidence (Tyrie et al. 2013a, para 7). There were ten members of the Tyrie Committee, including Lord Lawson (former Chancellor of the Exchequer), the Archbishop of Canterbury and Lord Turnbull. It was a cross-party committee. This report and accompanying interviews were critical to this research.

As explained earlier, whistleblower Paul Moore was the Head of Group Regulatory Risk at HBOS, and warned of the problems of aggressive risk-taking, but was dismissed by the CEO in 2004, in spite of a significant track record of skill and professionalism. Evidence of his experience and key documents are studied extensively in this chapter, and they reveal the inner workings and tensions of risk management in practice. Moore cooperated fully with this research, as his evidence had been protected by parliamentary privilege. Such was the power of his testimony to the government that it led to the resignation of the deputy chairman of the Financial Services Authority (FSA) and even threatened to bring down Prime Minister Gordon Brown (Pagano 2009). The chief executive of HBOS, James Crosby, was appointed to the Board of the principal regulator, the FSA in early 2004, at a time when the bank was already in trouble with the regulators due to its aggressive growth strategy. Later, he was promoted to become its deputy chairman in 2007. We will see later that, rather paradoxically, the non-executive chairman of the Risk Committee admitted his illiteracy in the area of risk and also his lack of banking experience. In fact, the evidence showed that the Board was far too comfortable and rarely challenged the executive – even business strategy was never approved by the non-executive, and instead they were very quick to challenge the regulators and push them away. HBOS therefore provides us with rare insights into the culture and politics of risk management.

We now turn to examine in detail the practice of, and skills and resources for, risk management at HBOS.

Risk Management at HBOS

The bank's approach to risk management was the popular three lines of defence model: first at the level of each division, second at the level of Group oversight, and finally, by Internal Audit which sit above the Group risk functions (Moore 2012). There was constant tension between the divisions and the Group oversight – the divisions saw Group risk officers as evaluating their performance, when their aim was to monitor the adherence to Group policy. Moore explains:

> (This model) was at the absolute heart of the dysfunctionality of risk and compliance, checks and balances, and governance, for a whole range of reasons. Group Internal Audit, which sits at the apex of this process, did not have the skills and competence to check whether Group Regulatory Risk or Group Financial Risk were doing their jobs properly. They knew standard audit methodology – internal audit was narrowly defined in terms of accounting. They never had the content speciality in all the areas – their primary role was checking as opposed to understanding and effective assurance. They were never capable of saying is that the right policy or the right process for the critical risk – and they ignored culture entirely. So the third line of defence, Group Internal Audit, which was supposed to keep everyone safe, just didn't work as they did not have that expertise. The first line of defence were the risk management and compliance

officers in the operating divisions who had a reporting line to their local Chief Executives and a functional line to the specialists. This meant that they had split loyalties. The people who would be providing the proper leadership for the work they were doing was not being done by anyone who was competent inside the local divisions. It was at the Group level that the competence was based, but there was insufficient power to influence local risk management practices.

According to Moore, this model was common in most large banks at that time – but was not fit for purpose. And there was a lot of duplication of effort and resulting ineffectiveness in the management of risk. In their final report on the review of banking standards, Tyrie et al. (2013c) noted that the three lines of defence model was ineffective (para 143):

> … Responsibilities have been blurred, accountability diluted, and officers in risk, compliance and internal audit have lacked the status to challenge front-line staff effectively. Much of the system became a box-ticking exercise whereby processes were followed, but judgement was absent.

Appointed to HBOS from KPMG, where Moore was a highly successful partner in 2002, Moore set to work immediately, as Head of Risk for the Insurance and Investment division which was the second largest in HBOS. Moore observed:

> The Group Finance Director, was running Finance and also the Chief Risk Officer, the person I reported to. I think this is ridiculous – a direct conflict of interest as the same person is responsible for revenue as well as control. The Finance Director was subservient to the CEO – he was a lieutenant to deliver the numbers that his boss had asked him to – he did not challenge on strategy. Comments like we have a 'low risk appetite' were completely ludicrous, coming from the CRO. They were an oxymoron. You cannot have a growth strategy that outstrips the market in the way HBOS was growing without taking on higher risk. The market risk is the same for everyone. You don't need to be a mathematician to know this.

Risk and return are directly connected – high risk can bring high returns, but it can also create high losses if risks are badly managed. At HBOS, the CEO deliberately adopted a high-risk strategy. According to Moore, there was little Board debate or discussion about the link between the growth strategy and excessive risk-taking:

> There were a lot of words used and a lot of pieces of paper in which the Finance Director would write our 'risk appetite is low'. There was a veneer of the discussion of risk within the context of the business strategy – it was rarely a substantive discussion. It was obvious that the growth strategy was

not a low risk strategy – it was the focus on growth that led to the downfall.

... The long-term incentive packages for HBOS executives were all focussed on the share price and by how much more the total share-holder return beat the competition – they were not adjusted for risk. So in order to get their bonuses, they had to deliver the growth strategy they had promised. The reported performance exceeded the competition by a considerable margin. For three years in a row, the performance was 6% above the competition for each year, so the Executives got 200% of their conditional shares at the price when the bonus plan was set – a huge bonus.

From the above, we see that the executive were strongly motivated in the risk-taking by the bonus scheme, yet in the minutes and papers recorded that they had a 'low risk appetite'. The non-executive, whose responsibility it is to comment on strategy, did not appear to challenge this.

On the day-to-day politics of risk management, monitoring and assurance, Moore had this to say:

There are two levels of review and investigation – one is to find out where you are so you can do things and move on, without holding people to account, and the other is to hold people into account. We made it expli-citly clear at the beginning of every single interview that this was not an investigation for the purpose of holding people to account – it was simply to understand exactly where we were so we could move on. That didn't work as the culture was one of fear and blame, so the risk-takers ended up thinking that we were there to investigate and blame.

In 2003, the Financial Services Authority (FSA) were very concerned about the fast-paced growth of HBOS and conducted a full ARROW assessment – Advanced Risk Operating Framework. The prognosis was very bleak, with many areas seen as high or medium risk. So concerned were they that they raised the Group capital requirement by 1%, which is a very serious demand, and costly for the bank. Price Waterhouse Coopers (2004) were commissioned to do a detailed s.166 review of the competence of risk officers and the risk management system. So very early on in the history of HBOS, there was serious concern about risk raised by the regulator.

Overall, the PWC findings were mixed, with some positives and many areas for improvement – they emphasised the importance of challenge and 'teeth'. The wording and phraseology of this report appeared to be crafted not to displease the management who had paid for the review. For example, 'high level of engagement in risk management' by the Board says nothing about competence – which was later found to be very weak. However, the Board minute recorded that '... PWC were clearly satisfied that Risk Management within HBOS was effective and satisfactory' (Tyrie et al. 2013a).

After this report, Paul Moore was promoted to Group Head of Regulatory Risk by James Crosby, the Group CEO, to appease the FSA and show that HBOS took them seriously. Moore said:

> I was given this role because I had a very strong relationship with the regulator [of] the FSA due to my previous track record. At KPMG, I had led some of the biggest regulatory remedial projects in the retail sector. The primary areas of growth at HBOS at the time were retail and insurance and investment divisions. Corporate was not big at that time. I put together an operating plan for the Board and the Group Audit Committee which I called 'The Regulatory Challenge – A key strategic driver'. When I was appointed as Head of Group Regulatory Risk, the single most important thing I wanted to do was to conduct more rigorous oversight and assurance inside HBOS.

So here we have a diligent professional with high skills, standards and determination promoted because of his regulatory relationships and reputation. Unfortunately, Moore encountered many challenges within HBOS and did not get the support he needed to be effective. In an email to the Group Finance Director (and CRO), Moore wrote in June 2004:

> We have spoken at some length this morning ... about the current issues in dealing with Retail. We really do have to do something ... .and you may wish to lead this ... to change the whole tone of engagement. This is not a battle of wits but a joint attempt to do what is right for the organisation. ... Some behaviours are going to need to change, particularly the sentiment that constantly questions the competence and intentions of Group Regulatory Risk carrying out its formal accountabilities for oversight plus the ever present need to be able to prove beyond reasonable doubt as if we were operating in a formal judicial environment. The more we adopt this approach, the more adversarial it all becomes, the more emotional it becomes, the more personal it becomes and the worse the relationship becomes. It is a vicious circle which needs to be broken. We need you and Andy Hornby (Director of Retail Bank) to intervene here to create a watershed here so we can move on from the issues of the past.

Moore explained:

> ... The Group Finance Director to whom I reported failed constantly to provide adequate support when issues arose. He strongly reprimanded me for suggesting at a Group Audit Committee that a person with my role should be protected by having a direct reporting line to the non-executive in case they had to raise criticisms of the executive.

The detailed investigation by the PRA (2015a) devoted a whole chapter to risk management and governance, and the findings were very critical. Here are some examples:

A crucial weakness of HBOS's strategic approach was that it was developed and pursued in the absence of a clearly defined risk appetite statement for the Group as a whole and the ability to aggregate risks at Group level. … discussions about the firms strategy and risk appetite tended to focus on performance targets. (para 84)

… risk management was regarded as a constraint on the business rather than integral to it. … (para 86)

… Challenge from Group Internal Audit was limited, with some evidence that internal audit reports could be upgraded based on promises from the business to make improvements. The Audit Committee and the Corporate and International divisional Risk Control Committees did not provide effective challenge on issues that were brought to their attention … (para 88)

The ineffectiveness of HBOS's risk management framework was a consequence of a culture within the firm that prioritised growth aspirations over the consideration of risk. HBOS's weak risk culture was evident at all levels of the firm, with the Board-approved emphasis on growth setting the tone for the rest of the organisation. (para 91)

Much later, in October 2008, the PRA (2015a, para 764) uncovered another similar incident where the senior risk officers were silenced and ignored. This is the time when huge losses were being incurred, and decisions needed to be made about the level of provisioning. The suggestion made by the senior risk officers was that it should be between £1.7 and £3.6 billion. At an urgent meeting to discuss this on 5th October, the Head of Group Credit Risk was completely excluded from this meeting, and no minutes were taken. The decision was to take the lowest estimate of £1.7 billion losses. The cheating and cover-ups were happening in the height of the crisis, so the behaviour that Moore uncovered had got worse, it seems. In practice, it later turned out that even £3.6 billion was very conservative.

All the above independently echoes what Moore has said. There was no clear Group 'risk appetite', and risk performance was not consolidated – it seems even risk was divided and ruled by the Board. This is a truly shocking way to manage a banking institution. It is negligence at the highest level. The third and most important 'line of defence', internal audit, clearly was being manipulated or overshadowed by promises to make improvements. Risk discussions were performance-related, which shows how risk was subservient to targets about growth and profits. Inside the heart of the organisation, the drive was towards growth and profits at any cost, and the restraints which were set to control and monitor were failing miserably. As to setting an appropriate risk culture, something which Moore really tried to do, there was little attempt, as it directly conflicted with sales and growth targets. In such a large organisation, the Board deliberately undermined culture, a critical ingredient of success. The rhetoric in the annual reports, like most corporate reports, is that our people matter, and we place a lot of emphasis on managing and retaining talent. The reality often is that profits override people – corporates are primarily highly materialistic organisations.

Removing the Risk of Challenge

In November 2004, Moore was suddenly fired by James Crosby, the CEO. The CEO clearly stated that 'the decision was his and his alone' (Moore 2012). Moore was personally devastated by this and complained to the FSA and HBOS through his lawyers. The FSA were equally concerned, given that he was such a senior risk officer and one whom they respected highly and relied upon after the PWC s.166 review of people and systems. Also, in the rule book such dismissals should be seen as red alarms and had to be investigated. The Board requested KPMG to investigate this dismissal, who concluded that Moore's claims for being fired because he was 'too good at his job' were not justified (KPMG 2005). More on this will be discussed in the later section on KPMG.

Paul Moore was replaced by an internal candidate, who came from a sales background and had no prior experience of risk management. An 'independent' process was followed with head hunters, but she was seen as the best candidate for the job. KPMG endorsed this appointment in their investigation (KPMG 2005). She barely lasted a year in the job, and was replaced by another novice to risk management. Paragraph 64 of Tyrie et al. (2013a) notes:

> Successive Group Risk Directors were fatally weakened in carrying out their duties by their lack of expertise and experience in carrying out a risk function, by the fact that the centre of gravity lay with the divisions themselves rather than the group risk function, and by the knowledge that their hopes for career progression lay elsewhere in the bank. The degradation of the risk function was an important factor in explaining why the high risk activities of the Corporate, International and Treasury Divisions were not properly analysed or checked at the highest levels in the bank.

The CEO with the cooperation of the Board completely reduced the power and influence of the risk management function after dismissing Moore – presumably to eliminate any challenge from this direction. Through influence over key appointments, risk management forms and processes may be retained, but their substance can be undermined. In this case, the CEO was the chief risk-taker and decided wilfully to fire the risk manager, going above the finance director (who was the chief risk officer). The routine approach of the FSA to rely on the Big 4 accounting firms to conduct special investigations – in the above case we saw the use of PWC and KPMG – demonstrates, at the very least, poor regulatory strategy and enforcement, as the firms are not independent of big financial institutions and earn significant fees from them, directly or indirectly. The fact that this work is paid for by the 'regulatees' also compromises the contents significantly – similar to the conflict of interest between auditors and their real audit clients (shareholders) that is commonly exposed in the literature (see e.g. Sikka 2009).

PRA (2015a, section 4) records a decline in risk management functions and practice since Moore's departure. Six months after Moore left, another senior risk officer, Dr Angela Smith, departed, and she too raised serious concerns about HBOS's risk management. Risk governance, culture and resources were being deliberately undermined, Smith argued. Subsequent investigations by PWC of Group Internal Audit also exposed many weaknesses and deficiencies. So there were plenty of signals, but, somehow, there was little muscle to provide regulatory challenge and be very firm. This aspect is explored in detail in Chapter 5.

Many years after the HBOS collapse, in a detailed investigation of risk management at the Bank of Scotland (significant HBOS subsidiary), the FSA (FSA 2012) noted that there were serious deficiencies in the processes, systems, culture, leadership and governance of the bank. The targets set incentivised managers to increase their risk appetite and regard risk management as a constraint on the business rather than integral to it. There were failures at the Group level in conducting effective oversight and assurance over the risks undertaken by the Bank of Scotland. This evidence confirms Moore's thesis and his early warnings about systemic and cultural failures. A forensic analysis of Moore's whistleblowing claims by Dewing and Russell (2014) finds that both KPMG and the regulators were wrong in ignoring his appeals at that time. In fact, subsequent to the collapse, huge fines were imposed by the FCA on the retail sales culture and mis-selling at HBOS to the newly merged bank Lloyds. The aggressive culture had persisted even after the crash.

From the above, we can see that there were fundamental structural problems with risk management, conflicts of interest and cultural and political barriers. A new position was created to manage the 'regulatory risk' – which really would not arise if risk is managed properly in the first place. The internal description of 'low risk appetite' was simply untrue. Management saw risk systems and processes as being necessary to appease the regulators, but a nuisance to their growth and expansion ambitions. This is in line with Power's cynicism about the real motives and agendas for risk management. Process and form were more important than substance, and if lies could be recorded to cover up the truth and show a 'low risk appetite', or manage the 'regulatory risk', this was done without any expressed leadership concern.

Regulators are not the only people overseeing the banks. In the next section, we examine the effectiveness of independent risk monitoring – the governance, audit and regulatory framework and the market. We examine their role in the case of HBOS in the next section.

Independent Risk Monitoring – Non-executive Directors, the FSA, Auditors and Financial Markets

Non-executive Directors

One of the last and most critical lines of defence in a company where the executives abuse their power is the non-executives. Tyrie et al. (2013a) spent considerable effort grilling them, especially the chairman, Lord Stevenson, who was in this position throughout the life of HBOS. As we have already seen, their challenge of business strategy and risk was negligible. Here are some observations from the PRA (2015a) report:

> As is still common for banks, certain key group functions were not represented on the Board by a dedicated director. In particular, Risk was represented by the Group CEO ...
>
> There were also deep flaws in the way the Board was structured and oversight was done. The structure was federated with the result that there were only two people who had complete oversight of the Group – the CEO and the Group Finance Director. (para 804, 806)
>
> While the role of Chairman was part-time and non-executive, the Annual Reports and Accounts during the Review Period made it clear that he was *'not independent'* and *'played an active role in influencing the strategic direction of the Group and ensuring overall performance delivery'* [emphasis added]. On this basis, the Chairman participated in the firm's long-term performance related incentive plan as well as receiving a base fee. This was different to chairmen at most other UK banks and may have contributed to the Chairman becoming too closely aligned to the Executive. (para 810)

From the above a pattern emerges of structural mismanagement right at the top, and a deliberate undermining of the importance of risk management and prudence at the highest level of the organisation. The fact that the chairman's incentives were aligned with growth is highly unusual and directly conflicts with his independence – and this was known and allowed by the auditors and regulators. It also means that the chairman was not too concerned about risk if profits were at stake. This echoes the interview evidence from Lord Stevenson unearthed in both the Tyrie and PRA reports.

It is common practice in Britain that the CEO has a key influence on Board appointments (Shah 2012). In spite of several corporate governance reviews, this has not changed, and there is no real independence. This also makes management biased and reduces genuine independence and governance. In terms of culture, we noted earlier that the NEDs were very comfortable with one another – again, not a positive signal given that their primary job is to challenge.

Moore was asked about the Board Risk Committee:

> The Chairman of Retail Risk Committee confided in me that he was in the wrong job. He did say to me I am not entirely sure how to be the Chairman of the Risk Committee – he had no technical knowledge, nor did he have a personality which would challenge. I am astonished as to why he was given this role. Another NED member confided in me that this appointment was totally wrong.

There has been evidence of personal disciplinary actions by the FSA in the past against approved persons (Dewing and Russell 2008). So in pursuing his concerns, Moore was also fulfilling his legal duty and protecting himself against prosecution for professional incompetence.

The extensive parliamentary investigation of banking noted (McFall et al. 2009a, para 158):

> We believe that the scale of the current banking crisis stands as testament to the fact that risk has not been well managed by the boards of banks across the globe. It is vital that non-executive directors in particular exercise more effective oversight and resist the urge to ally themselves too closely with the managers they are charged with scrutinizing. We believe that within banks, the risk management function should report directly to the non-executive members of the board.

We now look at the regulatory work of the FSA in relation to HBOS.

The Financial Services Authority

The FSA had a primary responsibility for the supervision of large financial institutions. It was a body set up by the Financial Services and Markets Act 2000 and accountable to government. It was the 'New Labour' government who created it, with a primary motive to protect the individual savers and investors. For the first time, financial regulation in Britain became state controlled, and gave the FSA powers of discipline and enforcement. Funding for the work of the FSA came from the financial institutions it supervised, and Board appointments were approved by government. In the case of HBOS, the FSA did some good work at the early stages, identified many critical areas, but, somehow, this level of focus and scrutiny slowed down after 2004. This is puzzling. The Tyrie investigation revealed that they had a team of about five to six people supervising HBOS. The liaison with a senior member of the HBOS management was done by a relatively junior member of the FSA.

Banks must have a culture of respect for regulators, as their very licence and existence depends on good regulation and governance. However, what we find is that the leaders from the outset seemed to have a disdain for regulators. When in early 2004 concerns were raised by the FSA about risk management, controls and fast-paced growth, the Board minutes recorded (Tyrie et al. 2013a, B Ev 283):

> ...It was essential, however, that the Group's responses to the FSA continue to be measured and robust. ... the conclusions drawn by the FSA would be disputed strenuously.

Regulation was seen as something to be relationship managed and pushed back. There was also evidence in the Hornby interview (Tyrie et al. 2013a) where he explained how Crosby 'went ballistic and raised the broader point that if the FSA were to be continually concerned about volume, they should understand the products better.'

Tyrie et al. (2013a) summarised the work of the FSA as follows (para 83):

> The picture that emerges is that the FSA's regulation of HBOS was thoroughly inadequate. In the three years following the merger the FSA identified some of the issues that would eventually contribute to the Group's downfall, notably the risk that controls would fail to keep pace with aggressive growth and the Group's reliance on wholesale funding. The FSA failed to follow through on these concerns and was too easily satisfied that they had been resolved. The FSA took too much comfort from reports prepared by third parties whose interests were not aligned with those of the FSA.

During the period 2005 to 2007, after Moore's departure, when things at HBOS actually got much worse, the risk management focus had been on negotiating with the FSA to obtain a lower capital requirement, in order to reduce capital costs. Tyrie et al. (2013a, para 73) notes:

> A huge amount of regulatory time and attention, in relation to HBOS as with other banks, was devoted to the Basel II model approval process, whereby banks could apply for a waiver to be permitted to use their own internal models to calculate capital adequacy requirements.

FSA Director Michael Foot described Basel II as 'immensely complex and immensely resource demanding and a complete waste of time' (Tyrie et al. 2013a, para 75). In January 2004, James Crosby joined the Board of the FSA and later became deputy chairman (Fraser 2012). 'After 15th January 2004, all fines from the regulator mysteriously dry up and the regulator basically gives up any attempt to properly regulate HBOS' (Fraser 2012).

Moore explains it in this way:

> The FSA wanted to appoint a non-executive from Industry, and they decided to appoint James Crosby. That was clearly and totally wrong in my view. These key appointments should be subjected to proper political oversight and scrutiny – and not just made by the principal private secretary to the Chancellor of the Exchequer. It should be subject to the approval of the Treasury Select Committee.
>
> I told them everything when I was fired from HBOS. It is completely extraordinary that the regulator when faced with my allegations and the subsequent things that happened should back off. After the KPMG report on my dismissal was issued, they accepted it as read instead of calling to ask me what I thought about it. There has got to be an inference that because the HBOS CEO was on the Board one of two things happened – either he explicitly intervened to stop the FSA from investigating or his mere

presence on the Board put the FSA in a position which made it very difficult for the FSA to challenge HBOS and Crosby.

Moore further notes:

> The operational regulators at the FSA were very good – they got it, and made the warnings. There must have been some corruption among the senior leadership for them not to pursue my warnings – Crosby was on the Board of the FSA at that time. I think regulators want a quiet life – they couldn't face challenging Crosby about his growth strategy. There is very specific guidance in the FSA rules about people who mistreat 'whistle-blowers' who have raised legitimate concerns about protected disclosures. It would call into question the threshold authorised conditions for HBOS itself and the approved persons status of the individual who fired the whistleblower. When KPMG issued a report saying basically that I was wrong and it is OK for them to employ a sales manager as Group Risk Director, the FSA may have thought – Oh great, we can blame KPMG now if anything goes wrong.

So we see powerful people using their status and influence, not only to remove any internal critique of their risk-taking and business strategy, but also to diminish the influence of auditors and external regulators. This was the breadth and depth of the power and influence of one man – the founding CEO of HBOS. It was he who brought in the chairman, and the future CEO, the three key people who were responsible for the collapse of HBOS (Tyrie et al. 2013a). In fact, it is puzzling that he was appointed to the FSA Board in the first place because the FSA had already identified serious weakness in risk management at HBOS. Given that the FSA was entirely funded by the industry it regulates, scope for influence by industry always existed (Shaw 2012). Even after the crash, the newly reformed Financial Conduct Authority is funded by industry. This secrecy and concentration of power in the City of London has been prevalent for a long time, with very real implications for the conduct of finance and the levels of risk undertaken (Shaxson 2012). And politically, Britain has latterly been very keen to encourage the global dominance of the City and work with its bankers to appease and gain influence (Moran 1991).

When the FSA gave evidence to the Treasury Select Committee in 2009, they admitted that as a matter of principle, they did not question whether banks had appropriate strategies (McFall et al. 2009b). They adhered to the free-market ideology that banks behave rationally – their only role was to make sure that the people, structures, systems and processes of the FSA were sound. It wasn't proper for them to challenge banks about whether they were growing too fast, or borrowing too much. This directly contradicts what they did in the case of HBOS – they questioned the strategy as early as 2003. The CEO of the FSA admitted that their Approved Persons regime was primarily focused on checking whether applicants had criminal records – and not on their experience and capability. Lord Turner (FSA Chairman, post-2007 crash) also admitted that neither the FSA nor the Bank of England had legal responsibility for maintaining the stability and solvency of the financial system (McFall et al. 2009b). Thus regulatory weakness, incompetence and capture encouraged risk-taking by financial institutions at the expense of a safe society and stable economy.

In the next section, we focus on the work of KPMG in relation to HBOS.

KPMG – The Auditors and Advisors of HBOS

According to British Company Law, the auditors are responsible for ensuring that the annual financial statements give a 'true and fair view'. KPMG, the HBOS auditors from 2001 to 2008, did not qualify any of the audits, in spite of the significant risk-taking, management incompetence and loan losses. Given that KPMG are a very 'prestigious' and well-known global firm, with skills and competence in risk management, as they have teams which advise clients about it (Moore used to lead some of them), this weakness in audit quality seems questionable. The KPMG name on an audit report gives credibility to the contents and subtly endorses the conduct of management. Fraser (2012) notes:

> For its pains KPMG, whose audit partner on HBOS was Guy Bainbridge, received £55.8m in audit fees and £45.1m in non-audit fees from HBOS. The other fees included consultancy work, tax advisory, advising on the abortive acquisition of Abbey National in 2004 and handling corporate insolvencies of bankrupt HBOS clients. There was massive scope for conflicts of interest in these assignments.

To date, six years after the event, there has been no independent investigation into the quality of the HBOS audit by the Financial Reporting Council, nor has there been any sanctioning of audit partners by their profession. Fines and law suits against KPMG and its lack of independence and weak auditing have quite a history (Fraser 2009). More recently, questions are being raised about the KPMG audits of 'The Co-op Bank', a major UK bank in serious financial difficulty (Sunderland 2013). An FRC investigation into the audit of Co-op Bank by KPMG has now been launched (Financial Reporting Council 2014).

Tyrie et al. (2013a), in spite of calling many executives in front of the Parliamentary Committee, did not interrogate the HBOS auditors. Even after the collapse of HBOS, the senior partner in charge of the HBOS audit is still a partner at KPMG. Moore, himself a former KPMG senior partner, explains:

> The auditors knew things were really wrong at HBOS. They knew that this business is a serious risk to the financial system. They had access to so many private conversations, they knew exactly what I was saying, but their goals are plainly commercial. In my view, the audits were deeply flawed. The loan losses from 2008 were astronomical, and the auditors never noticed how seriously bad the loan credits were.

After Moore was fired by the chief executive, he raised a complaint for unfair dismissal and whistleblowing through his lawyers with both HBOS and the FSA (Hamilton 2004). The Board did a very unusual thing – they asked KPMG, the HBOS auditors, to investigate this, and what is even more surprising is that KPMG accepted, in spite of the fact that Moore was a previous senior employee of theirs. The FSA were aware of this and chose to rely on the KPMG report, even though the selection of KPMG was not done independently of HBOS. HBOS paid KPMG for the report. In their report, KPMG (2005) basically said that there was no damage to the method and operation of risk management in HBOS and 'on the basis of the work we have done we believe that the quality of Mr. Moore's relationships with the key stakeholders ... was a key factor in him being asked to leave the group ... we have seen no evidence to suggest that Mr. Moore's redundancy was in response to him performing his job too well' (para 6.7).

From the above, it was KPMG (commissioned by the HBOS Audit Committee chair, Tony Hobson) who agreed to do an investigation on behalf of HBOS as to whether or not it was right for them to make Paul Moore redundant, and whether or not his whistleblowing claims were legitimate. When we examine the Board minutes closely, we can see that Moore had problems because he was challenging divisional directors and other senior risk-takers – and that was his job, so if relationships were damaged by this, he should have been supported by the CEO and not penalised. The Tyrie investigation picked up on this and repeatedly asked Crosby and Stevenson to clarify but did not get straight answers. KPMG also endorsed the appointment of the new Group risk director, even though she had no prior experience of risk management and came from a sales background. Moore explains:

> When I finally did talk after the collapse of HBOS, I was protected by parliamentary privilege ... . The vast majority of people at HBOS if they were able to speak up, would have been on my side. One NED said that the decision to fire me was unconscionable. By firing me, the CEO had proved that anyone who spoke up would be removed, so everyone kept quiet.

Not only did the auditors witness all that, but they sanctioned it through their report on the dismissal of Paul Moore which is now a public document due to the Parliamentary investigation (KPMG 2005). In his carefully worded written testimony to the Parliamentary Commission (Bainbridge 2012), the KPMG senior partner in charge of the audit admitted that no serious concerns had been raised about the adequacy of the systems and controls at HBOS, in relation to the two core problem areas, retail mortgages and commercial banking. He was also asked about Board competence and admitted that this was never evaluated by KPMG. Bainbridge admitted that in the five years he had been the lead audit partner at KPMG, not once had he met the full Board of HBOS. This is most surprising given the fact that the Board is primarily responsible for the preparation of the accounts on which the audit is performed. Also, between

September 2001 and February 2008, only two meetings had been held with the FSA on the subject of HBOS Group.

The Financial Reporting Council is the independent watchdog legally tasked with monitoring the quality and content of financial reporting, and conducting any investigations on the auditors. Since 2008, they have been promising to investigate KPMG, but, even in 2014, no such report has been issued or fine has been charged. Finally, after much lobbying, they agreed to do a very limited investigation in 2016 – see Chapter 5. Evidence showed that seven senior members of the watchdog were current or former employees of KPMG (Salmon 2013). Thus Big 4 audit firms are hugely influential in their own right, due to their size and alumni links. Chapter 4 is devoted to the detailed examination of the audit failure and its politics.

The next section examines the market failure in monitoring the fundamental risks of HBOS.

The Market Monitoring of Risk

The finance literature assumes that markets are efficient at processing information and effective at self-regulating any bad behaviour or misleading information (Das 2011).

Tyrie et al. (2013a, para 126) reported:

> Many of the principal causes of the HBOS failure and the weaknesses in its business model were known to financial markets. Public disclosures by the Group showed the pace of asset growth, key distinctive features of the Corporate Division's assets (including the exposures to commercial real estate, leveraged finance and equity and joint ventures), the pace of the International Divisions growth and its concentration in commercial real estate, and the overall Group reliance on wholesale funding. Nevertheless, the financial markets as a whole, including shareholders, debt-holders, analysts and rating agencies, also failed to discipline the company's growth until it was too late. When they did, the Group had become a serious threat to financial stability.

In spite of disclosures about the exposures and risks of HBOS, there was no penalty from the market – implying that either the risks were not understood, or they were simply ignored. This flies in the face of the efficient markets hypothesis. A herd mentality seemed to prevail – rather than a rational approach to investment appraisal. Tyrie et al. (2013a) even argued that the size of HBOS and its influence was such that through its vast investment in retail mortgage finance, it fuelled the UK property bubble and increased risk for the UK economy. One can argue that there was both a market failure and an intellectual capture of risk – something which may pervade to this day. Somehow, experts managed to persuade everyone that risks were contained and efficiently dealt with by the all-knowing market. Credit-rating agencies are paid by the issuer of the credit, so there were significant conflicts of interest in the favourable ratings they gave to complex securities, which turned out to be grossly inaccurate (McFall et al. 2009a).

This 'intellectual capture' of risk management is serious. When risks are not acknowledged and professionally endorsed, in spite of being known to be real and in existence, society has little hope of mitigation. The ignorance of the politics of risk management in the finance literature could also be a critical element of its intellectual capture by powerful interests. Rajan (2005), a director of research at the IMF, warned about the increased risks of financialisation, but these warnings were ignored and dismissed by powerful members in the audience (Ferguson 2010). Rajan demonstrated that derivatives, instead of reducing risk, were actually increasing risk in the markets and institutions.

The above evidence shows a regulatory failure and market failure in the monitoring and penalising of excessive risk-taking. Power's thesis of the capture of risk definition and the practical challenges of effective management can be extended to the potential for market and regulatory capture of the risk process by 'too big to fail' and 'too powerful to challenge' financial institutions. Market fundamentalism also contributed to the failure of risk monitoring and timely market penalty, in spite of the fact that risks at HBOS were revealed in the accounts and not complex to interpret or foresee. In the next section, we examine the substance of risk measurement and management as compared to its form. The finance literature focuses exclusively on technical measurement, by using historic models and making unrealistic assumptions about probabilities and the absence of systemic correlations (McSweeney 2009).

The Politics of Risk Judgement and Response

In the context of the Banking Crash and HBOS, Tyrie et al. (2013a, para 123) noted:

> Poor asset quality was the direct result of the company's strategy, which pursued asset growth in higher risk areas. This asset growth was compounded by a risky funding strategy. The combination of higher risk assets and risky funding represents a fundamentally flawed business model and a colossal failure of senior management and of the Board.

From the evidence presented so far, we can see that there was emphasis on implementing risk management processes and monitoring systems, with the primary aim of keeping regulators off HBOS's back – managing the 'regulatory risk'. Somehow, the substantive fact that the quality and quantity of risks, the people and culture were dangerous and unconstrained seemed to have escaped the Board, auditors, markets and the regulators. Process and appeasement were more important than substance, although, in actual fact, both process and culture were flawed. Measurement and audit relationships were more important than management and containment of risk. Also the technical complexity of measuring and managing the overall and systemic risk of HBOS was not given due importance. In fact, there was no evidence from the Tyrie investigation which revealed any concern whatsoever by the Board over the systemic consequences of their actions – HBOS appears to have acted very selfishly. The Board actively adopted a strategy of 'managing the regulators' rather than substantively managing the business and operational risk – probably due to the bonus targets and incentives of executives. The creation of Group Regulatory Risk was designed to appease the FSA and hopefully keep them off HBOS's back. This strikes at the heart of the politics and economics of risk management in banking, yet is also an issue which is all too often buried under the carpet.

As we saw earlier, one issue which took a lot of time of HBOS risk officers and senior management after 2004 was complying with Basel II – the new capital adequacy regulation regime, which was admitted to be a total time-waster by one of the FSA's directors, Michael Foot (Tyrie et al. 2013a). It is possible that given the huge power and influence of large and systemically important banks, the regulators deliberately used form to hide from substance, as dealing with the significant risk-taking was proving challenging, uncomfortable and unsuccessful.

Tyrie et al. (2013a) interviewed key directors of the FSA responsible for supervising HBOS. Michael Foot said in his testimony:

> Many risk officers I have come across, not just in the UK, are or have been until recently, quite junior people. It has been very difficult to find a significant number of people who have the right kind of CV, because you are asking people to have expertise in operational risk, credit risk, market risk and macro-economics.

So here we have a senior regulator from the FSA publicly admitting that the quality of risk officers is generally weak. This is true even where this is such a critical role and reliance placed on them by the regulators and their legal framework – this implies that the FSA were approving risk officers whom they believed were incompetent, simply because the banks wanted and needed them. The industry was ruling the regulator! Foot also goes on to admit the internal tensions and politics of risk management – so the regulators were fully aware of this, yet naïve, too, as they failed to take remedial action. Tyrie et al. (2013a, para 85) notes:

> Too much supervision was undertaken at too low a level – without sufficient engagement of the senior leadership within the FSA. The regulatory approach encouraged a focus on box-ticking which detracted from consideration of the fundamental issues with the potential to bring the bank down.

The evidence suggests that the FSA, even though they had a combination of principles and rules-based regulation, did not engage in a sustained way with substantive issues like aggressive management and poor risk monitoring.

Where judgement is involved, relative power and confidence becomes very relevant. Whose judgement is the right one? Who wins and loses from the risk-taking decisions? What are the personal and institutional consequences of challenge? Could it be that the FSA were highly politicised in their behaviour and influenced (captured?) by the banking industry, but spoke in the technical language of rules and regulations to justify their actions, and be seen to be doing something – was form used as a defence of substance?

Moore explained what happened inside HBOS:

> There is a big difference between risk measurement and risk management. ... I felt that Group Financial Risk sat in their ivory towers with marvellous risk calculations and policies and threw them over the fence to the operating divisions and expected them to apply them and get on with them, without actually making sure that this was done. I cannot believe that any properly designed system can deliver the level of loss that actually came to prevail at HBOS. Either the policies were badly designed or changed – the Group Head of Financial Risk was also dismissed in 2005, and they completely dismantled the credit risk measurement system, or the Corporate Division just ignored them or arbitraged them. The Chief Executive of the Corporate Division was also the Chairman of the Credit Risk Committee within Corporate – a clear conflict of interest. ... It is also true that there are many risk managers and advisors in the financial sector who think that their primary job is regulatory arbitrage – to help their firms avoid the regulations. There is often no culture of respect for regulation.

From the above we see that anyone who tries to engage with the fundamental substance of risk – be it internal risk officers or the regulators – can hit the powerful politics and influence of the industry leaders, government and risk-takers. Where judgement is involved, politics not substance determines the outcome. The regulators did not have the muscle to challenge the status quo, and were captured both by the banks and the government. When forced to take a decision about the firing of Moore, they chose to pass the buck onto KPMG and protect their own skin, instead of dealing with the seriousness of the problem and the real source of the risk mismanagement (the HBOS leadership). Surprisingly, KPMG complied with this, despite the obvious potential risks of doing so. Fundamentally, banking is a money-manufacturing industry and through its power and influence is able to borrow huge sums of money at very low interest rates, adding to the vast financial resources available to the executive. It is therefore required to be managed very prudently. This is a critical reason why regulation is so important, but also one where regulation can be easily managed, exploited and undermined – by the very power given to the banks by the licensing authorities. It is possible, as Miller et al. (2008) have suggested, that the hybrid and subtle collusion of the FSA, KPMG, HBOS, FRC and credit-rating agencies operated in a 'comfortable and comforting' way. We will see in the next section when we look at the political environment around risk and regulation in London at that time that the Labour government fell over backwards to praise and please the bankers, before the 2008 crash. In the next section, we examine the macro-politics prevailing in Britain at that time, and how HBOS's power and influence was obtained and sustained.

Risk Ignorance and Denial – British Political Climate and the Financial Sector: 2001–8

The state is the de facto risk manager and guarantor of the financial system. In the case of HBOS, the evidence is clear that it failed in this task. Why did it fail? Was it because, as above, it was afraid to challenge the status quo? Or was it because, like the Board of HBOS, it was busy enjoying the 'returns' of a risky strategy – through higher taxes and an economic bubble – and got carried away by the hubris? Was the government captured by the finance industry? We investigate these questions in this section.

The Labour Party led by Tony Blair was in power throughout this period, and Gordon Brown was the Chancellor of the Exchequer, becoming Prime Minister in 2007. This was a time of economic boom – in fact, Gordon Brown famously declared it the 'end of boom and bust' (Shaw 2012). He also congratulated the bankers for their huge contribution to the economy in a now infamous speech at Mansion House (Brown 2006). There was a rising property market and a global boom in finance, with declining interest rates. Whilst the US was dishing out generous mortgages to those who could not afford to pay, the British financial sector was busy mis-selling a range of products, including Personal Protection Insurance and loans to small businesses (HBOS has been subsequently fined heavily for this mis-selling). Fraud and corruption was rampant in this sector but tucked away and hidden – or known, but not addressed. After the crash in 2008, the bubble burst and the truth started to come out – and is still coming out. The extent of scandals in London has been significant, with the rigging of LIBOR, foreign exchange rates and other key indices in markets like energy, the mis-selling of insurance products and loans both to small businesses and retail customers, and insider trading.

During that period, the general ideology of 'light-touch regulation' prevailed both in North America and in the UK. There was a belief that free markets would somehow be self-regulating and did not need any strong state intervention or oversight. In terms of financial innovation and securitisation, there was a feeling that, if anything, these products distributed and reduced risk, thereby making institutions and the system more stable. Despite evidence of the complexities of financial instruments, and management weaknesses in understanding and monitoring them, London and the FSA allowed the significant growth and proprietary trading of derivatives by banks, without any serious restraint. In fact, when the Treasury Select Committee interrogated the Bank of England governor and the chairman of the FSA about which institution was legally responsible for ensuring the stability and security of the financial system, the answer was clear – neither (Treasury Committee 2009). So there was no

Chief Risk Officer or Risk Monitoring Institution acting on behalf of the government.

Interviewed about the reason why regulators did not act in time, the Bank of England governor, Sir Mervyn King, replied (McFall et al. 2009a):

> The people in the banks would have said, 'Well, who are you to say we are taking too big risks? We have got far brighter and more qualified risk assessors than you have got. We have made massive profits every year for almost ten years. We have paid big bonuses. The City is the most successful part of the UK economy. How dare you tell us that we should stop taking such risks? Can you prove to us that the risks we are taking will necessarily end in tears?' and of course [the FSA] could not ... Any bank that had been threatened by a regulator because it was taking excessive risks would have had PR machines out in full force, Westminster and the Government would have been lobbied, it would have been a pretty lonely job being a regulator.

From the above, we can see that significant political pressure was applied by the banks in those heady days. Not only Paul Moore operating inside one organisation, but even the regulator, whose task it was to externally monitor and supervise, seemed toothless against the avalanche of risk and power.

In his famous Mansion House speech of 2006 (Brown 2006), where the audience was packed with the great and good of the City of London, Brown heartily congratulated the bankers for their contribution to economic growth, and their ingenuity and innovation. He spoke with great pride, excitement, arrogance even, as if Labour had conquered the root problems of the economy with the help of business. The general philosophy he espoused was that Britain is a change agent and world catalyst for globalisation, with the City of London at its epicentre. There was no mention of any financial concern or insecurity, in spite of the Asian crash, nor about the localisation of global risk through this strategy. The speech assumed the ideology of rational self-correcting financial markets. It also went completely against the traditional roots of labour – the defence of the working class.

Gordon Brown boasted about the huge growth and importance of London as a Global Financial Centre (Brown 2006). By inviting the world to London, and to build its financial businesses here, there was a strong desire to boost the UK economy and revive the story of Great Britain as a global superpower that it once was. For Brown, the City showed that the UK was embracing globalisation with open arms, and not fearful of or resistant to it. He wholeheartedly endorsed liberalisation, deregulation and free trade:

> (We want) stability through a stable and competitive tax regime, and stability through a predictable and light touch regulatory environment.
>   ... no advanced industrial economy facing global competition can either shelter their old industries or services, nor can they neglect the big, serious

and long term challenges that arise from this new phase of globalisation: The challenge of resisting all forms of protectionism and instead breaking down the barriers to an open trading global economy ...

There was little foresight about the impending crash, or the potential for significantly increasing the risk of the financial system by globalising it. Hutton (2010) is very critical of the ignorance of all the signs of an asset bubble and an impending financial crash by Brown's government.

As the City of London was such a huge contributor to the UK economy, in order to compete globally to attract financial institutions, its regulatory environment was a critical factor which was leveraged to attract global financial institutions (Moran 1991). Globalisation has increased competition among states and regulatory agencies, with many predicting a race to the bottom. Britain's historic role in financial institutions and management has made it attractive to firms from all over the world, and Labour was keen to build on this. The general culture of regulation in the UK had been based on the philosophy of self-regulation, with the City having a direct influence on its rules and policing. Soon after the Labour Party was elected, it announced in 1997 the creation of an independent Bank of England and a state-run Financial Services Authority (Shaw 2012). This was a major step in taking regulation out of the hands of the City, but the experience has shown that the influence of the private sector in the administration and enforcement of the Financial Services and Markets Act 2000 did not wane. The remit of the Act stipulated that it had to consider the international mobility of financial businesses and avoid damaging the UK's competitiveness. The funding of the Financial Services Authority was entirely from the private sector – thereby increasing the potential for 'regulatory capture'.

Labour had made a Faustian Pact with the City (Shaw 2012): their policy of light-touch financial regulation both rested on and reflected its commitment to a financial growth model inherited from the Conservatives. The reasons for the adoption of light-touch regulation were as much ideological as structural and institutional (Way 2005). Shaw (2012) notes:

> In June 2005, after a speech in which the Prime Minister had expressed concern about the inhibiting effects of excessive regulation, the FSA Chairman was happy to reassure him 'that the FSA applied to the supervision of its largest banks only a fraction of the resource applied by US regulators ...'

Given the huge economic and political power of the City, confronting it would have been a risky political enterprise for Labour, as its tentacles and reach were formidable.

As Gordon Brown was both the Chancellor of the Exchequer (until 2007) and then Prime Minister throughout the short life of HBOS, we can safely say that the state had the same 'Chief Risk Officer' for its financial sector. Just like HBOS, he was both finance director and CRO – a clear conflict of interest.

And even more specifically in the context of this study, he was a close personal friend of the founding HBOS CEO and cultural architect, James Crosby – who was knighted for his services to the banking industry in 2006 (Pagano 2009). This was a further conflict of interest for Brown.

The Conservative-Liberal Coalition government took power from Labour in 2010. Previously, when the Conservatives were in power in the 1980s, the focus was on self-regulation. After the crash, two new institutions have been created to regulate the City and replace the FSA – the Financial Conduct Authority and the Prudential Regulatory Authority. The first chairman of the Financial Conduct Authority is Sir John Griffith-Jones, an old Etonian (the prestigious upper-class public school from where the current Prime Minister and Chancellor come) and former head of KPMG. Sir Griffith-Jones was head of KPMG when it audited HBOS, Bradford & Bingley and Singer & Friedlander, all of which were rescued by the taxpayer (Aldrick 2013). This shows how serious the UK government is about independent regulation of the City. There have since been many calls for the resignation of Sir Griffith-Jones (Sunderland 2013).

Sir Mervyn King, the governor of the Bank of England, explained (Tyrie et al. 2013b, para 19):

> Certainly (bank executives) have easier access to the people at the very top than the regulators have. I remember before 2007 that the only time there was a speech about regulation from the Prime Minister was when there was an attack on the FSA for over-bureaucratic regulation. That was the climate in which regulators operated then. It was extraordinarily difficult. They knew that if they were tough on a bank, the chief executive would go straight to No. 10 or No. 11 and say this was an attack on the UK's most successful industry – even when it was a perfectly reasonable application of the regulations. The climate has clearly changed since then, but the access probably has not.

For the state to effectively manage financial system risk, it needs to recognise it, understand it, measure and monitor it and have pro-active risk management and assurance policies and practices. It would also need a capable, respectable and influential Chief Risk Officer, qualities which are not easy to find, especially when the industry it is trying to regulate is so huge and so powerful. McFall et al. (2009a, para 114) noted:

> … Where responsibility lies for strategic decisions and executive action was, and remains, a muddle. The Treasury's design of the institutional framework for financial stability must bear in mind that, when the dust eventually settles on a new system, the question that we, and others, will ask is 'Who gets fired?' if and when the next crisis occurs.

From the above, it appears that systemic risk was never a serious concern for government, and the institution created to monitor the City, the FSA, was, if anything, a micro-risk manager rather than a macro one. It was also subject to political and corporate influence and interference. There were significant warnings about the inherent instability of the global financial markets by Keynesian writers of the time, and even George Soros warned of the dangers, but the Labour government was unwilling to challenge or take action (Shaw 2012). Perhaps Labour feared that it would be 'fired' by the City. In the case of HBOS, Moore acted out of conscience, but no such conscience or whistle-blower existed in the British government. In fact, Lee (2009) demonstrates that Brown's overall leadership as Prime Minister was very weak and ineffective. There is fundamental personal insecurity among political leaders to challenge the power and might of financial markets and institutions (Way 2005). Though Moore was prepared to lose his job through his conscience, UK political leaders were not. It is people, not institutions, who can have a conscience – for some reason, no powerful person spoke loud enough about the systemic risk of the City of London.

Conclusion and Implications for Future Research

As Douglas and Wildavsky (1982) had predicted, this case study evidence shows that, fundamentally, financial risk is a social, cultural and political concept, not a technical one. The huge emphasis by the finance academy on the mathematical techniques of risk measurement, and by banking organisations on the structures and three-line defences of risk management, are at best misguided and at worst deliberately designed to disguise and deny the real risks, as Power has suggested. Banks seem to be institutionally motivated to minimise the fear of risk in order to maximise the opportunity for gain. The social and economic cost of bank risk-taking has been immense. This makes the political ignorance and naiveté of the finance literature very misleading and costly. The evidence echoes Power's cynicism about the growing industry of risk management.

Before risk can be measured and controlled, it needs to be understood and acknowledged. Systems and processes depend on people, incentives, governance, culture and politics. HBOS governors, including the chairman of the Risk Committee, 'did not get it', in spite of the fact that at HBOS the risks were not technically complex. The governors are the primary source of challenge to the executive, and have a legal responsibility to ensure that the business is being managed prudently (Financial Reporting Council 2014). They are the last line of defence in the chain of risk. Their appointment was influenced by the executive, and competence approved by the FSA. The HBOS chairman did play a significant role in challenging the regulator – not his executive. In fact, even after the collapse, he was still blaming market forces. Thus the non-executive directors colluded with the executive and enabled the aggressive and imprudent risk-taking. Even after the collapse of HBOS, none of the key responsible executives have suffered any fines or prison sentences (apart from one director). More generally, there was a significant failure of governance and the internal control and audit systems. As we have seen, the Board discussions and agenda were tightly controlled to avoid conflict, the chairman was incentivised to benefit from growth, and a few people colluded and undermined any challenge through changing Board processes and responsibilities. There was very little Group-level oversight of overall risk. When we know that there are flaws in finance theory in terms of risk measurement, financial institutions are always on a risk tightrope, especially where the business and transactions are complex and inter-dependent.

When we look closely at the specific risks mismanaged by HBOS, we find that credit risk was incorrectly measured and not managed effectively; liquidity risk was highlighted, but little was done to remedy it; and systemic risk was ignored totally – it was not a worry for the bank that its collapse would have a ripple effect on the whole system. A major risk in HBOS was 'people risk' – incompetent people were in powerful positions and played a key role in the downfall of HBOS. Nowhere in the contemporary finance literature is there mention of 'people risk' or even 'ethical leadership', in spite of its critical importance. Given that the implementation of effective risk management depends on people, this risk should be given due importance in the academic literature. Once this is acknowledged, we can see how politics plays a key role in the financial risk management of institutions.

Power's (2007) work on the dilemmas of 'organising' risk and 'managing' it is relevant here. There was tension between the risk-takers and risk managers. This was resolved through power and authority, and not through rational dialogue and reconciliation. Risk management was ultimately a political matter, a nuisance to the growth ambitions of the CEO and the Prime Minister or Chancellor. Although measurement processes were maintained, their influence and authority were deliberately undermined. The culture and power of the HBOS management had an overriding influence on the organisational response to risk information. Firing a senior risk officer was an extreme act, but it was permitted and endorsed by a professional firm, the Board and the regulatory body. All the evidence here implies that risk management can be more ritual than real, especially when it conflicts with management profit targets and bonuses. Power foresaw this.

In his evidence to Parliament, Professor John Kay explained very accurately the banking culture and attitude to compliance officers and regulators (Tyrie et al. 2013a):

> If you go into financial institution after financial institution, you will see firstly that regulation is regarded unequivocally as a nuisance, and secondly, that regulation is largely entrusted to a department whose job it is to deal with regulation, and that department itself is regarded as a nuisance.

The HBOS evidence confirms this – the whole attitude to regulation was misguided and prejudicial, and the Board encouraged non-compliance.

The evidence above suggests that there was significant concentration and abuse of power among the leadership at HBOS. Tett (2010) finds evidence of a broader herd mentality among bank executives keen to report significant growth and profits in order to match competitors, and, in this madness, risk was ignored. People who objected or resisted were fired – Moore being a classic example, but not the only one. The regulators somehow missed the CEO domination, or colluded with it by not challenging it early enough. Politicians seemed to like and trust James Crosby and brought him into government – in April 2008, during the height of the financial crisis, he was asked by Prime Minister Gordon Brown to chair a working group to examine the UK's rapidly shrinking mortgage market (Fraser 2012). Politicians effectively supported and endorsed the growth and expansion of HBOS. More recently, evidence has emerged of the collusion of senior Labour party leaders with the failed Co-op Bank, spread over a large number of years, with the bank giving significant loans and funding to the party (Tweedie 2013). As in the case of HBOS, an incompetent chairman at Co-op Bank, Reverend Paul Flowers, was in position over many years. This case study exposes collusion between the independent FSA, government and Big 4 firms in the interpretation and enforcement of regulation – lending support to the hybrid theory propounded by Miller et al. (2008).

Key evidence for this study came from a whistleblower, someone who was not afraid to challenge, in spite of adverse personal consequences. It seems he was initially promoted by the CEO to appease the FSA, as it had raised concerns about risk management and had good respect for Moore – a 'political' motive. But when Moore challenged Group's strategy, he was seen by the CEO as a threat instead of an asset. Challenge is critical to effective risk management, both at the institutional level and at the state level. In this study we saw the huge personal cost of challenge – Moore lost his job and had great difficulty for many years in finding another job. Tett (2010) found similar evidence amongst other large international banks – those who warned about the risks were either ignored or fired. The finance literature is silent on the relevance and importance of the 'conscience' of the risk officer or manager. I had asked Moore whether he was politically naïve in accepting the role of Head of Group Regulatory Risk inside HBOS. He explained:

> Yes and No. When I was asked to do the top job as Head of Group Regulatory Risk, I knew it was a very tough and risky job. I went to the Chief Risk Officer and spent two and a half hours explaining what needed to be done and told him that I was bound to upset people in doing my job properly. ... He said of course that is what we want you to do Paul. My naiveté was that I believed him. My naiveté was that I believed the truth would always prevail, and that if there was evidence, I would be alright. ... I thought I was doing what needed to be done for HBOS. Why did the CEO not think that I would be risking my career for a fundamental reason?

Both politicians and the regulators have since admitted that they did not understand or anticipate the systemic risk of modern banking and finance. Even finance academics by and large failed in predicting the systemic crisis. But is that the real story? There have been many global experiences of systemic crises in recent history – the latest being the Asian crash of 1997–8. Why were these ignored? Why did they allow themselves to be persuaded by the flawed ideology of free and efficient markets? How could they have believed that derivatives and securitisation reduce risk, when in fact they multiplied it? Or is the real story that finance scholars too were enjoying the short-term fruits of risk-taking and blinded by the wealth and power, just like HBOS executives? The finance academy has been captured by its own ideology (McSweeney 2009). The award-winning film on the crash, *Inside Job* (Ferguson 2010), provides evidence of a number of influential academics, including world-renowned Harvard Economist Professor Larry Summers allegedly earning significant consultancy income from financial institutions. When in 2005 Professor Raghuram Rajan presented a paper (Rajan 2005) warning about the huge risks in bank portfolios to an eminent audience of global central bankers, it was Summers who dismissed it as being impossible. According to the film, the governor of the Bank of England, Sir Mervyn King, was in the audience in Washington during this research presentation. When eminent lawyer Brooksley Born, chair of the Commodities and Futures Trading Commission in Chicago, wanted to increase the regulation of derivatives, she was rebuffed and eventually resigned in 1999 (*Inside Job*). Hence even the state and the collective might of financial institutions have a way of silencing whistleblowers to serve their own interests. There was no official Chief Financial Risk Officer for the UK state, nor were the two key institutions, the FSA and the Bank of England, legally responsible for ensuring systemic stability. There was micro-regulation as opposed to macro-oversight, and this seemed politically convenient at the time.

Does 'too big to fail' mean 'too powerful to challenge' by auditors and regulators? The FSA had power and authority to challenge, and had gathered the evidence to do so, but when it came to critiquing the Board and the CEO, they shied away. This happened because they appear to have been 'captured' by the financial and political influence of one man – the HBOS CEO. It is possible that the FSA deliberately used KPMG as a scapegoat in defending its decision to fire Moore, as it could not face having to dismiss the CEO or put HBOS under special notice – acts which would have required the need to defend their judgement, have confidence in their authority and deal with the consequences of the judgement. This study shows that even when armed with the knowledge of adverse risk practices, regulators and auditors can be 'politically and economically captured' and prevented from acting decisively.

There is also a psychology of internal challenge – it requires courage, self-belief and a willingness to sacrifice power and position, even jobs and income. This needs to be analysed in the financial risk management literature – instead of being ignored. Cultural and gender difference can be a critical source of challenge, though there was little cultural diversity in the Boards of HBOS or the FSA. In fact, British Boards have generally been very weak in terms of cultural and gender diversity in spite of the unique diversity of the British population (Shah 2012). As Moore experienced, whistleblowing against a large firm is often a no-win proposition – they have all the power and resources to silence. In the UK, there is very little government protection for whistleblowers. More research needs to be done around the psychology of challenge, especially in the banking context where there is a huge imbalance of power and influence. Tyrie et al. (2013c) have recommended special protection and rights for whistleblowers in the future.

In the case of HBOS, a lot of the earlier regulatory challenges were done secretly – most documents were marked 'strictly confidential' – as information would be market sensitive. The extent to which such secrecy is important and its influence on the nature and extent of the challenge process needs to be studied. How does secrecy undermine power? Does it help banks gain political advantage without proper scrutiny and enforcement? Even where challenge is the duty and responsibility of regulatory bodies like the Financial Conduct Authority or the Prudential Regulatory Authority, it does depend on the ethics, quality and self-confidence of the leadership to mount an effective challenge. Having legal powers is simply not enough, as we saw in the case of the FSA. Does this market sensitivity of regulatory challenge make it easier for large banks to take risks and get away with them? This needs to be studied further.

The most important finding from the evidence in this chapter is that the political explanations for the methods and influences of practices of financial risk management turned out to be much more relevant than the technical ones of any calculative failures. The powerful people were unwilling to face or acknowledge the economic reality, and used their networks and influence to ensure that they got away without any reprimand. They pro-actively 'managed' the regulators and the auditors, thereby reducing any restraints on their excessive risk-taking. Tett (2010) documents similar case studies of significant political in-fighting within banks, with those earning the higher profits and returns gaining unquestioned authority, in spite of the significant risk and gambles they were taking on behalf of the firm. In some cases, they got away with hiding the real risks by misleading management or not reporting them at all. Even Moore now acknowledges that in spite of being a highly talented and accomplished risk management expert, he was politically naïve. The founding CEO garnered significant political influence with the Labour leadership, and this helped shelter HBOS during its risky years. This case study shows that it is possible to 'capture' the risk management process, both internally within a firm and externally with regulators or politicians.

In the case of systemic failure of financial institutions in a particular country, it is not clear which particular individual stands to lose significantly by their inaction – so moral hazard is profoundly pervasive. The potential of conscience to mitigate against unethical or excessive risk is removed, as it is group-think and institutions which dominate play. In the case of HBOS, the Board appeared to have no systemic concern and were earning significant bonuses from risk-taking. Government leaders also got significant short-term rewards in terms of status and political party funding, and only lost their political power after the failure of the system. It is a fact that under the UK political system, the five-year term of office is a significant barrier to longer-term and systemic concerns. While the going was good, no one took system failure risks with any degree of seriousness. The eminent long-standing governor of the Bank of England, Sir Mervyn King, failed to warn about the crisis. When he finally stepped down in 2013, he was given a hero's farewell even though his theories turned out to be hopelessly misguided (Martin 2013). Just like bankers, one can argue that politicians have a lot to gain from the upside of risk-taking, and little to lose personally from the downside – so why would they be discouraged in the risk-taking? In future, a government Chief Financial Risk Officer may take systemic risk more seriously, though Power (2005b) is suspicious of the real influence of such roles. It is also not clear whether one person would be willing to or is capable of bearing the ultimate responsibility for this.

Research shows that the science of financial risk is far from exact or inclusive of all relevant risks (Shah 1997b). A major new 'World Scientific Series' book on financial risk management published post-crash (Roggi and Altman 2013) has only one rambling article on the problems of risk definition – all the rest are dedicated to risk measurement, ignoring the very uncertainty of risk itself. There is no mention in the book about the psychology or politics of risk management – implying that it is irrelevant. There is no reference to risk literature in other well-established scientific fields like psychology, sociology and anthropology. Finance theory uses omission to disguise its political and market fundamentalist ideology.

Could it be true that just as there were political and boundary conflicts inside HBOS in the area of risk management, the same applies to the finance academy? It wants to keep a rational 'economic' and 'measurable' boundary over its discipline and find ways to exclude any 'aberrations', as politics or psychology are not strictly economics (Kay 2011; 2015). Its appetite is to publish more papers in distinguished journals rather than to engage with empirical truth, substance and politics – something that can be judged as a 'low risk appetite' for the academy but a very high-risk one for society. The emphasis on risk calculation and measurement can be perceived as a strategy of 'colonising' the discipline and ring-fencing it from critique due to the complexity of the mathematics – it is often dubbed a field dominated by physicists and rocket scientists. For example, pretence around the accuracy of measurement of complex derivative risk can serve to legitimate their use, even when the truthfulness and accuracy of the models is highly suspect. At the same time, the complex maths can be used as a defence of its scientism. As the film *Inside Job* has shown, this appetite has been quite lucrative for the finance academy – their position, remuneration and rank inside business schools all over the world is still very significant. Jobs are also plentiful, and credibility is decided by publication in 'mainstream' finance journals. In the author's experience, the engagement of finance academics with other colleagues within a business school has been very limited. Just as bankers have been proved to live in a 'bubble' of their own making, so has the finance academy (Das 2011). Frankfurter and McGoun (2002) have exposed the deep flaws in both the ideology and methodology of finance – but this does not seem to have affected the academy in the slightest. Some have even argued that finance theories and models shape markets (Mackenzie 2006), that rather than reflecting reality, they create it. Banks have been allowed to take on risks and increase uncertainty, without academic challenge or regulatory enforcement. Future research is needed to explore the extent to which this 'intellectual capture' of the finance academy is deliberate, strategic and politically motivated to support the power and influence of the finance industry and exploit society in the process. If not, why has it prevailed for so long, and does it continue to flourish?

Just as the science of financial risk measurement is far from perfect, so is the science of risk 'management'. The common model applied in the banking industry – three lines of defence – was found to be woefully inadequate and inefficient. It completely ignores the realpolitik of management, and somehow assumes that overlapping structure will solve the problems, when in reality it is wasteful of resources and ineffective in risk mitigation. In fact, the word 'defence' now seems to be more rhetorical than real, supporting the scepticism of Power (2007). At the top of this pyramid, the Chief Risk Officer of HBOS was also finance director of the bank – a huge conflict of interest. In him lay the boundary between risk-taking and risk management, and it was non-existent. According to Moore, 'assurance' is critical to the implementation of policy – when mathematicians dominate risk management, they often fail in oversight. The risk-takers were allowed to dominate. The FSA failed in implementing its oversight of 'approved persons'. They allowed a highly talented and experienced senior risk officer to be fired and replaced by inexperienced people. The FSA did not fully challenge the business strategy of HBOS. Knowing that there was a generically poor skill base of risk managers, it continued to approve them and rely on them to manage and oversee significant financial institutions. The classification of regulation as 'risk' by HBOS also tells us a lot about the corporate attitude to regulation – even inside a systemically important banking organisation. It promoted a culture of regulation management as opposed to risk management. This is yet more evidence of the political capture of both the regulatory process and its outcome.

There is a very real political tension between rule-based risk regulation and principles-based risk regulation which becomes apparent from this case study. Rule-based regulation is open to multiple interpretations and arbitrage – the active exploitation of gaps in rules, rampant in the banking industry. So in crises, there is a reversion to principles-based regulation. However, the difficulty with such an approach is that it relies on human judgement, both at the institutional level and at the regulatory level. The FSA chose to comply more with form rather than substance even though it had a principles-based framework for regulation. Ultimately, the decision as to when to apply rules and when to use principles becomes political – a matter of who has most power and influence, and in what situations and circumstances. Also the differing interpretations of principles have the potential to increase subjectivity and political influence on the outcomes of risk calculations and management – so the politics would not go away. It is also likely that this is a rhetorical response to the findings of the banking scandals – even though principles-based regulation was enshrined in the Financial Services and Markets Act 2000, it appears not to have been applied and enforced in the case of HBOS.

This chapter also throws light on the politics of systemic risk. Systemic risk relates to the risk of failure of a whole financial system in a country – which includes institutions and markets. Global systemic risk arises when global financial systems are inter-connected and inter-dependent, and there is concern that there would be failure of the whole system of global financial markets and institutions. Systems are affected by correlations of risks, not just individual market or operational risks. When we move from micro-risk monitoring to macro-risk monitoring, there is a different range of skills and oversight that would become necessary. At a global level, it is unclear which global institution exists to supervise systemic crises and the related risks (Germain 2010; Shah 1996e, 1997a). Prior to the 2008 crash, the prevailing ideology among central bankers was that systemic risk did not exist, at country level as well as at a global level. There is now greater recognition of its existence, though the means of definition, measuring, monitoring and enforcement are far from clear or universally accepted. Once we go to global supervision and oversight, the matter becomes even more political as nations need to agree on corrective actions from the advice of non-state institutions, and the international regulatory architecture is very fuzzy and overlapping (Germain 2010). Given the need for prompt attention in the event of a systemic crisis, this is a very serious flaw in the global management of financial risk. It has also provided huge opportunities for regulatory arbitrage over decades (Shah 1996e; Shaxson 2012).

In their research on what they call 'The Finance Curse', Shaxson and Christensen (2013) argue that a significant financial sector (as London is) is often a curse even though it is promoted as a boon for a number of reasons, risk and fraud being key concerns. They argue that it leads to 'country capture' where the entire political system of a country can be subverted and controlled by powerful financial institutions. In the above case study, the evidence corroborates this. The effectiveness of managing regulatory and systemic risk depends on the extent of country capture. Paradoxically, it appears that the larger the financial sector in any country, and the more global it is, the more likely it is for the state to be captured by financial interests, rendering state-based regulation and governance ineffective.

The evidence earlier showed that neither the FSA nor the Bank of England was legally responsible for the overall supervision of the banking system at the time of the 2008 crash. Even if they were legally responsible, it is not clear how the leaders in these organisations would have exercised this responsibility, given the political capture of the industry. Several years after the crash, the same applies. Sir Mervyn King said that the Bank of England do not want any reserve powers in relation to the financial sector as a whole, because that decision ought to be taken by parliament (Tyrie et al. 2013b). King explains:

In my judgement, the trouble with doing this for the sector as a whole is that this reserve power is pretty much equivalent to primary legislation which ought to be the responsibility of Parliament. I would worry that enormous pressure would be brought to bear on the regulator, and there would be a lot of lobbying.

So not only is there no personal Chief Risk Officer for the UK financial sector, there is no institutional one either. A new independent 'Financial Policy Committee' has instead been set up tasked 'with a primary objective of identifying, monitoring and taking action to remove or reduce systemic risks with a view to protecting and enhancing the resilience of the UK financial system.' Even after the huge systemic crisis of 2008, we have no person or institution willing to take responsibility for overseeing the financial system and be accountable for it. The preventable dangers continue to lurk, at the expense of society.

The next chapter turns to examining the audit failure at HBOS – which meant that there were no early warnings from independent experts of the underlying problems and risks. It examines the key people, relationships and the quality of auditing and challenge which hampered public revelations. In the process, the independence and integrity of KPMG has been put into doubt, and their actions seemed to have been motivated by the networks and fees rather than objective analysis. We also examine closely KPMG's leadership and governance processes. Evidence for all this is pieced together from a variety of sources. A detailed interview of a senior partner in the firm exposes the deep contradictions that exist in such giant multi-national professional conglomerates.

4   The Chemistry of Audit Failure

Commonly perceived as technical and neutral, accounting is in reality a sub-jective and political practice, which can and often has been used to disguise, deceive and manipulate. The Big 4 firms have grown in size and influence in the era of globalisation, and collectively generate billions of dollars of revenues every year, and operate in over 150 countries (total revenues over $100 billion) (Humphrey et al. 2009). Their activities began from the statutory requirement for auditing, which gave them privileged access to the top of large and powerful corporations, but have now extended into many other areas of advisory work such as taxation, management consulting, forensics, fraud investigation, policy and strategy, and governments also have become their clients. Globalisation and financialisation have been hugely beneficial to their growth and expansion. They have also openly moved from being professional, ethical firms to entrepre-neurial businesses, without any apology, and do not see any conflict between business and professional values (Zeff 2003; West 2003; Sikka 2008).

Unique among accounting academics, Professor Prem Sikka has been notable in his consistent challenge to their growth, practices, conflicts of interest and political influence. Mitchell and Sikka (2011) use the phrase 'Pin-stripe Mafia' to describe their work and damage to economies and societies. They argue that in the UK:

> Successive governments have failed to investigate the firms, or prosecute their partners. Instead, the partners of major accountancy firms are given peerages, knighthoods, public accolades and government consultancies, all funded by taxpayers. The same firms have colonised regulatory bodies, fund political parties and provide jobs for former and potential ministers. This penetration of the state has bought them political insurance.

The US Forbes blogger Francine McKenna in *re: The Auditors*, writes regular blogs revealing the power, frauds and subversion conducted by the Big 4 and calls them the 'Button Down Mafia' (McKenna 2011). For her, their work is not different from organised crime, and she identifies political influence as a key part of their business agenda in the United States, shielding them from rigorous scrutiny or even failure. In summary, McKenna says: 'When it comes to the Big 4 public accounting firms, the official word is still, "Too few to fail. Too powerful to call to account.'"

Accounting scholars have generally been reluctant to analyse this power and influence, or have been looking away from the real-world practice of accounting, at a huge cost to society (Arnold 2009). Hopwood (2009) has explained (p. 550):

> The diffusion of technologies of financial calculation has played an important role in the creation of the financial and economic environment in which we now operate, but one that still remains poorly understood not only in historical and institutional terms but in terms of the wider consequences this has had.

The UK House of Lords conducted a detailed investigation of the size and oligopolistic influence of the Big 4 firms and expressed serious concerns about their oligopoly, collusion and audit quality (House of Lords 2011). They have ordered an investigation into their practices by the UK Competition and Markets Authority.

Arnold (2009) calls for a detailed examination of the role and influence of the Big 4 on the 2008 Global Financial Crisis. Demonstrating the significant revenues made by these firms from financial institutions, through providing an array of audit and advisory services, she questions their influence on the crisis, and lack of any warnings about the systemic risk of the sector. She notes:

> The financialisation of the economy over the past quarter century created profitable niches not only for investment banks and other financial inter-mediaries, but also for the major accounting firms. Over the past two decades, economic and political power with the international accounting industry was consolidated in the hands of a small oligopoly of firms based in the US and UK.

This chapter focuses on the failure of the fifth largest UK bank – HBOS, and the role played by its only auditor, KPMG, who provided consistent unqualified audit reports and no warnings of the impending risks, or the serious and systemic failure of risk management inside the firm (Shah 2015a). The parliamentary investigation (Tyrie et al. 2013a) discovered simple and pervasive failures in risk management which would have been easily discovered through a quality audit. Hitherto, in spite of several announcements by the Financial Reporting Council that they will be investigating the KPMG audit, no action has been taken. KPMG has been making one vacuous public statement throughout – 'we stand by our audit of HBOS' – without providing any evidence for this, and blocking any investigation of their audit files and process. As is usual with such cases, direct evidence through the interview of key personnel within audit firms is usually unavailable due to the veil of client confidentiality. I requested an interview with the KPMG chairman about their audit of HBOS in July

2014 but was denied the opportunity – they were somehow unwilling to 'stand by' their audit in front of this researcher. Instead, I was given a generic interview with their senior partner and Head of Quality and Risk, whose answers have been very revealing for this research study. The responses reveal the significant contradictions and flawed rhetoric of the firm.

Traditionally, this lack of cooperation has been a major barrier to research on the political economy of auditing. It is often very difficult to get at the truth of why particular decisions are made and why challenge is avoided in specific circumstances. When audit partners agree to cooperate in research, it is usually only in general or abstract terms, and very rarely in terms of specific contexts and named clients (Humphrey 2008). But the naming of audit clients and key individuals involved in the Board, audit and regulatory process elucidates the wider social, economic and political context. Key individuals involved in decision-making may also be public figures, helping us understand the role of status, influence and skills in audit leadership, politics and governance processes. This study also exposes the revolving doors in the machinery of audit, regulation and government and the deep conflicts of interest that are generated through individuals having multiple roles or histories and power networks.

The findings reveal the depth and range of the conflicts of interest, the reach of KPMG's alumni networks, political and regulatory influence and the methods by which it covered up its failure and successfully avoided investigation over the failed audit of HBOS. It exposes the corruption of accounting by professionals abusing their status, expertise and influence. KPMG's private and commercial values dominate professional ethics, even though the firm promotes itself as a top professional services advisor with a strong public interest. KPMG's rhetoric of transparency, public interest and independence is exposed to be flawed and contradictory. In fact, the professional title and audit licence are being exploited to gain maximum commercial advantage. In spite of being a regulator itself, there is a pro-active and strategic process of 'regulatory risk management' by KPMG. There is doubt as to whether the firm sees and understands its own profound contradictions. Far from mitigating risk, the research shows how their practices increased risk to society for which a huge multi-billion pound price has already been paid just in this one case. The evidence provides us with a rich understanding of the method of operation of the firm, and the importance it attaches to political networks and regulatory influence. It demonstrates that techniques of 'regulatory risk management' are being used to pro-actively obtain political insurance, and save money in professional indemnity. It is likely that the significant political influence built by KPMG in the UK in recent decades may have contributed to a blasé attitude to audit quality in the face of significant and strategically important clients. Profitable client appeasement becomes easier when a firm has such strong risk insurance.

In the UK, KPMG approved the accounts of major failed banks such as HBOS, Co-op Bank (for which it is currently under investigation by the Financial Reporting Council) and Bradford & Bingley. The firm also audited other major financial institutions such as: Countrywide (US), Kaupthing (UK and Iceland), Hypo Real Estate (Germany), Independent Insurance (UK), Fannie Mae (US), Fortis (Belgium), New Century Financial (US) and Wachovia (US), all of which suffered huge losses from the financial crisis. Although globally they are one brand, they operate largely as independent legal entities in each country, with some exceptions.

This chapter is organised as follows. First, we review the academic literature and develop key themes for this study and justify and explain the research method. Next, we identify the key facts about KPMG in the UK. We then examine the reasons why KPMG failed to qualify the audits of HBOS and warn regulators about the dangers during the critical years before the crisis – we show evidence that suggests that instead of being an arms-length relationship, it was a strategic partnership. Next, we focus on the quality, professionalism, conflicts of interest, degree of challenge and the political and regulatory influence of the firm prevailing at the time. We highlight the evidence from a key early whistleblower, who raised serious concerns about HBOS risk controls but was dismissed by management, with the collusion of KPMG. Detailed examination of this episode provides breakthrough revelations about the conduct and real motives of KPMG. The very problems Moore had warned about turned out to be the cause of the multi-billion pound downfall of HBOS – aggressive sales culture and growth trajectory with weak risk controls. We next focus on the role of the regulators in the HBOS cover-up, and KPMG's influence over this. We then analyse professional scepticism, independence and conflicts of interest over HBOS in more detail. We also identify the revolving doors between KPMG, HBOS and the regulatory establishment. The political insurance used to cover for weak auditing is identified next. Finally, we report on a generic interview with the KPMG Head of Risk and Quality on its culture, ethics and audit quality and independence controls. In the concluding section, we highlight the lessons and implications of this research for the study of accounting, and identify new avenues for research.

Theoretical Framework

In the professional accounting literature, accounting is discussed and taught as apolitical, objective and neutral – a technical practice, often devoid of theory or pedagogy (West 2003). The role of audit is to independently evaluate the reported financial performance in order to give a 'true and fair view'. It is a legal requirement for all large UK corporations, and auditors are members of professional bodies, with the Institute of Chartered Accountants in England and Wales being the oldest and most prestigious. The quality of audit is regulated by the Financial Reporting Council. Good corporate governance requires firms to have audit committees to oversee the relationship with auditors, and ensure independence, quality and integrity. Auditors are expected to be motivated by ethics and professionalism, and not greed and expediency. Membership of their professional bodies requires this, and they are supposed to be policed, reprimanded and fined for errant behaviour.

In truth, the accounting profession is a business that pursues profit, and is opportunistic and strategic in its desire to accumulate capital (Hanlon 1994). Sikka (2008) demonstrates the increasing willingness of Big 4 firms to generate profits through price fixing, bribery, corruption, money laundering and practices that show scant regard for social consequences. 'How can capitalists regulate one another?', Sikka (2009) pertinently asks. His account of the number of failed financial institutions attaining clean audit reports is shocking. Flaws in the current auditing model which make auditors financially dependent upon companies, and the neglect of the organisational and social context in discussions of audit quality, are discussed extensively in Sikka et al. (2009). Little is known about how audits are produced or manufactured within auditing firms, and rarely do they provide information about their internal culture and relationships with company directors. There is evidence which suggests that audit partner incentives are not risk-adjusted and based on revenue generation (Burrows and Black 1998).

Brunsson (2002) proposes a theory of hypocrisy, where organisations have two different logics which run side-by-side — an action-oriented model where the organisation pro-actively helps to transform its environment, and a political logic which embeds the organisation as dependent on its environment, with no clear boundaries. He suggests that these two logics often run side-by-side, and can be used to explain and justify different actions and scenarios. For example, the audit rhetoric of the Big 4 has an action and independence orientation, whilst at the same time, their response to the financial crisis was very political — it was the environment which caused bank failure, and we could have done nothing about it. Different logics can be used to defend organisational legitimacy, depending on the situation. They may also co-exist quite comfortably — the behaviour of most large organisations is difficult to understand if we do not allow for both models, Brunsson argues.

Hopwood (1998, p. 516) explains:

> So much remains to be known of the economic and social structures of the audit and consultancy industries, their modes of internal organisation and processes of management.

Given their huge size, reach and influence, Hopwood requests more detailed research on their behaviours, cultures, structures, incentives and practices. In an extensive review of the 'international financial architecture', Humphrey et al. (2009) demonstrate close cooperation between bank regulators, auditors and standard-setting bodies and find it very difficult to disentangle them. Could it be that even audit firms pro-actively manage their own regulatory risk in such a way as to minimise sanction, by maintaining good relations with the regulators? The boundary between the regulator and the regulated is increasingly becoming blurred in the financial arena, and it appears that the Big 4 pro-actively increase this blurring, to their commercial advantage. Professionalism is used as a shield to gain and retain business as opposed to a method of policing companies and protecting the public interest. As Hopwood predicted, the privileges of the 'professional' licence are very valuable in a commercial setting.

In their review essay on accounting and regulation, Cooper and Robson (2006, p. 415) write:

> We suggest that these (Big 4) are important sites where accounting practices are themselves standardised and regulated, where accounting rules and standards are translated into practice, where professional identities are mediated and transformed, and where important conceptions of personal, professional and corporate governance and management are transmitted.

The Big 4 firms play an influential role in the global financial architecture, and they succeeded in avoiding blame or responsibility for the financial crisis through pro-active responses, individually, collectively and via global professional networks and regulatory institutions (Humphrey et al. 2009; Sikka 2009). There is an emerging regulatory partnership between firms, regulatory bodies and professional organisations, which raises questions about the status and quality of auditing and the precise interests being served in the rhetoric of 'public interest'. Humphrey et al. (2009, p. 822) conclude:

> The global audit regulatory arena is a complex, intricate and shifting domain and one that is often absent or poorly depicted in audit regulation papers.

In a comprehensive multi-disciplinary review essay on auditing theory and practice research, Humphrey (2008) calls for more qualitative studies which expose the politics of auditing and notes that (pp. 193–4):

> ... at the same time as criticising research for being too divorced from practice, audit firms remain quite cagey and sensitive in terms of providing researchers with access to study the development and implementation of audit practices at close-hand, on grounds of client or commercial sensitivity ... . There is real merit in studying the practical, political realities of regulatory processes.

From the above review of theory and literature, the following core concerns affect the behaviour and performance of the Big 4 in an age of financialisation:

- independence and scepticism;
- audit quality;
- hypocrisy;
- professionalism, ethics and public interest;
- regulatory and political capture;
- conflicts of interest.

The above themes will be investigated in detail through this case study, and the findings analysed in the concluding section. Parker and Guthrie (2014) have cogently defended the inter-disciplinary paradigm in accounting, and the need for research to reflect pressing public policy issues and to connect with its practice. They also echo Hopwood (2007) and warn against theoretical traps in accounting which make it too conservative and distant from major issues of social and public concern.

Research Method

Hopwood (2007, p. 1370–1) explains rather lucidly:

> …accounting as a practice, can be and indeed should be constantly examined, re-examined, interrogated, and criticised within the world of knowledge. Rather than being a discipline in its own right, accounting needs to draw on a variety of sources of illumination and understanding. It has been and must continue to be a site of interdisciplinary inquiry.

The approach used in this case study is to examine the public evidence available about KPMG and, more specifically, its audit and relationship with HBOS and its regulators. It is motivated by a normative concern and interpretivist (Parker 2008), examining practice in close detail to inform our understanding of auditing. Parker argues that in our desire to pursue rigorous research, we should be careful not to miss the opportunity of 'seeking the new, the different, the risky, the dangerous' (p. 912). The focus in this chapter is on analysing the evidence from themes developed in the literature presented earlier.

Once again, use is made of the high-quality probing investigation done by the Parliamentary Committee on Banking Standards (Tyrie et al. 2013a) and PRA (2015a), which also questioned KPMG, and the cooperation of a key early HBOS whistleblower has been critical to the findings of this research. The forensic investigation exposed primary internal documents, meetings, information and correspondence within HBOS which would not have been publicly available otherwise. Professional barristers were hired to interview the participants. Minutes of Board meetings and the correspondence between HBOS and the FSA reveal how much the auditors should have known about the problems with internal controls and risk management. Other sources of information used in this research include KPMG annual reports, transparency reports, public interest reports, code of conduct and other reviews and reports published by KPMG. The KPMG website was also a major source of information for this research, and press reports on KPMG conduct, audit quality and ethics were also examined. Annual Audit Quality inspection reports conducted by the FRC of Big 4 firms and KPMG were also examined. The House of Lords (2011) investigation into the Big 4 firms and their conflicts of interest was also closely analysed. Varied sources of evidence are pieced together to examine the nature of the relationship between KPMG, regulators and HBOS to expose the ways in which independence was compromised. In the process, the political power and economic influence of KPMG in the City of London is revealed.

As before, a critical source of evidence for this research is the full cooperation of whistleblower Paul Moore, who was Head of Group Regulatory Risk at HBOS and also a former KPMG partner, through detailed interviews and supporting documents and evidence. Moore was very good at keeping records of internal HBOS reports and correspondence, and very responsive to our interviews and questioning. He even revealed previously confidential reports which have now been protected under parliamentary privilege due to the HBOS collapse. His evidence to parliament in 2009 resulted in global media coverage, and at one point even threatened to bring down the Prime Minister (Pagano 2009). Moore had provided a very early warning of the dangers of HBOS's culture and risk appetite, but was dismissed by the CEO in 2004 for being too challenging. Surprisingly, KPMG was asked by the Group Audit Chairman (NED) to investigate this dismissal, and accepted this request even though it was not totally independent.

In conducting this analysis, HBOS is used as a primary case study, but other evidence from KPMG and its regulators about its conduct, ethics, accounting and key leaders and revolving doors of political and commercial influence are also brought together to help us understand the generic influences on its audit quality and independence. Towards the end of this research process, we managed to obtain an opportunity to interview Mr David Matthews, KPMG UK's Head of Quality and Risk, and raise a number of questions related to the findings of this research. The results of this interview are presented in detail to help us understand their side of the story and rationale for audit quality, and the hugely conflicted and unprofessional behaviours and practices.

The next section presents a micro-context for the case study, something which researchers have identified as critical to understanding audit quality, judgements and processes.

HBOS and KPMG – A Strategic Partnership

HBOS collapsed on 16th September 2008, two days after the Lehman Brothers bankruptcy, with a £198 billion gap between its lending and its deposits, and was rescued by Lloyds TSB with the support and intervention of the UK government. Significant bad debts hidden in HBOS's loan books appeared much later – amounting to 20% of the 2008 Corporate Loan Book – at least £25 billion (Tyrie et al. 2013a, p. 12). The 2008 unqualified audit opinion approved loan loss provisions of £370 million. In 2012, the FSA investigated the causes of this serious risk management failure, and issued a Final Notice which would have involved a multi-million pound fine, were it not for the collapse of the bank in 2008 (FSA 2012). The report details the serious failings in the Bank of Scotland risk management and control practices. Throughout its existence, HBOS had the same firm of auditors, KPMG, for the entire group of companies and subsidiaries. Throughout the critical period 2003–7, there was one senior audit partner who led the audit – Guy Bainbridge. The declared revenues they made from the firm over the period were £55.8 million in audit fees and £45.1 million in consultancy fees – a sizable amount (Fraser 2012). This does not include other income they may have made indirectly through the firm – e.g. through insolvency work for HBOS clients who had borrowed money from them.

In the UK, the regulatory architecture for banking and bank auditing during that period was dominated by the Financial Services Authority (FSA), the Financial Reporting Council and the Big 4 firms through their mandatory independent audits of financial institutions. The chief executive of HBOS also sat on the Board of the FSA and later became its deputy chairman.

From the outset, HBOS had a strong rhetoric of aggressive competition against the established four major British banks. James Crosby gave a public target for the new Group to increase the return on equity from 17% in 2001 to 20% in 2004. As we saw in Chapter 3, risk and culture were at the very heart of the collapse – even the market failed to detect the problems until it was too late. There was a failure of leadership and governance, a failure of regulation and a failure of risk management (Tyrie et al. 2013; Shah 2014). There were pro-active policies and practices of risk management and control – 150 professionals were involved in this area across HBOS Retail Bank alone and reported to Moore (Moore interview, 2013). There was a Non-Executive Board of Directors whose primary job it is to govern, by approving business strategy and overseeing culture, risk and regulatory compliance. Spin appeared to have been applied in the management of HBOS communications led by the same person throughout – who won an award for his communications in 2008 (Fraser 2012). The FSA were concerned at the outset, and took some remedial actions, but later somehow acquiesced.

By size, KPMG is the largest accounting firm in the world, and in 2013 the UK arm earned total revenues of £1.55 billion and profits of £455 million, of which the audit share was 39%. £542 million was generated from financial services work (35% of the annual revenue). On their website, there is an A–Z list of services, and the total number of services listed here exceeds fifty different types – it is a supermarket of consultancy and professional services. The annual report (KPMG 2013 report, p. 1) states:

> KPMG in the UK is one of the largest member firms of KPMG's global network providing Audit, Tax and Advisory services. In the UK we have 583 partners and over 10,500 outstanding professionals working together to deliver value to our clients across our 22 offices.

The chairman's report explains (emphasis added):

> *Audit is the foundation stone of our business.* We branch out proudly into other areas but, at its roots, our job is about providing assurance in the widest sense. We are governed by only one standard: our public, professional and deep personal interest in providing assurance of the highest

quality. We wake thinking about these things; it is the very heartbeat of what we do. We know that building trust takes years, and that if we lose that trust our brand may be irreparably damaged. We are not prepared to see that happen.

... [we have] *one clear ambition – to dominate professional services in the UK.* (KPMG 2013 report, p. 12)

Having been a financial sector auditor for decades, KPMG amassed considerable skill and experience in the sector. They benefited hugely from the growth of London as a global financial centre. Given the complexity of modern banking, they have created special risk and advisory arms for the financial sector, publishing reports and research papers on various topics. In 2014, they issued a 'Reinvention of UK Banking' report which included benchmarking of the banks through an analysis of 2013 results (KPMG 2014 report). Their work is not simply reactive to the needs of the financial sector – it is pro-active too. It is a combination of a think-tank, an advisory and policy unit and a global professional skills bank. In terms of values, it is unabashedly a commercial organisation.

One key aspect of any audit is an examination of the internal control system, and assessment of its quality and reliability (Auditing Practices Board 1999). In the case of banks, particular attention should be paid by auditors to the evaluation of risk management systems and processes under the Banking Act 1987. According to Tyrie et al. (2013a), the FSA had shown concerns about this, and in 2003 ordered an independent s.166 investigation of the risk systems by PWC. There was a real fear that the pace of growth of the new firm would outstrip its ability to manage its risk and culture – HBOS was deemed 'an accident waiting to happen'. They had also commissioned a credit risk review by KPMG. These concerns were repeated by them regularly since, and eventually became a serious reason for their downfall. All such correspondence between the FSA and HBOS had been copied to KPMG. KPMG lead auditor Bainbridge (2012) admitted that in spite of these weaknesses, no significant concerns were made to HBOS management about the overall quality and reliability of their risk management systems and processes throughout its life. Chairman of HBOS Lord Stevenson echoed this when he said (Tyrie et al. 2013a):

... I was never aware of any area where we were in disagreement with our auditors. ... I met alone with the auditors – the two main partners – at least once a year, and in our meeting, they could air anything they found difficult. Although we had interesting discussions – they were very helpful about the business – there were never any issues raised.

When Lord Stevenson, who was chairman of HBOS from its inception to its demise, says that throughout the life of HBOS, KPMG was never in disagreement, and to the contrary was 'very helpful', we have clear evidence of a culture of appeasement and partnership as opposed to one of independence and challenge.

This 'friendship' is also echoed by the chair of the HBOS Audit Committee Tony Hobson. This goes to the very heart of the hypocrisy of the firm in its claims of professionalism and independence.

The next section exposes a particular episode in their relationship which highlighted their inter-dependence and KPMG's true values and ethics.

KPMG'S Role in Sacking of the HBOS Risk Whistleblower

In 2002, a highly accomplished and respected KPMG consultancy partner left to lead risk management at HBOS, and was promoted to Head of Group Regulatory Risk on 1st January 2004 – a critical senior position where he led a team of 150 professionals. Tyrie et al. (2013a) and many others have now credited him as being a very important early critic of HBOS, who spotted the risks and problems, which later brought the huge multi-billion pound downfall and losses for the economy and society. However, in November 2004, he was suddenly fired by the HBOS CEO because of his challenging questioning and critique of the firm's sales and growth strategy. He filed a complaint about this to the firm and to the FSA. The HBOS Board then appointed KPMG to investigate the dismissal, and KPMG accepted the appointment, knowing that Moore was a former colleague and accomplished partner of theirs. To add insult to injury, their report concluded that Paul Moore's dismissal was justified – they independently sided with their client. Moore has cooperated fully with this present research and explained exactly what happened. This episode reveals the conflicts of interest which arise in such large multi-disciplinary firms, and how KPMG agreed to appease and protect the CEO and satisfy the FSA through this report.

During our research interview, Paul Moore explained:

> I am a lawyer by profession, but got involved in financial sector regulation from 1984. Most people think that regulation is not really risk management, but I disagree. Risk and regulation are very closely connected – I am not a mathematician, nor am I an expert in financial risk management. I do know the basics of it, but I am not an actuary. My focus has always been around systems and controls – setting the right risk framework, policies and process to mitigate the risks, and setting thorough risk assurance to check that risk management policies are being carried out. If I was looking at a particular area of risk where I did not have the content speciality, I would bring the content specialist into the meeting with me. Everything I have done throughout my career has something to do with risk management.
>
> I joined KPMG in 1995 and stayed there till 2002. I was one of the top performing partners in the whole of the UK. I was often involved in projects where clients had got into terrible trouble with their risk man-agement and we had to go in and sort them out – they were very high paying engagements. With one client, we turned over £14mn of fees in ten months – we had 140 people working on it. It was always insurance

companies, banks, asset management. My expertise was on the retail and insurance side, but the same basic principles applied in any risk management context: Do you know what the risks are? Do you know what policies you have to mitigate those risks? Do you know what processes you have to implement proper checks and balances? What is the level of assurance around the implementation and execution of those policies? My final appraisal at KPMG was – you are one of KPMG's most outstanding performers.

I joined HBOS in 2002 as the Head of Risk for the Insurance and Investment division – second largest division. I wanted to put into practice everything I had learnt over many years about how to do it properly. The two key things to me are – 1. Having the right people who are the risk management advisors (I don't call them risk managers) and 2. Leading a culture of openness, ethics and excellence, in which fear, blame and pride have no part.

Risk culture to me is critical. In the past, risk managers and risk-takers had a very unsatisfactory and tenuous relationship – risk managers, compliance officers and auditors were always thought of as saying – 'the answer is no, now what is the question'.

I joined HBOS with a view to setting up a new cognizance framework for risk management advisors and a new way of relating with the risk-takers – the executive. We did that very successfully in the 18 months that I worked in that division, and got absolutely outstanding feedback for my work both from the executive and the non-executive and that is all fully documented. In 2003, this new way of working on risk management was evaluated by the FSA in their full ARROW assessment – ARROW means Advanced Risk Operating Framework – this was the new way for the new regulatory regime, used to assess where they should focus their work in terms of supervision, investigation and enforcement.

The FSA were very concerned because HBOS was outgrowing its competitors at a rate which was extraordinary given its size. Due to these concerns, HBOS wanted somebody else to lead the Group Regulatory Risk function and appease the regulators, and I was promoted to this job after the critical ARROW assessments. It was the CEO James Crosby who appointed me. This was in mid-September 2003 after I had been there for a year and received fantastic feedback and one of the highest bonuses.

I was given this role because I had a very strong relationship with the regulator [of] the FSA due to my previous track record. At KPMG, I had led some of the biggest regulatory remedial projects in the retail sector. The primary areas of growth at HBOS at the time were retail and insurance and investment divisions. I put together an operating plan for the Board and the Group Audit Committee which I called 'The Regulatory Challenge – A key strategic driver'.

My experience at KPMG taught me to work with auditors in designing proper investigations and assurance reviews – we focused on four key things: 1. What is the Business Strategy; 2. What are the policies and processes for risk management; 3. What are the people like; 4. What is the culture like. We looked at things in a holistic sense. Would the process set out deliver the compliance objectives for mitigation of relevant risks? Or was the correct process not implemented properly? We worked on both sides of the coin – the setup, policies and processes, and the assurance.

When I was appointed as Head of Group Regulatory Risk, the single most important thing I wanted to do was to conduct more rigorous oversight and assurance inside HBOS.

In spite of all the warnings from one of their own former partners, whose skills and qualities KPMG were fully aware of, it is clear from the Board minutes and the evidence given in Bainbridge (2012) that KPMG did not sufficiently challenge their audit client HBOS about its aggressive sales culture and weak risk management systems and processes. Due to the challenges that he posed to senior staff within the bank, the CEO James Crosby dismissed Moore at the end of 2004, soon after he himself had promoted Moore to the headship of Group Regulatory Risk. Instead, a former sales executive, with little experience of risk management, was promoted to the position of Group Risk Director. This should have raised a regulatory red flag without any doubt.

Disgruntled by his sudden dismissal, Moore lodged an official complaint both with the FSA and HBOS. HBOS asked KPMG to investigate it, who accepted this role in spite of conflicts of interest with ex-partner Moore, and a confidential report was filed on 28th April 2005 (KPMG 2005), which basically exonerated HBOS from unfair dismissal, and said:

> We have seen no evidence to suggest that Mr. Moore's redundancy was in response to him performing his job too well ... (para 6.7)
>
> It is inevitable that the Group, because of its size and diversity, will continue to have ongoing regulatory issues that need to be actively addressed. ... the evidence suggests that the Group does understand, accept and take its regulatory responsibilities seriously. (para 6.6)
>
> ... we do not believe that the evidence reviewed suggests that Ms. Dawson is not fit and proper to undertake the Group Risk Director role. (para 6.4)

We look closely at their audit of HBOS in the next section.

Audit Negligence and Bias

Tyrie et al. (2013a) devoted a whole chapter to 'A failure of internal control' and noted (para 64):

> The risk function in HBOS was a cardinal area of weakness in the bank. The status of the Group risk functions was low relative to the operating

divisions. Successive Group Risk Directors were fatally weakened in carrying out their duties by their lack of expertise and experience in carrying out a risk function, by the fact that the centre of gravity lay with the divisions themselves rather than the group risk function, and by the knowledge that their hopes for career progression lay elsewhere in the bank. The degradation of the risk function was an important factor in explaining why the high risk activities of the Corporate, International and Treasury Divisions were not properly analysed or checked at the highest levels in the bank.

This suggests that KPMG's audit was deeply flawed for many years before the financial crisis, due to a lack of any serious challenge. The evaluation of risk management and internal control systems is a key part of any audit, and required by the standards. We asked Moore:

When KPMG did their investigation of your 'whistleblowing' dismissal complaints on behalf of the FSA, there were two conflicts of interest – one that you were a former senior KPMG partner, and two that they were the auditors and advisors of HBOS and therefore not completely independent. Why did KPMG accept the job from the FSA?

It is extraordinary and even worse than that – I knew the people who were investigating and they knew me. A friend and KPMG partner at the time told me on the phone that it was completely wrong of KPMG to accept that engagement. What we never realised was that the report would be accepted by the FSA – they didn't allow me to check the facts. We were supposed to agree the terms of reference with them – but discovered that they had already agreed these with HBOS and merely pretended to listen to me. I later proved this to John Griffith-Jones, the KPMG senior partner at the time. They never sent me the draft of the factual findings before issuing the report, they didn't ask me to comment on the draft report before it was finalised, and just delivered it. The fee on the project was estimated to be £1.2mn, a huge amount for a small piece of work (a fifth of the entire Group audit fee). After the report was published, we wrote to HBOS saying that there were a number of problems with it – one complaining about the conduct of the KPMG whistleblowing investigation, and the other about the findings of the report. HBOS immediately contacted us saying that they wanted to settle my grievances, and they gave me a sizable amount and I had to sign a Non-Disclosure Agreement. It is a very unequal battle – they have all the financial resources, so I had to accept.

... There is no shadow of a doubt that the auditors knew things were really wrong at HBOS. They knew that this business is a serious risk to the financial system. They had access to so much private conversations, they knew exactly what I was saying, but their goals are plainly commercial.

When I finally did talk after the collapse of HBOS, I was protected by parliamentary privilege. The CEO lied to parliament when he said that I was not fired because of my incompetence, but because I was not needed after the restructuring. It is a lie because in a reorganisation, you do not replace a critical risk management job with someone who had no expertise – my job could not be made redundant as it was a requirement of the FSA that there was a senior risk manager – Control Functions 10 and 11. One non-executive director said that the decision to fire me was unconscionable, and one other executive said that was the worst decision James Crosby ever made in his life. By firing me, he had proved that anyone who spoke up would be removed, so everyone kept quiet.

In his rebuttal letter to the KPMG report (dated 13th May 2005), Moore's lawyer wrote:

> In our negotiations, you should be aware that we consider that the KPMG Report has materially failed to take into account the evidence given by Paul to the investigation team in key areas. In our view, therefore, the Report is imbalanced and has arrived at conclusions which, if reviewed by an external independent tribunal, would not be supported.
>
> The mere fact that the report states that its findings are consistent with the oral briefing given to the March Audit Committee which took place a full ten days before Paul submitted his final eleven page written evidence to KPMG is strongly indicative that KPMG had already 'made up their minds' and did not take into account any of the subsequent and important evidence given to the investigation team by Paul. It also demonstrates that the concerns we raised in our letter to Tony Hobson (Chair of HBOS Audit Committee) on the 24th February about the appropriateness of the adversarial approach adopted by KPMG in a case involving serious allegations of whistle-blowing were, in fact, justified even though, at the time, they were totally rejected. We are also very concerned to understand why, if KPMG had already made up their minds as to the outcome of the investigation by the March Audit Committee, why it took two months for them to finalise their short report?
>
> In addition, the Report simply fails to deal with all the issues raised by Paul in the Outline Case. For example, it fails to deal with the issues of the total lack of support by Mike Ellis (Group Finance Director and Chief Risk Officer). Failing to have the clear and unequivocal support of one's direct line manager was bound to affect the confidence of other executives and non-executives. The Report also fails to deal with his approach to Board Minutes and, in particular, his severe written reprimand of Paul for tabling the full version of the Sales Culture Review Report at the October Audit Committee meeting.

Independent research by Dewing and Russell (2014) corroborates Moore's whistleblowing claims and KPMG's bias in its investigation report. The above evidence shows the extent to which KPMG cooperated with the client – instead of challenging them on what later turned out to be a highly critical turning point for HBOS costing billions of pounds in the bailout.

In the next section, we examine the role of the FSA whose responsibility it was to closely supervise large financial institutions and prevent systemic failure.

KPMG and the Regulators – Collusion to Deceive

Such was the power and impact of Moore's subsequent revelations (many years later) about HBOS to parliament that Crosby immediately resigned his position as vice-chairman of the FSA on 11th February 2009 (Hume 2009). Moore received widespread and global media coverage about his time at HBOS.

In their parliamentary investigation, Chairman Tyrie probed Moore about his dismissal by HBOS (Tyrie et al. 2013a):

> But when you were dismissed, if the FSA was taking comfort in the PWC report, you would have thought they might have said, 'Yes, but you have pulled away the key prop that was going to make this system work.' But what then happens, as I understand it–and this is from the FSA's own account–is that KPMG, with the agreement of the FSA, is appointed by the audit committee to review this, and KPMG reports that there was no evidence in the report that Mr Moore was dismissed due to being excessively robust. So the FSA, with the help of KPMG, seemed to take this view, and did not raise objections to your dismissal. The FSA did not say, 'He was absolutely crucial to the implementation of the advice we gave.' That comes back to my point that, at that point, there is a visible diminution of pressure, which then goes on after your time to 2006, when the FSA come back, and writes that there are things to improve but basically the main structure is sound. The management have taken great comfort from the fact that the FSA went along with your dismissal, did not raise objections to it, and then wrote the subsequent report in 2006. It seems to me that the management would have thought, 'Phew–seen them off.' Then, we get to 2012 and the decision notice on the Bank of Scotland. One of the things it says is that the management of risk in the company was defective.

Tyrie continues:

(BQ85) CHAIR: So my hypothesis is that, by not pursuing this vigorously around 2006, the FSA gave false comfort, and then allowed another two or three years of aggressive lending and selling to continue.

PAUL MOORE: Yes.

(BQ86) CHAIR: It then came back, and, although it did not actually say, 'We wish we had been more vigorous in 2006', it did say that the company's risk systems were defective. That does not seem to be a very satisfactory story.

PAUL MOORE: It is not satisfactory at all. It is perfectly clear that KPMG could not have been independent in investigating my allegations-they were the auditors. We made complaints throughout the entire process about the way they conducted things. We wrote one rebuttal letter to the KPMG investigation, but the FSA never called me back in to say, 'Well, what do you say to the KPMG report?' The KPMG report did the opposite – in summary, it said that I was a lunatic and that they were right. So we have an entire system that doesn't really work.

The evidence above suggests that as a multi-disciplinary firm, KPMG did have the expertise to evaluate the effectiveness of the internal controls and risk management of HBOS. The Audit Inspection Unit (2011) found in its inspection of audit working papers sporadic use of expert advisors in complex areas by Big 4 firms – there was little consistency. In fact, when the evidence of this KPMG endorsement of Moore's dismissal came out during the parliamentary investigations, both KPMG and the FSA were quick to blame each other – with the FSA arguing that they relied on this report, and KPMG saying that it was a very 'narrow' and limited investigation (Jones 2009a, 2009b).

Moore (2012) wrote a strong letter of complaint to the Financial Reporting Council about the conduct of KPMG, requesting an investigation into their behaviour. Here are some key extracts:

> From a personal perspective, I can testify to having been in meetings while at KPMG, in which I have raised statutory duties to report, when it has been extremely difficult, even though the evidence has been very strong, to persuade the Audit Partner concerned to fulfil their duty because of the risks to the 'client relationship' (i.e. fees).
> On one occasion, I was actually asked by the lawyers of a client 'what it would take' for me to agree not to write a report required under our terms of engagement containing evidence of serious regulatory breaches in a client. When I refused to agree to this, I was asked by KPMG to give up my role as the engagement Partner of the project.
> ... I publicly challenged the independence of the (KPMG report about my dismissal) to the media, alleging either gross incompetence or even dishonesty. Since doing so neither Sir James Crosby, nor the FSA nor KPMG itself have made any rebuttal to my allegations. But what is even more extraordinary is that neither the ICAEW nor the FRC have considered it appropriate to investigate or ask me about the allegations I made even though they were clearly a matter of great public interest and even though the Prime Minister Gordon Brown MP himself said in Parliament that my allegations were serious and should be investigated.

In the next section we look at the extent to which KPMG was investigative and sceptical about HBOS in the course of its audit.

Professional Scepticism: (Not) Challenging the Client

The Banking Act 1987 and the Financial Services Act 1986 and the Financial Services and Markets Act 2000 prevailed at that time. There are various legal clauses about the role and importance of auditors, and their duties to report. One key legal issue is the competence of the Board. The Auditing Practices Board provided guidance for Bank Audits and Practice Note 19 is directly relevant here (Auditing Practices Board 1999). There are guidelines about the auditor's duty to report to the FSA where it sees incompetence – no such reports were ever filed with the FSA. KPMG's Bainbridge (2012) explained:

> In forming our audit opinion, I did not formally consider the level of banking expertise (on the Board) ... I do not recall however, as a matter of fact that HBOS had non-executives with significant retail or corporate banking experience.

The note gives detailed guidance on the mitigation of audit risk by requiring a thorough evaluation of the internal control and risk monitoring systems of the client. Paragraph 80 states: 'It is important for auditors to understand the multi-dimensional nature and extent of the financial and business risks which are integral to a banking environment, and how the bank's systems record and address these risks.' The risks include credit risk, liquidity risk, interest rate risk, currency risk, market risk, operational risk, legal risk and regulatory risk.

Section 47 of the Banking Act 1987 gives auditors the statutory right to report to the FSA and protects them from any breach of client confidentiality in doing so, provided they act in good faith. In certain specific circumstances (e.g. when there is a risk of failure of the institution), there is a legal duty for the auditors to report this to the FSA. No such powers were exercised, even though we now know how serious the problems were and what the auditors were aware of. It appears from the evidence that not only did KPMG not challenge the client, they never even considered reporting them to the regulator. Sir David Tweedie publicly questioned why the auditing guideline requiring auditors to report to the regulator fell into disuse (Tyrie et al. 2013b). Lord Lawson, who had himself introduced this clause in the legislation, was really baffled by the lack of dialogue between auditors and regulators – explaining that as a member of the Barclays audit committee, he saw auditors discussing a wide range of issues with the client which does not get out to shareholders (Jones 2011).

One of the severest areas of losses (tens of billions) came from the Bank of Scotland, which was where HBOS Corporate Banking was located. The FSA had made consistent and repeated concerns about the quality of risk management in this area, and all such correspondence had been copied to the auditors KPMG. Internally, there were also various issues regarding challenging the corporate team on risk matters, which came out in the Tyrie report. The reputation on the street was that corporate were willing to lend to people and businesses who had been refused by others, often for risky projects where the bank took both a debt and an equity stake. This was unusual for banks, and later evidence showed that the focus on equity stakes reduced the level of risk monitoring on the debt side. There is evidence that KPMG were also invited to attend key risk review meetings. In spite of all this, the audits were unqualified, and little challenge was made to the level of provisioning in corporate.

KPMG lead partner for HBOS Group (years ending 2003–7), Guy Bainbridge, did not appear before the Tyrie Parliamentary Committee investigating HBOS, even though many other prominent people, including HBOS Board members and FSA directors, did appear. A live appearance would have meant accurate and truthful responses in front of a live Parliamentary Committee – but unlike the US, in the UK there is no legal power of subpoena for people to appear. Instead, he supplied written answers to specific questions (Bainbridge 2012). Here is a summary of the answers Bainbridge gave which are relevant to this study:

- 'I do not recall being aware of any significant concerns regarding the adequacy of the disclosures in the financial statements during the period of my involvement with the HBOS audit.'
- No significant concerns were raised relating to the control framework and risk management at HBOS except in relation to the Life & Pensions business. Bainbridge admits that he was aware of the KPMG report on Moore's whistleblowing claims (KPMG 2005).
- When asked about Board competence and relationships, Bainbridge said that KPMG never met the full Board of HBOS, nor did they formally consider the levels of banking experience of the directors. The relationship was primarily with the Audit Committee and the Chief Financial Officer, whom he met regularly.
- Between September 2001 and February 2008, only two meetings were held with the FSA to discuss HBOS – one in March 2002 and the other in January 2008.
- Loan loss provisions, a critical area of any bank audit, and hugely critical in the case of the subsequent collapse of HBOS, were also consistently endorsed by KPMG.

In their evidence to parliament, both the HBOS chairman Lord Stevenson, and the Audit Committee chairman Tony Hobson, said they had excellent relationships with the auditors (Tyrie et al. 2013a). There appears to have been no independent or adversarial relationship with key leaders of HBOS in spite of the excessive risk-taking. In fact, Hobson said (Tyrie et al. 2013a):

I think that where we got to (regarding loan loss provisions) was … absolutely supported by the auditors – by the way, I would say that the audit committee and the board had consistent, very productive and very constructive relationships with the auditors. This was not a situation in which there were disagreements.

More specifically, Bainbridge (2012) noted:

> I met the Chair of the Audit Committee around four times a year, often a few days before an Audit Committee meeting to discuss financial reporting, auditing and other matters less formally and help him prepare for the meeting.

When the PRA (2015a) report came out, there were a few references to the audit, although the PRA excluded a full investigation, leaving this to the FRC who had decided not to investigate. Loan loss provisions are a very key area of the audit of any bank, as this is often where the risks are either hidden or realised. Auditors are meant to spend a lot of time and expert resources on this area. However, a key change in the accounting standards prevailing at the time had meant that only incurred losses need to be provided for – so prudence had been thrown out of the window, and the risks of auditing were reduced as a result of this standard. What KPMG did in the case of HBOS was to focus on its 'Bad Book' – loans which HBOS had identified which had already gone bad and needed to be provided for. What the PRA unearthed through its enquiries was that KPMG ignored the 'Good Book' – where, in actual fact, some loans had been misclassified and had already started going bad. This is very weak and negligent auditing (see PRA 2015a, para 730).

There is also further revelation about the nature and outcomes of negotiations on loan loss provisions with the auditors (see PRA 2015a, paras 726–30). According to KPMG reports, the loan loss provisions were 'within the acceptable range', and Board members said they placed reliance on these reports to approve the provisions. This was severely reprimanded in the Tyrie and PRA reports, as Board members are supposed to make their own judgements about risk and accounting, and not rely on what the auditors have accepted. They were deflecting responsibility. This is yet another example of how professional firms are happy to be used to provide guidance for a fee, thereby helping companies, Boards and regulators to shift blame. In UK history, there have been very few times when Big 4 auditors have been found to be negligent and punished or fined. Somehow, they have managed to deflect their litigation risk consistently. Once the global financial crisis started in earnest, from late 2007 onwards, KPMG became more challenging about loan loss provisions.

In the next section, we look closely at the conflicts of interest, and to what extent KPMG sees them as conflicts or commercial advantages, and a method of regulatory risk management.

Professional Chameleons – Pro–Active Regulatory Risk Management

UK Bank Auditing Standard SAS 300 defines regulatory risk as 'the risk of restriction or withdrawal of authorisation to conduct for some or all of the bank's activities' (Auditing Practices Board 1999). The UK Financial Reporting

Council has the ultimate authority to remove this licence from an audit firm. The Big 4 provide extensive consultancy services around regulatory risk, and Paul Moore was leading teams whilst at KPMG advising clients of this. He had a good name and relationship with the FSA as he explains above. The FSA investigations and early penalties led HBOS to create this separate position and appoint Paul Moore the first head of 'Group Regulatory Risk'. At around the same time, James Crosby was appointed to the main Board of the FSA, and later promoted to deputy chairman.

On its UK website, KPMG explicitly announces its strengths in helping financial services clients manage regulatory risk by way of:

- integration of financial and regulatory risk specialists;
- emphasising their training and secondment experience within regulators as an asset which gives them exceptional insight into their expectations and perspective.

The firm also highlights its multi-disciplinary skills, and the knowledge it has gained from other financial sector clients as something it is willing to sell, without any fear of breach of client confidentiality or even accusations of corporate espionage.

On page 34 of their 2013 UK annual report, KPMG identified their own key 'regulatory' risks as:

- major or multiple audit failures;
- failure of maintaining good relationships with key regulators;
- major litigation or regulatory investigation;
- major regulatory change impacting on their business model.

Thus the firm sees regulatory risk as being very critical to its entire operation, and pro-actively manages it.

Professional Ethics, Conduct and Revolving Doors

KPMG (2012 report) have produced a UK Code of Conduct document with a foreword from the present chairman, Simon Collins. As with most such documents, it is long on the usual rhetoric about 'leading by example', integrity and professionalism and short on rules, sanctions and practical advice. There is no advice on how to deal with conflicts of interest, or information on 'Chinese Walls', and how to uphold them and ensure confidential information relating to clients is kept ring-fenced. The code pushes a lot of ethical responsibility onto the individual – which is not satisfactory, as individuals are not responsible for leadership conduct and corporate culture. It also places a huge burden on employees and compromises them, inducing a blame culture when things actually do go wrong. There are no example scenarios or case studies, nor is there a specific committee charged with dealing with ethical concerns. If members encounter problems, they are asked to speak to 'relevant' senior staff – and there is a whistleblowing service based in Canada staff can contact in exceptional circumstances, without fear of retribution. The advice here does not deal with the obvious and fundamental conflict between professional values and commercial goals, or the cultural differences between audit and consultancy, nor does it abjectly encourage forensic audit processes or scepticism. It protects the importance of client confidentiality which means that others cannot find out what KPMG does for its clients, even investigative journalists or researchers. There is nothing about how to deal with political power imbalances or undue influence on material concerns like reported accounting numbers and policies or fraud and manipulation. There is no mention of an internal ethics hotline if employees feel unsure or conflicted. This suggests that the firm does not wish to get drawn into ethical dilemmas.

The FRC's Audit Inspection Unit (2011) investigated several audit firms, including KPMG and reported that (para 3.3.16):

> A range of ethical issues continued to be identified, the more significant of which related to the provision of non-audit services.

And that (para 3.3.21):

> The AIU also continues to see evidence in appraisal and promotion documentation that senior staff believe, contrary to the requirements of the Ethical Standards, that success in selling non-audit services to audited entities is a factor influencing remuneration and promotion decisions.

This is further evidence of the ineffectiveness of internal policing and enforcement of ethics and conflicts of interest among Big 4 accounting firms. In their specific investigation of a small sample of KPMG audit files and processes (Financial Reporting Council 2013b), the conclusions and recommendations drawn include:

- to undertake a detailed review of the firm's ethical policies, procedures, guidance and training and ensure that improvements are achieved in the awareness of and attention to ethical matters and in dealing with them in practice. On three audits, there was insufficient evidence that the audit team had given appropriate consideration to the threats and safeguards relating to the provision of non-audit services;
- to ensure that loan loss provisions for banking clients are carefully reviewed, and sufficient challenge and evidence is given in the case of questionable decisions. They had found problems with all the three audit files of UK banks they had reviewed – the entire sample had deficiencies;
- to strengthen the firm's policies and procedures in relation to quality control reviews;

- on five out of a sample of partner appraisals reviewed, there was insufficient evidence that adverse audit quality metrics had been taken into account in arriving at the partner's year-end grading;
- there was no independent pre-issuance review of financial statements by KPMG's Department of Professional Practice, in spite of this recommendation being made by the FRC in the previous year.

Even many years after the crash, some of the critical issues prevailing prior to the crash continue to exist. This suggests that the firm's culture and values do not take audit seriously, in spite of the spin and rhetoric, and actually seem more interested on the advisory roles and revenues. There may also be cost pressures on audit which compromise audit quality.

Given its size and alumni network, KPMG also has a significant presence in the financial services industry. Here is an example of the additional 'revolving doors' of KPMG in relation to HBOS:

Dr Andrew Smith, an ex-KPMG partner (1993–9), was Head of Group Financial Risk at HBOS. He left in 2005 to head up KPMG's Risk Consultancy Practice.

Guy Bainbridge was the lead KPMG audit partner of HBOS for each of the five years ended 31st December 2003 to 2007 (Bainbridge 2012). On 1st October 2007, he was appointed to the inaugural Board of KPMG Europe where he remained until 2012. He was chair of the Audit Committee. In 2010, he was appointed as lead audit partner of HSBC, one of the world's largest banks. Sharp (2013) noted investor concern about his appointment after the HBOS scandal, and wrote: 'Douglas Flint, the Glaswegian who chairs HSBC, said: "Guy Bainbridge has been our lead audit partner since 2010 and the audit committee [has] judged his performance to be extraordinarily diligent and of high integrity."'

Douglas Flint, the Chairman of HSBC, was a former employee and partner in the London offices of KPMG.

John Griffith-Jones, the first chairman of the new Financial Conduct Authority (set up to replace the FSA after the crisis), was senior partner and chairman of KPMG during the period it audited HBOS. He also became the first chairman of KPMG Europe from its formation in 2007.

The Financial Reporting Council, the key regulatory body for accountants and auditors, with the ability to fine or censure them, has so far not investigated KPMG about their conduct of the audit, despite repeated complaints and strong evidence of serious regulatory and governance failure. Their director of conduct, Paul George, was a former partner at KPMG. Salmon (2013) reported that in all, seven senior members of the FRC are current or former staff members of KPMG.

The FRC appointed Lord Sharman to produce a critical report with reform recommendations on lessons learned from the banking crisis regarding 'Going concern and liquidity risks' (Sharman 2012). This was a key 'defence' document responding to the concern about poor auditing and lack of warnings prior to the crisis. Lord Sharman was formally a senior partner and chairman of KPMG UK (and KPMG International), and key architect of its transformation to an entrepreneurial advisory firm in the 90s.

Mr Adam Bates was KPMG partner in charge of the KPMG forensic investigation of HBOS's dismissal of Paul Moore. From 2003 to 2010, he was global head of KPMG forensics, and he then joined the KPMG global think-tank from December 2012 and became UK Head of Creative Thinking, according to his LinkedIn profile.

Sir Steve Robson, the 'independent' chair of KPMG Europe's new Public Interest Committee (2012–), was formerly a permanent secretary in the Treasury, a non-executive Board member of RBS (chair of their Audit Committee) which collapsed spectacularly, and a non-executive Board member of the Financial Reporting Council.

In the next section, we look more closely at how this political insurance was obtained.

Political Insurance – A Cover for Audit Negligence?

At a meeting in September 2012 regarding an investigation into the collapse of HBOS, the Financial Conduct Authority specifically excluded an investigation of KPMG, and Mr Griffith-Jones (former head of KPMG and chairman of the FCA) was present. It said it would 'take account of input from the auditors but not review their work nor seek to opine on relevant accounting standards and their application' (Aldrick 2013). One way of deflecting difficult investigations is for regulators to argue that they are not strictly responsible for oversight on that particular industry or issue. Of course, this process can also be actively managed by parties directly interested in avoiding investigation. More generally, we have already seen how the Big 4 audit firms succeeded globally in avoiding an investigation into their conduct before the financial crisis (Sikka 2009).

The history and geography of the City of London (also known as the square mile) makes it easily susceptible to political capture. In fact, its history reveals how it is virtually an 'independent state' within the UK, with its own rules and powers, and the government dare not interfere with it (Shaxson 2012). Some like Sikka, Shaxson and Richard Murphy have even called it an 'offshore secrecy and tax haven' right in the heart of Britain. In terms of political influence, it has been shown to have the highest concentration of power anywhere in the world (Shaw 2012). The Big 4 firms are either located in the City or within close proximity of it. Given the size of their professional manpower, the work they do and services they provide, they are often working hand in hand with and for the government. The Institute of Chartered Accountants in England and Wales is also headquartered in the heart of the City and is an influential guild in the running and governance of the City, with some previous Lord Mayors coming from its ranks. Thus the physical and spatial concentration of financial, professional and regulatory power is very significant.

A specific event in relation to HBOS is relevant here. The first public testimony from whistleblower Paul Moore came when he was invited to appear before the Treasury Select Committee in 2009. Prior to that, he was sworn to secrecy by a confidentiality agreement with HBOS, as a result of which he could not publicly reveal how and why he was dismissed. However, Andrew Tyrie, an eminent conservative member of the cross-party panel, confided in Moore that there was significant pressure from the Labour party to block his appearance, and it was Tyrie who pursued the matter and ensured that Moore appeared before the panel (Moore interview, 2014). This is evidence of attempted political capture. Moore said:

> The Labour party were trying desperately to exclude my appearance and evidence as it would flip back on Prime Minister Gordon Brown. I sent my evidence in on Friday morning. The clerk thought it was explosive and did not send it to committee members as it would be leaked. He gave a copy to the Chairman and leader of each political party on the committee.

Both HBOS pioneers James Crosby and Lord Stevenson had very close ties with the leadership of the Labour party which governed throughout HBOS's life – Tony Blair, Peter Mandelson and Gordon Brown (Perman 2012; Rawstone and Salmon 2012). One of the most influential positions Lord Stevenson occupied was as chair of the Arts and Media Honours Committee – the committee decided which people are awarded honours like knighthoods. It is possible that such political influence was a major attraction to KPMG in terms of retaining and appeasing a client like HBOS.

The services provided by the Big 4 to central government include auditing, advisory work on large capital projects, consultancy and out-sourced services for central government and large public institutions and quangos. KPMG has also had significant political influence over decades. One way in which such influence is obtained is through senior staff secondments, something which KPMG openly admits to having done with all three main political parties 'to underpin the fact that KPMG has a strong interest in good and practical public policy' (McClenaghan 2012). Major allegations have been made about the influence of the Big 4 on the HMRC, tax policy and tax enforcement, a key area through which client tax liabilities can be reduced, negotiated or avoided. Blogger Richard Murphy of the Tax Research UK has been a strong and consistent critic of this influence (www.taxresearch.org.uk). The chairwoman of the House of Commons Public Accounts Committee (Margaret Hodge MP) has also strongly complained about the Big 4's influence on tax policy (Houlder 2013). The Big 4 earn nearly £2 billion a year from tax advisory work – a significant proportion of their total income (Houlder 2013). Such political influence can be an important source of business, as it is powerful people who decide on major consultancy, tax and audit contracts, and the costs of these do not come directly out of the pockets of the politicians.

Another abject example of 'political insurance' was a secret meeting between leaders of the Big 4 firms and Lord Myners, the City Minister in the Labour government, seeking assurances that the government will stand by failing banks and thereby support audit firms in giving a clean audit report (Jones 2010). This was held at the request of the Big 4, on the eve of the crash. This information accidently came out during the House of Lords enquiry into the Big 4. Lord Myners did assure them in writing that the government will do everything in its powers to protect depositors. When the House of Lords (2011) heard about this, they became very angry. They saw it as an attempt by the audit firms to insure themselves, rather than to do a proper and diligent audit and make their own judgement and be prepared to defend it. They also saw it as the auditors avoiding their duty to protect all stakeholders – negligence.

KPMG Response to Our Findings – Contradictions Galore

I sought an interview with the chairman of KPMG UK to ask questions about the HBOS audit and KPMG's culture and ethos. After some persistence, I was given an appointment in November 2014 with Mr David Matthews, a senior partner in the London office and executive head of Quality and Risk to discuss generic questions. I raised a number of queries around independence, conflicts of interest and the side-effects of a sweeping commercial culture – how it erodes public interest and reduces audit quality. The detailed answers are presented so as to give the reader an appreciation of the rhetoric used to defend their actions:

> *How is audit independence and public interest maintained given the size, reach and commercial culture of KPMG? How are conflicts between these two values reconciled?*
>
> We do not see a conflict between the two. Our primary public interest responsibility is in relation to the audit. Our clients are shareholders rather than the management of the company. There is a very clear awareness that our clients are in fact investors, and that is to whom we have responsibility. So quality of opinion is the highest objective. It is in our commercial interest to ensure that our audit quality is good otherwise investors would not hire us. Our reputation and success is dependent on the confidence of the capital markets in our ability to deliver a good audit. If we were to put our private interests above the public interests, then we would lose that confidence which would have a severe impact on our commercial prospects. I don't think the significance of these restraints should be underestimated. The training we give makes ethics, professionalism and integrity ingrained in our people. Serving the public interest is a core essential for our staff. Our Sentinel system is used to monitor all our client relationships and services and record them to ensure that we do not get into conflict of interest situations. Any project that we do will be processed by our Sentinel system which would flag up any conflicts. We do tread very carefully. We

maintain strict information protocols and ethical barriers e.g. by creating separation between teams where there is potential for conflicts of interest.

But you have had audit failures and you have survived?

Yes. We have been reflecting on the financial crisis. Our then Chairman John Griffith-Jones said shortly after the financial crisis in 2008 in a speech at the Mansion House after the crash that we need to learn from what has happened, but also recognise that it may be a limitation of what an audit actually is rather than an audit failure. We are very happy to engage in a discussion about whether audit is fit for purpose, or can be extended, but that is a very different question to whether the audit of the banks that we audited actually failed.

I was told that audit partners are not rewarded for generating non-audit revenue. I got a lot of process and systems-based answers about ethical policies, and professional integrity and quality controls, but they were standard rhetorical responses. I wondered whether marketing spin could resolve the brand problem. Why is it that so many previous scandals have not damaged their reputation? I was also told that the focus of attention now is on investors who are their primary audit clients – not the management of the firm. I did not dare ask how they meet these investors and engage with them as an audit firm. There was admission that the external environment has changed especially in areas like tax avoidance, although when I asked about the conflict between auditing the tax provision and giving tax advice, he was defensive.

> *It's interesting you mention tax. Tax illustrates exactly the conflict – if you advise companies to minimise tax liabilities, you are opening a range of conflicts. The public exchequer loses out significantly from this behaviour. Professionals are using their knowledge of the rules and regulations, to help companies escape the rules and regulations. Then there is the conflict over audit – you are effectively auditing the tax calculation which you have advised companies about – so you are auditing your own estimate. Surely there is a conflict between tax advice and a proper independent audit?*
>
> There are lots of different levels of that. When I was training, my tax lecturer said from the Duke of Westminster case that it was the right of every taxpayer to organise their affairs in the way that minimises their tax. That interpretation has changed rapidly over the last decade, to a view that tax planning that is not based on a valid business operation becomes artificial. This is a complicated debate. In the past we did advise companies about these schemes, but at that time to our knowledge they were in compliance with legal principles. We are one of the first firms to publish our tax principles on what we would and would not do for companies, in a way which reflects an appropriate balance between serving the client and the wider environment around tax fairness.
>
> There is a difference between tax compliance and tax planning and the bulk of our work is on the compliance side rather than the advisory side.

On the advisory side, the vast majority of it is in relation to some corporate activity like an acquisition. There are degrees and we spend a lot of time to try and engage in the debate around helping to get a consensus around what are difficult questions. Companies are incentivised to provide long-term growth to shareholders. Time has moved on and we need to look at modern circumstances and transparency.

In the case of auditing, I even heard the defence of the 'Expectations Gap'. Bank failures did not arise from bad auditing but from bad banking – accounts have limitations. This is such an old, out-of-date answer, but they clearly seem to think that it is still a current issue and used the phrase 'worth debating'.

I was told KPMG were keen to show transparency through their reports, and also concerned about maintaining ethical values:

What is the punishment for unethical behaviour? What are the rules for staff, e.g. in terms of limits to gifts or hospitality from clients?

We have policies, but not rules. It depends what the breach is – it is important that one is proportionate. The ultimate sanction is to exit the organisation, or there may be a reprimand or a financial penalty. We do not know how many times in the last year these sanctions have been applied. In our transparency report, we are more explicit about our transgressions and the investigations we have had. Our risk metric process is reported in the Transparency Report. We look at various indicators of quality – internal and external quality reviews, any claims against us which may be due to poor quality, and our core compliance. For each partner there is a green, amber or red metric, and anyone who gets a red has financial consequences. We have made these consequences more transparent to our partners. We also have external regulators looking at our work, and peer review from our global network. It is very clear that audit partners are not remunerated for non-audit fees generated. In our current remuneration system, there isn't any linkage with short-term performance and the system is directed towards longer-term achievements and successes.

However, my questions concerned systemic cultural and ethical problems, and the huge conflicts created by their structure, size and influence. The Code of Conduct document states clearly that 'each KPMG partner and employee is personally responsible for following the legal, professional and ethical standards that apply to his or her job function and level of responsibility' (KPMG 2012 report, p. 10). The policy of the firm is to get staff to sign off annually on their legal and ethical conduct, and this can mean that in the event of a crisis, the firm can blame individuals. The firm had an independent review of their ethics policies and practices, but the author was refused permission to see a copy of this. Transparency is defined by KPMG on its own terms.

Do you have a Public Affairs Unit? Do you help clients to deal with political issues, changes in legislation, influencing public policy – working in the relationship between private sector and government?

We help clients understand the impact of proposed legislation. Similarly we do work for clients that may be relevant to public debate e.g. review of HS2 (High-Speed Rail) economic benefits. In much of our work, we are helping inform their decision-making process through objective analysis. We do have individuals that work inside government departments by secondment when asked to do so. It helps government to understand private sector and also get private sector skills.

Given your size and influence, the line between the regulator or government and you is very blurred.

We would sometimes undertake specific projects for government and do this on an objective basis. It's not aimed at influencing a particular outcome, but helping inform the decision they are trying to make through objective analysis.

You openly advertise your closeness to regulators on your website. Why?

A deeper understanding of the regulatory intention creates a better opportunity to ensure compliance. Why is that not appropriate? If we designed a system to meet a clients' particular needs, and then influence government that would be wrong.

I then probed him about audit quality, regulatory arbitrage and independence.

The role of a professional is to have expert knowledge. When does this knowledge turn from compliance to arbitrage? Many professionals today use the rules to break the rules. At the very least there has to be very rigorous internal policing to ensure compliance. And commercialism corrupts the professional in my view. Also I notice when you talk about risk, you focus on risk to the firm. What about public risk – the risk imposed on society from a bad audit, or from tax avoidance or creative accounting? There is a private perspective on risk and public ignorance, at a huge cost to society. Prior to the financial crisis, you had 30% of the sector as your clients. Are you saying you knew nothing about it?

Most people did not see the crisis coming, not just us. We are very happy to engage in a debate about whether audit does what society needs it to do. The audit is on financial statements, and they generally report on a historical set of numbers. What drives investment is something that is completely different.

There is FRC evidence from a sample of KPMG audits that bad debt provisions were not challenged in a sample of audits. That is very serious as they are core to an audit. KPMG talks about professional scepticism but rarely applies it. Firms say that when they recruit graduates, they are looking for 'business advisors'. There is a big difference between a business advisor and an auditor/inspector. In my opinion, KPMG have a fundamental problem with its culture, ethics and values. How can professional ethics be sustained in a posh building like your UK headquarters in the Docklands?

Perhaps we won't agree on everything. Professional scepticism happens in the dialogues with clients, but is not always written down in audit files. There are whole rafts of things that happen – we have created an internal framework to help our staff think about challenging clients and to record these challenges. When there is disagreement with a client over a number of material items, compromises are reached, but this may not appear in the final accounts. That doesn't mean we have always been perfect. We would expect our staff to be robust in front of a client challenge. Material disagreements would lead to a qualification. All this rarely comes out in a public debate.

We have been involved in shaping integrated reporting, and trying to make it more investor relevant. We cannot enforce what we wish to have. I think the glass is half full. There is now more of an impetus about what is different and what can change. We need an alignment between regulators and investors, otherwise all that happens is we increase regulatory burden and cost. We are open to engaging and making a difference so I do feel hurt by your comments.

When the culture is a business culture, scepticism becomes very difficult. For example, if you have a very big client, then challenging them may result in a significant loss of future revenues if you lose the client. How do you deal with such situations?

It is generally very rare for a company to sack its auditors. There is an internal check on the management team which is the Audit Committee. Much is resolved before it even gets to the audit committee. We do have genuine disagreements over significant items with management. Much is resolved before the audited financial statements are published.

I also probed about their practical actions in terms of corporate social responsibility and concern for the public interest – which I felt from research were more spin and less substance:

It's normal practice to produce a separate CSR report for a firm of your size. Why does KPMG not do this?

We produce data on it in our annual report. We are fairly active. We have our KPMG Foundation with a capital sum to support charities, we have national charities, we do a variety of pro-bono work, we are actively involved in the Access Accountancy initiative to widen access to the profession for young people from disadvantaged backgrounds, we support the KPMG Hackney Academy, so there are a variety of strings to our CSR programme.

Research shows that financialisation has been hugely profitable for Big 4 firms in the last three decades. At the same time, financial literacy has declined whilst complexity has increased. This is a serious public interest issue. Does KPMG care about these people? Firms like yours who benefit from financialisation should actively take an interest in improving literacy.

I don't know what the statistics are – I recognise this is a national problem.

The KPMG Public Interest Report does not show a fundamental interest in the public in my opinion. The pro-bono charity is valued at your commercial charge-out rates of your staff. This is misleading.

There is no doubt that business complexity and size have increased. The principles of audit are still there. CAEVOP – Completeness, Accuracy, Evidence, Valuation, Objectivity and Presentation – have always been the core principles of auditing. Auditing is more difficult, and achieving the objectives is difficult, but the principles are unchanged.

I am keen to look at actions not words. How do you have an organisational conscience, and how do you monitor your conscience? You have alumni in so many critical organisations, like the FRC.

Ethics is at the forefront of our minds. Part of our challenge as a profession and a firm is to transparently communicate why that is the position – and it is not spin.

Are you too big to fail, and benefiting from protection from the state?

We are as big as we are because companies have grown big and global, and this requires an incredible scale. We need to be in at least 100 countries to be effective to our global clients. It's a challenge how clients can get more choice. This is not an easy question to address. I recognise the challenges that you pose. In the meantime, one has to work within the current model that prevails and make the best of it. It may be different tomorrow. We try to do the right thing, be transparent about it, and encouraging change towards better models.

I asked about the lack of independence of the independent chair of the Public Interest Committee – and he found that challenge to be surprising:

The independent Chair of the Public Interest Committee Sir Steve Robson was previously a permanent secretary at the Treasury and a Board member of FRC. How is this seen as independent? Why are prominent critics not asked to Chair the Public Interest Committee? Why is there remuneration for this post?

Why would that make them not challenging? What is wrong with them having been in the FRC?

Because he could pre-empt regulatory investigations, and help resolve them through his contacts. Is it a business decision to appoint a Chair with such contacts? This shows how problematic the business culture is within KPMG.

We do have critics on our committee – Mr David Pitt-Watson and Professor Laura Empson. They are very challenging. We wanted to get people with experience and challenge. We looked for people who would bring particular aspects to their challenge.

I also questioned the meaning of and focus on 'regulatory risk management' given that they themselves were regulators – an obvious contradiction:

How is regulatory risk managed? What resources and methods are used to manage it?

Understanding what the regulatory requirements are, and making sure we have policies and processes to address those, and the staffs are adequately trained about them. Globally we have a risk management manual with policies where all international firms have to comply with. It is a very thick manual. Nationally we would augment them with our own rules. Our quality control programmes all cover the breadth of it – there are three core processes for monitoring. The international peer review, self-assessment and we have client engagement quality performance reviews – these are the three key quality controls. This covers risk, ethics and quality.

Do you have professional indemnity cover?

Yes, all firms are required to do this. We do have cover, but do not comment on the nature of that cover.

At one level you are a 'regulator' by being auditor, and then you are also managing your regulatory risk – isn't there a contradiction?

We are not saying what non-compliance we can get away with – that is not what we mean by regulatory risk management. We want to ensure compliance with the regulations and that is what we mean by it. It is a commercial imperative – regulatory non-compliance damages our reputation. In comparison with our competitors, we are more expansive about our transparency and disclosures.

The general impression I got was that as a firm, they do not see any contradiction between their business and professional objectives, or where it exists – they think they have sufficient internal processes and safeguards to maintain independence and objectivity. When I asked how many people have been reprimanded due to their ethics or incompetence, I was shown their internal performance ranking method and data – which did not directly answer the question. So there are no clear sanctions for ethical weakness. Also there were no clear rules or limits for client gifts, entertainment or other rewards. I also questioned their size and relative influence, but they argued this cannot be helped, as some of their clients were very large and they needed the breadth to service them. Size is not seen as a problem for ethics, conscience or regulatory compliance for KPMG. I asked how they prevent using their knowledge of the rules to help clients break the rules and did not get a clear answer apart from a reliance on their ethical policies.

Overall, I got the impression that the firm is very big and powerful and difficult to challenge in any meaningful way. They also seem to have developed a skill of deflecting criticism. I also got the impression that they believe their own spin – even the partners. I did not get any sense that they were sufficiently reflective about their impact on society or the risk they impose on society (e.g. through the audit failure of HBOS) – most of their concerns were private to themselves. I could not detect a public conscience. The commercial culture seemed to overrule everything, and, as others have suggested, audit is an important source of client access to other more profitable services, but its quality and independence is not a priority. I sensed a prevailing culture of client appeasement rather than challenge, despite the rhetoric. The overwhelming conflicts of interest generated from size and market penetration were seen as things which could easily be dealt with through internal processes and controls. There were no restraints on growth – they have publicly stated they want to be 'the dominant professional services firm'.

Conclusions and Implications for Future Research

Given the size, reach and influence of the Big 4, this inter-disciplinary case study of a major firm has provided us with detailed insights into KPMG's mode of operation, and the various ways in which its conduct and behaviour has been highly compromised. This evidence is unusually rich and telling, and endorses Arnold's (2009) suspicions about their role, profiteering and influence on financialisation. It also demonstrates why scholars of accounting should focus on the conduct, professionalism and political influence of such firms on the profession, its regulation, economic impact and ethical character. The findings offer us rare possibilities to develop a range of insights and agendas for future research, based on an active social conscience.

The research in this chapter focused on KPMG's audit quality and independence credentials, to understand the role it played in regulating financial services firms during the critical period before and after the 2008 financial crash. The findings show a wide range of conflicts of interest, which were pro-actively and selectively used to generate considerable revenues, and cushion the firm against regulatory sanction, public critique, litigation or malfeasance. As Arnold (2009) had predicted, the firm played a strategic and pro-active role to profit from financialisation and to support the growth and expansion of HBOS in spite of fundamental cracks in its culture and risk management systems. From the start, the evidence suggests that the client was seen as a partner rather than an independent entity from whom objective and professional distance ought to be maintained. The public price of the collapse of HBOS was over £50 billion, but to date KPMG have not faced any sanctions over its audit and advisory relationship with the firm. On the contrary, KPMG has benefited from the financial crash, through new insolvency, advisory and regulatory work generated directly in its aftermath. It has not been asked to repay any of the earnings from HBOS.

The firing of HBOS whistleblower and Head of Risk, Paul Moore, a person whose considerable skills and expertise were well-known to the firm, is most surprising. In taking on the assignment itself, KPMG was highly conflicted due to Moore being an ex-partner of the firm, and due to KPMG being the firm's auditor and consultant. Far from challenging the client, the firm consistently supported and endorsed HBOS's performance and behaviour right to the very end. KPMG's sanctioning of Moore's dismissal was a very clear and objective conflict of interest which was overridden for commercial and political gain – helping both the client and the regulator out of a tricky situation. KPMG seemed all too keen to support and appease the senior management at HBOS. The evidence suggests that there was a poor culture of challenging the client within the firm – it seems to have been actively discouraged by the commercial and entrepreneurial values. The combination of financialisation and commercialisation prior to 2008 gave the Big 4 firms enormous power and profits. There seemed no desire to upset the gravy train in the build-up to the financial crisis. Given that KPMG had around 30% of the UK financial services market, it had a significant overview of what was happening in the financial services industry in the build-up to the crash. It did nothing to warn about the looming dangers, and, to the contrary, even did not qualify any of the audits of the failing institutions who were its clients. This evidence echoes Hopwood (2007, 2009) – Big 4 firms should be treated as normal businesses and professional roles, titles and licenses as being used to service commercial enterprise. When agents are controlled by two or more divergent interests, there is a tendency for the paymaster to dominate the compliance to norms, rules and regulations (Hechter 2008).

The conflicts of interest are not merely in relation to client–advisory relationships. They are much deeper and sophisticated, and extensive in their breadth and reach. This chapter highlights the evidence and shows the nuances. A crude and illegal way in which businesses can profit is through bribery and corruption. The evidence in this chapter shows that KPMG has been more subtle in its influence over client transactions, but also very strategic and aggressive. Its size, alumni network, talent pool, inter-disciplinary skill set, regulatory capture and reach are such that it has itself become 'too big to challenge'. It uses these networks and resources to protect itself from censure. Paradoxically, a firm that should be challenging to its clients has cushioned itself from serious challenge and reform. There were movements of KPMG people between various influential organisations at the heart of financialisation – the banks and financial institutions, the regulators (FSA and FRC), professional bodies, House of Lords, membership of advisory and reform committees, political parties, pro-bono parliamentary advisory – creating a large overlapping circle of influence. This became a huge asset in defending the firm against criticism after the 2008 crash. Through chameleon-like behaviour, the firm was able to get others to cover its back and prevent strong public criticism. Its networks were happy to cover for its errant behaviour. In fact, there are no perceived conflicts – only interests.

Audit quality somehow seems to have disappeared in the void. It is a grey and poorly defined arena, and therefore much easier to capture by powerful forces. The rhetoric that audit quality is policed by the market through KPMG's brand value and reputation was found to be wanting and evidenced to be untrue – in spite of many major scandals, the brand seems to have survived unscathed. Surprisingly, people in charge of the audit of HBOS after the crash got promoted to even more senior positions, like Board membership of KPMG Europe. There were no internal sanctions. There is consistent evidence that clients do not see much value in the pure audit and see it more as a hindrance than an asset. For a commercially aggressive firm, audit quality would not be a key strategic asset, especially if it were able to 'manage' its regulatory risk. Maintaining audit quality requires a culture of challenge and scepticism, something which the firm did not practice in the case of HBOS. Such a culture would fundamentally conflict with the advisory parts of the firm. It is also likely that for people working inside KPMG, especially at senior levels, pure audit would not be seen as a means of rising up the career ladder – its advisory and other kinds of work are noticed more and rewarded better.

Regulations, and changes in regulations, are likely to comprise a major source of revenue for these firms and a primary business strategy or opportunity. Through their reservoir of experts, contacts and experience, they become the one-stop shop for global businesses wishing to 'negotiate' the regulatory landscape – especially as they operate in an inter-disciplinary way. Also in terms of influencing governments about regulations, they also become an important conduit for businesses – and can easily sit on both sides of the fence, profiting from each side. Their contacts with business can help them advise governments, and their contacts with governments can help them advise business. The most extreme example of this is their role in tax avoidance – they help companies exploit the exchequer, and also provide consultancy services to government on a commercial basis.

In spite of being a regulator itself, KPMG openly talks about 'managing' its regulatory risk – as if its regulatory licence was a commercial commodity to be protected rather than a professional skill to be applied and quality controlled. We looked at certain key personnel involved in the work of HBOS and how they moved around in various influential circles, and were even promoted after the collapse. KPMG's stakes and alliances are so diverse that as a firm, it finds it difficult to understand and implement basic concepts of professional integrity and independence and somehow assumes that policies and processes are sufficient to transform ethics and culture. In actual fact, the lack of precise rules may itself be a strategy to deliberately allow a variety of ethical interpretations and enable conflicts to prevail.

As a firm, KPMG already have a large regulatory risk advisory practice – so the skill developed here can be transferred and applied to its own risk management. This is the commercial advantage of such giant institutions – their client base teaches them new skills and constantly expands their contact network, whilst generating revenues and profits at the same time. As Brunsson (2002) had predicted, they influence and are influenced by their environment at the same time, which makes them fundamentally hypocritical. So the 'political influence' cost is in fact low or non-existent – the clients subsidise it. This suggests that in order to pro-actively manage regulatory risk (RRM), big accountancy firms can have a number of strategies:

- limited liability partnerships and other legal structures to cushion different parts of the firm in the event of litigation so that failure is localised;
- manage relationships with professional and regulatory bodies to prevent any adverse opinions or sanctions;
- manage relationships with government policy makers, politicians and influential leaders, such that during crises, they protect the Big 4 from

threat or challenge. The risk or blame from audit failure can be spread more widely so that if KPMG is investigated, others would also have to be exposed, and if senior political figures are involved, this would be a priceless hedge. Through RRM, a firm could hedge its own political risk pro-actively;

- in the event of audit failure, stay under the radar and let the blame fall on the management and the Board of the client, as it is their responsibility to produce accurate accounts. The Tyrie report focused all its attention on the Board and its poor performance. This indirectly shields the auditors;
- strategically planting people in senior roles in regulatory bodies, both in executive and governance positions. In the UK, the HMRC (tax authority) is primarily governed by ex-partners in the Big 4 – the danger of this is that even regulatory policy is shaped by the Big 4 (Murphy 2013). Murphy even found secondees using their Big 4 email addresses to conduct government business;
- be pro-active in major potential liability areas, like an impending banking crash;
- if possible, get other people, organisations and institutions to speak in their favour and support, or to influence the debate and agenda through prominent third parties;
- try to shape the agenda of reaction and response – e.g. immediately after the crash, they took a pro-active interest in future reform (via the ICAEW this time) potentially to hide investigation of past failures, under the guise of the professional body and by cooperating with their other Big 4 competitors.

At root is the focus on commercial success and entrepreneurial values. No conflict is seen between this and professional independence, integrity and public interest protection.

The definition and management of regulatory risk throws up its own conundrums as we saw in this chapter. Yet in the financial sector, it is a major issue and source of profit for the Big 4. More work needs to be done around this category of risk, its definition, politics and impact on organisational culture and control mechanisms. When does risk management turn to regulatory arbitrage? Who gains and who loses from regulatory risk management? When does regulatory risk management turn into political and regulatory capture? What are the costs/benefits of this technique for the regulated organisation? What skills are required and applied in this field and what services are provided by the Big 4? These are all important questions worth exploring in future research.

Risk categories and management methods are often invented to serve different political masters and ends (Power 2005a; 2007; 2009). Power questions the ways in which risks are defined, designed and managed. The pro-active definition and management of regulatory risk by Big 4 firms should be seen in this light. It seems to be driven largely by commercial motives rather than professional or public interested ones. Firms seem to know very well how slow government and regulators are in reacting to problems or exploited loopholes, and, even after they respond, there is significant experience in influencing the response to favour themselves or their clients. The Big 4 seem to have mastered this dynamic through their decades of experience in dealing with their clients' tax affairs, but in recent decades have taken this to major new arenas like audit regulation, financial institutions and markets regulation, and global regulatory shopping, and even regulation making as was evident in the case of LLP legislation in Jersey (Sikka 2008). Research to unravel this expertise and knowledge inside the Big 4, the ways in which it is organised and utilised in the event of a crisis, and the commercial costs and benefits of doing so, would be most helpful. What are the economic and public consequences of institutionalised regulatory risk management? Does the phrase 'regulatory risk management' serve to legitimise political interference, regulatory arbitrage and capture, and rationalise this practice to other professionals within the firm? In this case the influence extended to preventing a detailed investigation by the regulators, with significant savings in terms of liabilities and professional indemnity insurance premiums. Further research on this would really help us understand the strategies, operations and motives of the Big 4.

There is a fundamental difference between entrepreneurial values and professional values (Carnegie and Napier 2010; Sikka 2008), though somehow the Big 4 do not admit it. Professional values comprise ethics, integrity, independence, a commitment to truth and fairness, objectivity, contentment and a lack of greed. The values exhibited by the Big 4, given their stated ambitions of growth in size and revenue, are primarily commercial, and this creates a fundamental value-based conflict of interest between ethics and professionalism and profit maximisation. In KPMG's public pronouncements and documents, the impression they give is that processes and words will somehow overcome fundamental flaws in behaviour and character. The firm's culture and operations seem transactional rather than value-based. As a very simple but lucid example, at the heart of their new 'Audit Quality Framework' diagram is 'Tone at the Top' (KPMG 2013 report). 'Tone' relates to words rather than behaviours or actions – it seems to suggest that leaders need to use the right words, even if actions are not synchronous with them – why have they not used 'character, values and behaviour at the top' as a focal point? This speaks volumes of how they are responding to significant public criticism about poor audit quality – they are improving the 'tone' at the top. The impression one gets is that as a firm, they have little concern for the 'public interest' and its leaders are keen to spin the notion of public concern with their rhetoric. As an example of this, a significant proportion of their CSR in the UK is done through pro-bono services provided by their staff, notionally valued at commercial charge-out rates. Unlike other big companies, they do not produce a separate CSR report, despite being such a significant employer in Britain.

What we consider to be 'conflicts' of interest are seen by KPMG as opportunities for profit, something very different. For example, they publicly do not see any conflicts in seconding staff to regulators and then selling this experience to firms needing regulatory advice and helping them with their regulatory risk management (RRM). In fact, the very importance and criticality of RRM may be developed and promoted by the firm as a means of generating business through promoting fear of regulatory sanction. They are unabashedly selling their experience gained from serving some large clients to other clients. Their defence of conflicts of interest is to say 'it is more a perception than a reality'! This does not answer the issue at all, as they do not provide any evidence to back this claim. It suggests that they do not see any real conflicts in the wide-ranging client and government service work they do. The evidence in this chapter shows how commercial values have eroded professional independence, audit quality and integrity.

In fact, size, alumni network and reach automatically generate plenty of con-flicts of interest, in a small country like the UK with a significant concentration of global companies and global business and financing networks. A firm has to pro-actively avoid conflicts if it wants to retain its professionalism and independence. The UK's geography is such that a strong professional and multi-skilled workforce presence in London can be a very effective way of having political and economic influence. To be effective, Big 4 firms need to be especially vigilant and forensic about monitoring and policing their conflicts of interest if they are to genuinely maintain independence. There are no restrictions on the size and growth ambitions of the Big 4. They do not appear to see any contradictions between growth, breadth and independence. When they speak above about a mis-perception, what they seem to be saying is that they wish to 'manage' the perception of the regulators and politicians. When power and spin combine, the effect can be lethal (Skapinker 2014). Skapinker questions how they consistently 'maintain a wholesome image while doing exactly what they want'.

Through serving such large and prestigious clients, KPMG and other Big 4 firms become a hub for information and knowledge about what is really happening in the commercial world, and this helps them advise regulators about the relative success of implementing particular policies and strategies. They de facto become the interpreters, implementers and enforcers of regula-tion. However, their commercial values push them more to side with their client firms (the paymasters) than with government. Also, they see regulatory dialogue as a positive business asset in serving their clients – it helps them to advise clients in managing any regulatory changes, breaches or arbitrage, for a fee of course. They may honorarily serve on regulatory committees, later to use these networks and knowledge to help clients. Margaret Hodge exposed evi-dence of this shocking conflict by all the Big 4 in the area of tax avoidance (Syal et al. 2013). Hodge exposed a particular Patent Box scheme where KPMG openly publicised its staff secondment advantage as a method of helping clients plan their tax avoidance in this area. This is the chameleon-like beha-viour which really smacks of unethical behaviour, but seems normal for the Big 4. As Mitchell and Sikka (2011) have suggested, the audit is a foot in the door for all kinds of other services from which significant profits can be made. It is no surprise that the Big 4 want to keep and preserve this licence, even when they do not appear to be committed to maintaining audit quality and effectiveness.

A successful large litigation against an audit firm can have serious economic consequences for the firm and its viability, as they do not retain much in the way of reserves in their audit subsidiaries. The too-big-to-fail concern has often been levelled at banks as a key reason for their protection and bailout. In recent years, the same issue has surfaced in relation to the Big 4 firms – after Arthur Andersen, it has been argued that society cannot afford the collapse of another large global accounting firm, as this would result in an even bigger monopoly for the remaining firms. The UK House of Lords (2011) did a special investigation of this issue, and so did the European Union. Unlike banks, accounting firms have no direct influence on the money supply or the confidence in the monetary system. However, they do play a key role in overseeing financial credibility, implementing regulation and supporting multi-national firms in their business activities. Even governments lean on them heavily for consultancy and support services. Just as systemic risk concern has for too long subsidised the poor management and abject greed of financial institutions, it seems the same is applying today to these multi-national firms. The indirect protection accorded to these firms is encouraging the kind of conflicted behaviour we are seeing in this case study. Beyond the rhetoric of independence and professionalism, these firms, like many large banks, have become untouchable today. Financialisation has potentially turned audit firms into influential and ungovernable institutions with a pervasive role in the financial sector.

Systemic risk in banking has been a huge regulatory concern, and a source of multi-billion pound losses for financial centres like London. Collecting and interpreting information about a system and network of banks and financial information is very difficult, and regulators like the FSA and the Bank of England have in the past failed to do this effectively. Large firms with a significant presence in the heart of the financial sector like KPMG by definition become very important conduits of knowledge and information about systemic risks and issues. They are party to very detailed information about what is happening in these financial institutions, and have a very significant skill set to advise and monitor. A central part of any audit is to monitor systems and processes. Despite their public interest remit, there was no warning given by these firms of systemic crises, nor did they use their powers to report individual firms to the regulators. The only time there was serious communication with the government was at the height of the crisis when the audit firms themselves became scared of litigation – an act which shows how self-interested they are. This is evidence of how conflicted they are, and how little 'public interest' they actually have. It is private interest which governs their culture and values – and the firm seems to think that by having selective processes about public interest, it fulfils the criteria.

The phrase 'regulatory arbitrage' has been used in the context of financial institutions avoiding regulatory compliance, in areas such as tax, accounting or capital, to their own commercial advantage (Shah 1997b). More research needs to be done about the nexus of regulatory arbitrage serviced by the Big 4 through their presence in London and the UK, and the wider damage this causes to economies and states in Europe, Middle East and Africa. Like Arnold, others have argued that the 'corporate services complex' is a major player in financialisation (Sassen 2001; 2012). As we have seen, Big 4 firms play an increasingly important knowledge creation and intermediation role in a fast-changing world of new products, markets and exchanges. A detailed examination of the strategic role of the Big 4 in facilitating regulatory arbitrage by multi-national corporations and thereby enabling them to avoid regulatory sanctions and even negotiate between governments for special allowances would be invaluable. In the significant area of taxation, there have been a number of recent studies like Mitchell and Sikka (2011) and Palan et al. (2010) which reveal this. The extent to which such attitudes and skills have been extended towards other regulatory constraints in the areas of accounting rules, financial governance, human rights, environmental regulation, investment incentives and political capture would be worthy of future research. If their monopoly of professional services has been ethically compromised, this is a very serious public interest issue.

In a famous article by Matt Taibbi (Taibbi 2009) on Goldman Sachs, Taibbi wrote:

> The first thing you need to know about Goldman Sachs is that it's every-where. The world's most powerful investment bank is a great vampire squid wrapped around the face of humanity … The bank is a huge, highly sophisticated engine for converting the useful, deployed wealth of society into the least useful, most wasteful and insoluble substance on Earth – pure profit for rich individuals.

When HBOS collapsed, it cost the taxpayer over £50 billion to bail out. This had real effects on ordinary people, their jobs and their pensions and savings. This chapter shows that KPMG's poor auditing and lack of independence played a key role in the unchecked greed and abuse by HBOS management. We also saw the extensive KPMG alumni network in key positions of power and influence. Whilst KPMG is not a financial institution, its activities and commercial culture are having a significant direct impact on the economy and society, and – like Goldman Sachs – it appears to be constantly getting away with it due to its significant power and influence. Like bankers, its bonus culture is opaque. By not warning about the banking crash, in spite of being in a position to do so, the firm may have aided and abetted the collapse of the UK economy, a significant act of economic vandalism. It completely failed in having any warning conversation with the FSA prior to the crash. By hiring some of the best young talent in the country and changing their values, by pretending to be independent and professional, by participating as government advisor and sitting on various regulatory boards either directly or through alumni networks, by helping clients avoid and minimise taxes, KPMG do not seem that different from what Taibbi is talking about. And like Goldman, they keep getting away with it.

A lot of knowledge systems and professions are taught along strict disciplinary lines. The Big 4 firms have developed the skills and resources to service firms using inter-disciplinary knowledge and methods. As clients grapple with increasingly complex problems and challenges, this skill base is very unique and commercially relevant. The Big 4 have become a warehouse of networks, skills and global regulatory systems and structures, operating in a global playing field. This potentially gives them a lot of strength and robustness, and at the same time reduces the potential for expert challenge from politicians and academics trained in specific disciplines and unable to see the larger picture. More research needs to be done to explore the role of the knowledge, skills development, networks and information systems inside these firms in giving them competitive and regulatory advantage.

Political geography is very critical in the case of KPMG and the UK. Right in front of the very eyes of the UK government and society, it is able to influence key regulatory and political decisions with multi-billion-pound consequences. We noted earlier how the City of London is a significant source of financialisation in the world, and the square mile is the largest concentration of such power anywhere in the world (Shaw 2012). Due to Britain's historic legacy of the commonwealth, the global reach and influence of the English language, a lot of high-end work relating to Europe, the Middle East and Africa is centred in the UK. The Big 4 firms in the UK are very active in these markets and therefore also export their knowledge, expertise, character and values through these interactions. Given the City of London's role in offshore secrecy and tax havens, and the close association of the Big 4 with such activities, we can see how significant the reach and influence of UK firms is, in terms of both politics and economics. Multi-national corporations have significant power and influence in the world given their size and reach, and many question their accountability and responsibility (see e.g. Hertz 2001; Korten 1995) – they are significant concentrations of economic influence, but have little democratic control or accountability. The Big 4 are both themselves multi-national and professional advisors to multi-nationals, giving them a unique position in this global milieu of political power and economic influence. Through audit, they have the power to improve transparency and accountability, but as the evidence in this case study shows (and other studies like Cooper and Robson 2006; Humphrey 2008), they rarely use this power to improve accountability, and, if anything, undermine it. Also, the generic weakness in corporate fraud and personal prosecution due to the British legal system has attracted a lot of business to the UK which firms like KPMG can profit from without fear of any personal sanction. The extent to which this is exploited as a commercial advantage needs further investigation.

The strongest indictment the Big 4 have been given by people like Sikka and McKenna is that they are centres of organised crime and corruption. This is a very serious view, one which they back with evidence, including the range of lawsuits they have lost in court. Crime is very far away from ethics, integrity and professionalism. Crime is a deliberate conflict of interest, a desire to exploit and profit from clients, governments and public institutions for their own private interest and with no public interest whatsoever. Organised crime is usually perpetrated by people who are very intelligent and sophisticated and powerful. If this is true, the public licence to audit corporate conduct should be reviewed.

In the next chapter, we examine in depth the regulatory failure at HBOS. Given the size of the bank, regulatory monitoring was supposed to be close and bear in mind the systemic and prudential risks of failure. This failed spectacularly to prevent what was in hindsight a simple bank failure with few complex risks and easily predictable consequences. We look at the people who cared and challenged but were dismissed or fired, like Paul Moore. We examine the role of personal and political networks in undermining or reducing regulatory challenge. In the process, the detailed politics of regulation and enforcement are revealed.

5 Regulatory Failure

The Financial Services Authority (FSA) was set up by law in 2002 as the principal regulator of banks and financial institutions through the determination and drive of then Chancellor Gordon Brown. Its creation was seen as a major breakthrough in the regulation of financial services, as previously in most major financial centres, this activity was fragmented and often regulators competed with one another rather than working cooperatively. For the first time, the policing and governance of finance came under one roof. The founding chairman, Sir Howard Davies, went all over the world sharing this major breakthrough in the first year of his appointment. Although the FSA was created by law, its principal funding came from the finance industry, through a levy. This meant that it had good representation from industry in its various Boards, and the financial dependence significantly reduced its real independence from the institutions its regulated. Whilst it created a perception of tough and smart regulation, it also was very hypocritical. Politics and compromise can influence the real impact of laws, principles and rules.

The FSA was responsible for both conduct and prudential regulation, using a combination of rules and principles, and had considerable powers to investigate banks. Boards of financial institutions were primarily responsible for monitoring business strategy and risk appetite on a day-to-day basis. In this way, it also reduced the need for active supervision, which is costly and may be seen to be interfering. However, what was key to this approach was that financial institutions took direct responsibility and created robust systems for internal control and monitoring, and had the right people in senior and responsible positions to police and enforce effectively. The FSA had a dedicated Enforcement Division to follow and pursue any breaches of rules, although it later transpired that it was very calculated about whom it would pursue. One of its key aspects was an Approved Persons regime, whereby leaders and managers in responsible positions needed pre-approval, and could also be fined, reprimanded or even banned from the industry for malfeasance. Sadly, this was also proven to be ineffective.

After Sir Howard Davies the FSA was chaired by Sir Callum McCarthy. For large institutions like HBOS, it had a dedicated full-time supervisory team of about seven staff whose role was close and continuous supervision of the bank (PRA 2015a). There were new powers to make senior people accountable for their actions and decisions, whose approval to lead could be granted or with-drawn by the FSA. Initially, this move was seen as very positive and hopeful in terms of effective regulation and enforcement, and some penalties, bans and fines were issued to senior managers in large institutions (Dewing and Russell, 2008).

However, the PRA Report (2015a, 2015b) found various structural failures in the FSA's supervision of systemic banks (paras 1120–1):

- Level and experience of supervisory resources devoted to large firms was inadequate.
- It was primarily reactive and placed undue reliance on assurances from Boards and senior management.
- It was not deemed the role of supervisors to question the business model of banks. Managers were left to follow specific principles and processes.
- HBOS was supervised by a manager and a team of about seven staff, who liaised directly with the CEO – they were always in an unequal position. Mr Clive Briault, the same managing director of retail markets throughout, had no meetings with HBOS Board members, even though he was ulti-mately in charge of HBOS supervision. FSA CEO Mr Tiner (para 1123) had assumed that he was having these meetings, though somehow he never verified this. It was usually the manager of the supervision team who would raise any concerns with Board directors.
- It was conflicted by the climate of light-touch regulation, with limited resource and budget – limiting resource can be a very powerful way of undermining the effectiveness of regulation.
- One manager and one team member responsible for HBOS supervision resigned from the FSA to join HBOS. In general, there was significant staff turnover in the supervision team after 2006. Paradoxically, this is the same time when HBOS got a regulatory dividend for maintaining good relationships with the FSA.
- The funding and liquidity gap in HBOS, which led to its downfall, was identified by the FSA and recorded as a critical risk from as early as 2005, but no enforcement action was undertaken to force them to reduce their levels of borrowing.
- There was hardly any discussion at FSA Board level about systemic and prudential risks, or monitoring of the overall health of the financial system, until the wider crisis started in 2007. This was seen as a dereliction of duty.

After the crash and subsequent investigations by parliament, it transpired that the Approved Persons regime was very weak and under-resourced, and did not analyse the banking skills and experience of senior management and Board members prior to approving them. It transpired that in the case of HBOS, none of the Board members had any significant senior-level banking experience, coming mainly from retail and commercial backgrounds, including the two CEOs. In the first few years, serious questions were being asked by the FSA about the aggressive growth strategy of the firm and the impact this was having on risk management and internal controls and monitoring. The FSA even dubbed it 'an accident waiting to happen' and raised concerns with the Board. Independent ARROW risk review reports were commissioned from Price Waterhouse Coopers (2004), and a penalty in the form of an increase in the Individual Capital Ratio by 0.5% was issued (p. 267).

Strategy and Enforcement

There seems a real tension when regulators start to question business strategy – this is where HBOS fought back like a viper, and managed to deflect attention. However, if the regulators are relying on internal systems and controls and the right leadership to ensure safety and soundness, then how can they avoid questioning business strategy? In fact, when we closely examine the reports, the FSA was bold in the early years in questioning HBOS's business strategy, although this lever was slackened in later years. Also timely and serious regulatory challenge requires skills and resources, and it seems here again, the political masters ensured that the FSA was not well resourced and was highly conflicted in its resourcing, which came primarily from the private sector it regulated. Weak regulation and enforcement was not just due to incompetence, but the political and ideological climate that prevailed.

HBOS CEO Sir James Crosby was appointed to the FSA Board in December 2003 and promoted to chairman of the FSA Audit Committee in 2005 (PRA 2015a). In December 2007 he became deputy chairman of the FSA Board. The PRA found no hard evidence that he unduly influenced the supervision of HBOS. However, his very presence within the FSA in such a senior position very early on would have helped in meeting key people, understanding the skills and resources with which the FSA had to challenge, and using this in the management of HBOS.

After the HBOS collapse, the FSA conducted another detailed investigation of HBOS, and issued two Final Notices in 2012 (FSA 2012) which blamed poor corporate lending, where huge risks were taken without proper controls and management, resulting in severe losses for the bank. A personal reprimand and fine was issued to Peter Cummings, the CEO of Bank of Scotland. Although the Tyrie et al. (2013a) investigation looked at the failure of HBOS in great detail, it did not investigate the enforcement failure, as this was already being investigated by the Prudential Regulatory Authority. The Treasury Select Committee (PRA 2015b) appointed an independent senior lawyer, Andrew Green QC, who found that the FSA Final Notices were flawed and biased, and failed to investigate the influential role and actions of the Group CEOs and chairman, Crosby, Hornby and Stevenson. Green wrote (p. 4):

> My conclusion, in summary, is that the scope of the FSA's enforcement investigations in relation to the failure of HBOS was not reasonable. The decision-making process adopted by the FSA was materially flawed; and the FSA should have conducted an investigation, or series of investigations,

wider in scope than merely into the conduct of Mr. Cummings and the Corporate Division.

There was no documentation to explain why the senior leaders (two CEOs and chairman) were not investigated prior to the time limits, and to explain a lack of information sharing between the supervision and enforcement teams. There was evidence to make a strong enforcement case against Andy Hornby, but this was somehow dismissed. As a result, the FSA were now time-barred from further personal enforcement and therefore the HBOS leadership were protected from fines, penalties or reprimands. Somehow, enforcement action against senior leaders, even after the collapse of HBOS, was severely compromised and even investigations of investigations could not uncover the real reasons for this lack of timely enforcement. There was a culture of not challenging and covering up for senior bankers, even after the crisis (PRA 2015b). Tyrie et al. (2015) found this whole episode very puzzling, and through forensic questioning discovered that even after the crash, the FSA leadership and culture was siloed and divorced from reality, preferring to intellectualise about a problem rather than to dig deep and expose the culprits. It is possible that the investigations were deliberately avoided as the FSA leadership would be dragged into them and found to be equally culpable – the decisions were deeply politicised.

One of the other reasons given for HBOS's regulatory failure was a significant turnover of the supervisory team staff. There was a further technical reason – the implementation of Basel II proved very complex and demanding for its staff, and led them to distract from core issues of supervision. Such was the power and impact of whistleblower Paul Moore's subsequent revelations to parliament (detailed in the next section) about HBOS that Crosby immediately resigned his position as vice-chairman of the FSA on 11th February 2009 (Hume 2009). Moore received widespread and global media coverage about his whistleblowing.

As we saw in Chapter 4, during the parliamentary enquiry into the failure of HBOS, Moore was quizzed about his dismissal, and we examined how it was dealt with by the Board of HBOS and the regulator, the FSA. In particular, there was detailed probing about the role of KPMG in 'independently' endorsing this dismissal, giving comfort to the HBOS Audit Committee, and also the FSA relying on this report, knowing that KPMG were also auditors of HBOS and therefore not entirely independent. The HBOS Board then relied on the FSA's inaction as approval of the CEO's action to dismiss Moore. Given that Moore was hired to appease the FSA's earlier concerns about risk management, and the fact that he was well-known to the FSA for his years of regulatory investigations, this response was truly shocking to Tyrie and his committee.

Paul Moore's dismissal enquiry was a business critical investigation, done at an important time in the history of HBOS, and allowed the management to continue with its aggressive and irresponsible risk-taking. In fact, when the evidence of this came out in 2009 during the parliamentary investigations, both

KPMG and the FSA were quick to blame each other – with the FSA arguing that they relied on this report, and KPMG saying that it was a very 'narrow' and limited investigation (Jones 2009a, 2009b).

In the PRA (2015a, pp. 322–4) investigation into Paul Moore's dismissal, the report noted that the FSA was wrong to rely on KPMG to investigate it given the obvious conflicts of interest, and broke its own rules in doing so. There was no evidence that other independent firms were approached to conduct this. Financial regulators in the UK rely extensively on Big 4 firms and get into blame-shifting when things go wrong. The next section focuses on Paul Moore's timely challenge and the conflicts of interest and regulatory bias that resulted in enforcement failure. The FSA did question the appointment of Jo Dawson as Group Risk Director, given her inexperience in risk management and conflicts of interest generated by the new role which involved monitoring her own previous department. However, HBOS executives pushed hard, and the FSA relented. After her appointment, they did continue to question the fast speed of growth as compared to the right systems and controls. Dr Angela Smith, the other senior risk officer, also left HBOS soon after Moore's departure, leaving the team very weak and inexperienced.

The key political issues around bank regulation are:

- striking the right balance between expanding the banking sector and generating tax revenues and controlling the regulatory risks this may bring;
- the right knowledge must be gathered by people with the ability and skill to interpret it in a timely fashion. Regulation of a powerful and fast-moving industry can be easily compromised by skills shortages and staff turnover, usually in one direction – experienced people are poached by the private sector to boost their own compliance functions. This has the overall effect of undermining the practice of regulation;
- this information should then be analysed for its implications;
- remedial action must be decided upon and taken in a timely fashion, without political interference or fear;
- enforcement proceedings should also be initiated if laws are breached, and sanctions imposed.

When we add all these aspects together in a hugely market-sensitive area such as a well-known big bank, the reality of effective regulation requires courage, confidence and fearlessness against powerful, well-connected people. Also for well-run banks, regulators can get a very easy ride and become quite cushy in their job, so when problems come up, it becomes difficult to be pro-active and firm. People and politics have a significant influence on the nature and practice of regulation.

Regulatory Challenge

Leaders, academics and professionals occupy responsible roles in protecting civic society from harm and deliberate exploitation, crime and abuse. The experience of the 2008 global financial crash has continued to have devastating repercussions for many societies and economies. There was a widespread regulatory failure, but little is known about why timely enforcement was not undertaken. Drawing upon research on the politics, capture and complexity of enforcement, this chapter focuses on the role of regulatory people and leaders who chose whether or not to act with a public conscience – and explores why and how they did so. It also analyses the consequences of their actions and how certain people and institutions responded to challenges to authority driven by public conscience. HBOS was the fifth largest UK commercial bank before its spectacular collapse in 2008. During its early years (2001–4), regulators were seriously concerned and called it 'an accident waiting to happen'. However, concerns dissipated at the time when it became even more aggressive and risqué. Even after its collapse, there were delays in regulatory investigations and enforcement actions. The findings in this chapter explain why it is not enough to just look at rules, institutions and processes – influential people and their actions matter in enforcement. Some people take great personal and professional risks when they critique and question behaviour and group-think. Challenge against a rising tide of profits and growth involves personal risk – as exhibited by HBOS in the early years through the sacking of a key whistleblower. The findings reveal the nuances and challenges of enforcement, and the critical roles played by powerful people and networks to undermine enforcement, in spite of laws and institutions. This research opens up questions about the need for courageous leadership, new risks introduced in the name of systemic protection, the importance of systemic whistleblowers and their safety net, and the real challenges of systemic conscience and its development and exercise. Much more research needs to be done to explore the role of personal and public conscience in effective regulation and enforcement.

Effective regulation can only work if there is timely and reliable enforcement – otherwise, a culture of ignorance of rules and principles can erode justice and fairness. Enforcement requires a will to challenge, prosecute and take risks. These risks may be personal, institutional or both. In the case of the regulation of large systemically important banks, leaders and regulators have often been easily captured, resulting in the undermining of enforcement (Germain 2010; Moran 1991). However, this is not always the case, and there have been some examples of people in corporations and regulatory authorities who have decided to challenge (Heffernan 2011). Often they do this without calculating the personal returns, driven by a public or civic conscience (Avakian and Roberts 2012). And there are many cases where their lives are ruined by these actions. Also, being human, regulators are fallible and may make mistakes in calculating and interpreting risks, or persuading others of the seriousness of the problem. With large banks, the complexities of group accountability and oversight may themselves lead to regulatory failure. Some have even argued that the financial crisis is an elite political debacle, arising from technical hubris and failure (Engelen et al. 2012). It is even possible that changes in regulations and regulators in the name of systemic protection can introduce new risks which can weaken effective governance and enforcement (Goodhart 2010). Leaders who have the big picture and the powers to enforce need to be talented, fearless and decisive at the right time.

Research shows that bank regulation cannot be studied without under-standing the international financial architecture, and the varieties of laws and institutions which regulate banking and financial reporting (Humphrey et al. 2009; Moran 1991). Since the 1990s there has been a growing concern with global systemic risk, and a desire to harmonise international bank regulation in the pursuit of financial stability (Arnold 2012). There has been a growing awareness of the power and influence of certain very large financial institutions, and a desire to prevent their failure. However, regulation has also become a complex technical minefield, with different institutions, standard-setters and global and local influences which are changing all the time. This complexity and change can also seriously undermine the effectiveness of regulation and its enforcement, because at a people level, skills, teamwork and training are required. 'Haphazard' is the phrase Tomasic (2011) used to describe UK civil and criminal enforcement actions before the crash. Enforcement can also easily be disrupted by staff turnover or revolving doors, especially if the private sector has more resources and funding to attract regulators with contacts and experience. In the process, regulatory skill and resources in the public sector can be easily and routinely undermined. The 'smart' people are often seen as the ones who generate business, not the ones who regulate it (Das 2011; Kay 2015), so the self-esteem and respect of regulators can be undermined by business leaders. Somehow, enforcement keeps on failing, and even after the 2008 crash, major financial misdemeanours continued in spite of huge criticism of bankers and banking.

The globalisation of banking restricted the capacity of any single national regulator to act (Kay 2015). Gatherings of regulators, instead of enhancing supervision and challenge, have become 'comfort' meetings, held in pleasant locations. Often regulators and politicians attending them use these opportunities to advance their own domestic interests, with lobbyists encouraging them to do so. Thus enforcement can be dampened by competing interests and the comfort factor provided by high finance which gambles 'other people's money', both to bankers and regulators. It is possible that this psychology of hubris and comfort explains regulatory failure at a personal and leadership level – it becomes very difficult to challenge economic booms and rich 'successful' bankers.

One of the major difficulties of studying enforcement failures is the avail-ability of credible evidence and information, especially in terms of access and interviews of key people involved in the enforcement process (Shah 2015a). There is often a hushed silence justified by 'ongoing investigations', regulatory football, zero access to external audit files and deliberate use of delay tactics to undermine credible research. However, Arnold (2009) makes a strong case for such investigative research, given the social and economic importance of banking and the need for academics to use their knowledge and skills to expose flaws and cracks in the bank regulatory process. Lessons must be learnt, she argues, and theory and research need to prioritise this arena. Arnold calls upon academics to take an ethical interest in preventing systemic crises, and move beyond positivism and post-modernism. Accounting academics are very well placed to conduct such research, she argues.

Theories of regulatory capture and regulatory space (Watson 2013) are helpful in understanding the very real dynamics of regulation and the people and groups who influence its agenda setting, legal rules, methods, resources, processes and outcomes. However, as Black (2002) has shown, they can also confuse and diffuse the fundamental meaning of regulation and enforcement which is to govern and challenge. It is critical that we learn from the failures of regulation and use the learning to transform institutions, policies, laws and standards. States and societies need to prevent capture by technocrats and professionals, and protect public interest through state intervention (Engelen et al. 2012).

Enforcement relies on a system of principles and rules, which are open to interpretation and creative compliance (McBarnet and Whelan 1992; Shah 1996a, 1997b). Experts can help in stretching the rules, exploiting gaps in the rules and thereby undermining effective regulation. Such regulatory arbitrage is common and widespread in banking, and often a major source of revenues and profits (Shaxson 2012). One of the critiques of principles-based regulation is precisely the uncertainty of interpretation, and the related abuse by regulatees, undermining the fundamental spirit of regulation (Black 2002; McBarnet and Whelan 1991). Some have even argued that for banks, regulatory arbitrage is an instinctive act, so we should not be surprised when regulation and enforcement fails.

What happens if someone in the regulatory process decides to speak up? Does this cut through regulatory capture and space and lead to real governance? Why and how is it that people 'knowingly' decide not to challenge and allow themselves to get compromised and captured in the process? Do regulatory institutions provide comfort as well as responsibility to individuals? Which is more overwhelming? What roles do the revolving doors of regulation play in the direct or covert undermining of enforcement? Such ethical questions are critical to the regulation of systemic banks, though not all of them can be answered in one study.

Contemporary finance theory virtually ignores the nuances, ethics and politics of this regulatory process, driven by its neo-liberal ideology of market-based regulation (McSweeney 2009; Frankfurter and McGoun 2002). Some have strongly argued that this ignorance has been compromised by significant academic conflicts of interest as reported in the film *Inside Job* (Ferguson 2010). Knowledge in business has become compromised by the business of knowledge. Beck (1992) has shown how experts often get corrupted by their expertise, and lose the notions of truth and fairness and instead of helping to prevent risks to society, they add to the risks faced by society. Some writers have suggested that finance academics should also bear responsibility for the financial crisis (Arnold 2009; Shah and Baker 2015). Concerns have also been raised about the emerging 'science' of macro-prudential regulation and its deep ideological and policy paradoxes (Baker 2014). While systemic risk may be real and important, we still know little about the huge ideological and policy implications of its management (Baker 2013), and the conflicts between different economic and political goals. Paradoxically, relying on the conscience and courage of senior leaders may be the only way we can 'muddle through' the complex arena of international finance and risk-taking. And this has been shown to be a very weak and problematic safety net.

This chapter is organised as follows: the next section explains the research method, followed by the background of HBOS and its collapse. We then focus on the actions of systemic people and networks, the FSA leadership and enforcement failures, whistleblower Paul Moore, Guy Bainbridge and KPMG, the Financial Reporting Council's deflection of enforcement and finally the challenges given to regulators by parliamentarian Andrew Tyrie. All of these help to understand how people in influential positions responded to the serious problems at HBOS. The final section draws on the above to help us understand why prudential enforcement fails and what signals and warning signs we should be looking for in the future.

Research Method

This chapter tries to study the actions and decisions of key people involved in the regulation of HBOS – such access to senior people, especially after a crisis, is usually impossible, but necessary. It uses an interpretive approach (Parker 2008) with an inter-disciplinary lens, motivated by a desire to unravel what we can learn about enforcement (Parker and Guthrie 2014). Fortunately, a number of parliamentary and regulatory enquiries conducted asked the questions we would have wanted to know the answers to. They also uncovered key primary documents relating to the management of HBOS and the roles and reports of professional auditors and advisors. This study relies on a combination of interview, documentary and primary evidence to piece together what really happened behind the scenes in the enforcement failure at HBOS. The author was also part of a team of experts who campaigned for an investigation into KPMG's audit failure, and in the process a lot was learnt about the dynamics of enforcement, and the behaviour of key agencies like the Financial Reporting Council. This study draws upon three major regulatory/parliamentary investigations, each of which lasted several years, and interviewed senior executives on the Board of HBOS and in the regulation of UK banking. These are:

- Tyrie et al. (2013a) – 'An accident waiting to happen: The failure of HBOS';
- PRA (2015a) – 'The failure of HBOS plc: A report by the Financial Conduct Authority and the Prudential Regulatory Authority, UK';
- PRA (2015b) – 'Report into the FSA's enforcement actions following the failure of HBOS';
- PRA (2015c) – 'Oral Evidence – Independent review of the report into the failure of HBOS'.

PRA (2015b) is unique in that it explicitly uses an independent legal expert team to examine whether the enforcement action taken by the FSA at the time was just and fair.

In total, the above reports cover over 1500 pages of evidence and analysis of the HBOS collapse, often obtained by forensic questioning by experts and legal counsel. For this research, they proved an invaluable source of evidence.

Hindsight is at one level easy, and what is difficult is to go back to a parti- cular point in time and look at the decisions taken in the light of what was known at that time. This study is conscious of this drawback, and tries to piece together evidence prevailing at certain points in time to understand how senior people dealt with systemic issues. Particular focus is placed around the time in 2004 when the aggressive growth strategy was being questioned by both reg- ulators and insiders of HBOS. The research also reveals who the key players were and their positions and decisions taken at critical times.

The Financial Reporting Council had exhausted all excuses to enforce, and were finally pushed in 2016 to investigate KPMG by Andrew Tyrie MP, chair of the Treasury Select Committee (TSC). A team of concerned people, including the present author, Professor Prem Sikka, Paul Moore and others campaigned actively and helped arm the TSC with the research needed (Shah 2015a) to support this investigation. The next section sets out the factual background of HBOS, the key people involved in the collapse of HBOS and their failure to exercise timely challenge, even where it was their role and duty to do so.

People and Power

In retrospect, it was a handful of people responsible for the downfall of HBOS – Lord Stevenson, James Crosby, Andy Hornby, Peter Cummings, Sir Callum McCarthy, Gordon Brown, Sir Mervyn King and Guy Bainbridge. They saw the risks, control failures and understood the systemic nature of banking and the critical importance of its prudent management and super- vision. Instead, they somehow chose to protect their personal power and status and did not exercise a public conscience in spite of knowing what they did – some like Stein (2011) and Das (2011) have argued that there was a culture of mania prevailing at the time. There is evidence to show that the paths of all these people crossed, sometimes on a regular basis.

Gordon Brown was, with Tony Blair, one of the chief architects of New Labour in Britain. He was Chancellor of the Exchequer from day one, and later rose to become Prime Minister, an ambition he never disguised. Son of a church minister, he was known for a moral compass and conscience. Some- how, the power of the finance industry and its hubris got to him (Lee 2009). Brown was euphoric about the economic boom and even congratulated elite bankers in a now infamous speech in the City of London (Brown 2006). Instead, the reality was that the bankers were perpetuating massive frauds, which continued well after the global crash of 2008. Finance had captured politics big time, and Brown seemed unaware of this capture, despite being a Labour politician. In parliament, Gordon Brown was grilled about his role in influencing HBOS conduct and mismanagement, and there were fears that he may have to resign over the scandal (Pagano 2009). The extent of scandals in London has been significant, with the rigging of LIBOR, foreign exchange rates and other key indices in markets like energy, the mis-selling of insurance products and loans both to small businesses and retail customers, and insider trading.

There was a prevailing ideology of 'light-touch regulation' which really perpetuated the belief in the perfection and ability of markets to be self-regulating. This went against the grain of British law, which was meant to keep a tough eye on financial institutions and regulate the quality of people, systems and risk management, and ensure customers were treated fairly. The hubris of boom completely transformed the interpretation, application and influence of the law regulating banks in Britain. Capturing politicians is one thing, but capturing their thinking and ideology is like game, set and match for the errant bankers, who only cared for the quickest way of maximising wealth. When the regulators were finally confronted about who was monitoring the safety and soundness of the financial system, they both said neither (Treasury Committee 2009). This means that no one was overseeing the whole system, in spite of having knowledge about banking crises and the systemic nature of financial crashes.

As noted in Chapter 3, when asked why regulators did not act in time, the Bank of England governor, Sir Mervyn King, replied (Mc Fall et al, 2009a):

> The people in the banks would have said, 'Well, who are you to say we are taking too big risks? We have got far brighter and more qualified risk assessors than you have got. We have made massive profits every year for almost ten years. We have paid big bonuses. The City is the most successful part of the UK economy. How dare you tell us that we should stop taking such risks? Can you prove to us that the risks we are taking will necessarily end in tears?' and of course [the FSA] could not ... Any bank that had been threatened by a regulator because it was taking excessive risks would have had PR machines out in full force, Westminster and the Government would have been lobbied, it would have been a pretty lonely job being a regulator.

Sir Mervyn King was the governor of the Bank of England throughout the HBOS period, and principal in charge of UK financial and monetary policy, although he denied responsibility for systemic prudential supervision and so did the FSA. The Bank of England had a long tradition, up until the 1980s, of being feared for their supervision, and bank leaders were invited for a 'cup of tea' if their bank was straying from prudent risk management (Moran 1991). That fear seems to have long gone, and here the governor appears to fear them! He did not provide any evidence of concerns he raised prior to the crash with the Chancellor or Prime Minister about the heating up of the banking system and the aggressive risks generated by banks. He was very influential and a former LSE professor and academic, but somehow failed to see the crisis brewing right under his nose. If there was such strong political interference from the bankers, he had the authority to challenge politicians and parliament, as the Bank of England was independent of government. He somehow chose not to respond strongly to lobbying pressure.

Sir King was present at a now famous meeting of world central bankers in the USA (Ferguson 2010) where Professor Raghuram Rajan gave serious warnings about the build-up of systemic risk in the financial system (Rajan 2005). After the crisis, there was no blame accorded to him, and he retired with a red carpet and was made a member of the House of Lords (Martin 2013). Subsequently, he has written a major book (King 2016) about how the global financial sector should be fundamentally reformed – though he did not do so when he was in charge.

Both people inside banks, like Paul Moore, and regulators, like the FSA, seemed powerless to restrain the risk juggernaut and man-made avalanche. Unlike Paul Moore or Andrew Tyrie, few people were prepared to risk their life and career and blow the whistle.

The Labour Party was really swept away by the high taxes coming from the City and got swamped by the idea of the City of London as a global capital of finance, from which Britain could stay great, irrespective of the greed and fraud which this continues to import and which make Britain a haven for tax and fraud. There was also a close personal friendship between Brown and Crosby (Pagano 2009).

Both HBOS pioneers James Crosby and Lord Stevenson had very close ties with the leadership of the Labour party which governed throughout HBOS's life – Tony Blair, Peter Mandelson and Gordon Brown (Perman 2012; Rawstone and Salmon 2012). One of the most influential positions Lord Stevenson occupied was as chair of the Arts and Media Honours Committee – the committee decided which people are awarded honours like knighthoods.

Guy Bainbridge was the lead KPMG audit partner of HBOS Group for each of the critical five years ended 31st December 2003 to 2007 (Bainbridge 2012). On 1st October 2007, he was promoted to the inaugural Board of KPMG Europe where he remained until 2012. He was made chair of the Audit Committee. In 2010, he was appointed as lead audit partner of HSBC Group, one of the world's largest banks.

Peter Cummings was the CEO of the Bank of Scotland, the commercial arm of HBOS which turned out to have made spectacular losses in its lending through poor risk assessment and controls. He was investigated and personally fined and reprimanded by the FSA (2012), although later investigation by the PRA (2015b) showed that it was wrong of the FSA to blame him solely for the losses, and senior Board leaders such as Hornby and Stevenson should also have been thoroughly investigated.

Andy Hornby was a senior retailer at ASDA before he was headhunted to join HBOS as director of retail banking and then promoted to the role of CEO upon the early retirement of James Crosby in 2006. He continued the push for constant growth started by James Crosby and encouraged aggressive risk-taking throughout the bank.

The next section focuses on the FSA whose primary role and duty it was to supervise and enforce the regulation of systemic banks like HBOS.

Whistleblower Paul Moore

To recap here, in 2002, a highly accomplished and respected KPMG regulatory consultancy partner left to lead risk management at HBOS, and was promoted to Head of Group Regulatory Risk on 1st January 2004 – a senior position where he led a team of 150 professionals. Tyrie et al. (2013a) and others have now credited him as being a very important early critic of HBOS, who spotted the risks and problems, which later brought the huge multi-billion-pound downfall and losses for the economy and society. However, in November 2004, he was suddenly fired by the HBOS CEO because of his challenging questioning and critique of the firm's sales and growth strategy. He filed a complaint about this to the firm and to the FSA. The HBOS Board then appointed KPMG to investigate the dismissal, and KPMG accepted the appointment, knowing that Moore was a former colleague and accomplished partner of theirs. Their report concluded that Paul Moore's dismissal was justified – they 'independently' sided with their client. Moore has written a whole book about his experiences at KPMG and HBOS (Moore 2015).

From earlier Chapters 3 and 4, the testimony of Moore shows a professional motivated by truth and fairness, and with significant skill in financial regulation and an ability to be forensic in his search for facts and evidence. He was not a technical expert in finance but had a deeper understanding of risk as being a matter concerned with people, systems and culture, not something that is simply measured and forgotten. Given this wealth of knowledge and experience, he chose not to be silent in the face of authority and power, and spoke about deep cultural problems and an aggressive growth strategy. He even took his concerns directly to some non-executive directors. In retrospect, it seems he was politically very naïve and did not calculate the consequences of his challenge, or fully fathom the huge power and executive authority of Crosby. He paid for this by losing his job and giving up his career, something which few people are ever willing to do. As a risk manager, he was not afraid to take personal risk – Moore did not separate his working life from his personal conscience and values. In this area, he did not calculate the personal risks to his life and career, even though he was capable of doing so. In the whole saga of HBOS we have seen time and again smart, capable people either neglecting their responsibility, or wilfully condoning bad behaviour, hoping somehow it would go away. It seems no one saw that in a short time, HBOS would go bust, and they would be held accountable.

One of the key documents which defended Moore's dismissal was the KPMG investigation, reported in detail earlier in Chapter 4. The relationship sounded more like a strategic alliance between KPMG and HBOS than an auditor–client professional and independent relationship. HBOS quickly settled with Moore financially after the report was presented, and this should also have been evidence to KPMG of an admission of guilt by their client. PRA (2015a, p. 324) revealed that James Crosby actually interfered in KPMG's investigation process of Paul Moore's dismissal, and the FSA were aware of this. They subsequently approved the appointment of Jo Dawson as new director of Group Risk, even though she had no prior risk governance experience. The FSA did scrutinise her appointment (PRA 2015a, pp. 320–1) and raised a number of concerns about her skills and competence, but 'somehow got persuaded' to approve it. According to Moore, the consequences of strong action from the FSA may have led to the dismissal of Crosby, which would be hugely market-sensitive and could possibly attract questioning and scrutiny of the FSA action. It did convey to internal staff at HBOS that anyone who speaks up can get fired – his equal colleague in risk management, Dr Angela Smith, left soon after Moore, and reported her concerns to the FSA. The FSA did increase the frequency of their meetings with Dawson from quarterly to monthly to keep a close watch on the strengths of risk supervision and control.

The next section looks into the role of the auditors and the knowledge and skills they had to exercise timely challenge.

KPMG – Independent Regulators?

In Chapter 4, we have seen in detail how KPMG was deeply compromised in its audit of HBOS. Throughout the core life of the HBOS Group, there was one lead auditor, Guy Bainbridge. He was a senior partner in the firm, and well-known and highly respected. To audit a large group is highly complex, especially given that it is growing very fast, and its management are so incompetent. KPMG would have access to warning letters issued by the FSA in the early years and concerns about 'an accident waiting to happen'. In addition, KPMG also benefited from highly lucrative consultancy contracts, and even though non-audit fees have to be reported in the HBOS accounts, it is not clear how complete and accurate these numbers were. For example, a crack team of thirty KPMG experts were hired at short notice to work on the HBOS acquisition of Abbey National, which was subsequently aborted – the fees for this would easily have been in the millions. Also where commercial clients of the Bank of Scotland were required to have due diligence by KPMG prior to loan approvals, the fees for this would come from the commercial customers rather than HBOS, so it need not be reported in the accounts. This work could also be hugely lucrative and cumulative, requiring little sales effort.

The literature is full of examples where auditors have failed to challenge their clients on critical and material issues, with serious consequences for the client (Humphrey 2008; Sikka et al. 2009; Sikka 2009). This literature also shows that matters like the 'public interest' and 'systemic concerns' have often not been demonstrated in practice. This could be for various reasons:

- They were unaware of the error or fraud or misjudged its materiality.
- They were aware but afraid to challenge.
- They were compromised by the allure of profits and motivated by greed and selfishness.
- They simply did not care about audit quality or accuracy and reliability or evaluated the audit risk to be insignificant.
- They had insufficient skills or resources to carry out a proper audit.

As we saw in Chapter 4, Guy Bainbridge was invited but did not appear before the Tyrie Parliamentary Committee investigating HBOS, even though many other prominent people, including HBOS Board members and FSA directors, did appear. Instead, KPMG supplied written answers to specific questions (Bainbridge 2012). The answers he gave raised serious concerns about the quality and independence of the audit, and the number of times challenges were raised at Board level. What is most surprising is that the auditors never met and addressed the full Board, even though in practice it is the Board which approves and authorises the annual report which KPMG audits. The auditors relied on management for accurate recording and internal policing and risk management, but never faced them as people, looking eye-to-eye. Had they demanded to do so, the Board could not refuse.

In their evidence to parliament, both the HBOS chairman Lord Stevenson and the Audit Committee chairman Tony Hobson said they had excellent relationships with the auditors (Tyrie et al. 2013a). When Lord Stevenson, who was chairman of HBOS from its inception to its demise, says that throughout the life of HBOS, KPMG was never in disagreement, and to the contrary was 'very helpful', we have clear evidence of a culture of appeasement and partnership as opposed to one of independence and challenge. This 'friendship' is also echoed by the chair of the HBOS Audit Committee Tony Hobson and Bainbridge (see Chapter 4).

From the Tyrie and PRA report documents, there is extensive correspondence between the FSA and HBOS, raising concerns about their systems and controls and risk management processes, especially between 2002 and 2006. All these letters were copied to KPMG. This shows that the FSA wanted all key matters to be reported to the auditors, although we know that KPMG did not meet them to discuss any concerns over HBOS. KPMG were reluctant to exercise their authority to speak directly to the regulator, even where they had ample opportunity for this.

The above answers at the very least demonstrate that the audit did not follow crucial rules and guidelines, and management were not challenged nor were critical matters reported or discussed with the FSA. They imply a cosy relationship with the Board, with a pro-active management of the relationship by the audit partners.

After the crash, Guy Bainbridge was promoted to the newly created Board of KPMG Europe and continues to be a senior partner at the firm. He was also put in charge of the group audit of HSBC, even though HSBC shareholders raised complaints about his appointment given the failure of HBOS (Sharp 2013). KPMG's head at the time of the HBOS audit failure was Sir John Griffith-Jones, who then went on to be the head of KPMG Europe after the crash. In 2013, he was appointed to head the newly created Financial Conduct Authority, and no questions about the failure of major banks audited by the firm under his leadership were asked by parliament in the appointment hearing and clearance (Treasury Committee 2013). The next section focuses on the role of the accounting and corporate governance regulator, the FRC, in enforcement failure over HBOS and KPMG.

Kicking It All into the Long Grass – The Financial Reporting Council (FRC)

The UK's Financial Reporting Council has a wide remit to monitor and enforce corporate governance of quoted companies, including supervision of Big 4 firms and their audit performance (Financial Reporting Council 2014). It carries out annual inspections of their audit quality and has the power to revoke the licence to audit. In the event of corporate scandals, it has the authority to investigate and penalise audit firms. It also oversees independent personal disciplinary arrangements for public interest cases involving accountants. Despite the huge banking crisis, where a number of very large UK banks failed, it did not conduct any investigation on the audits of the failed banks conducted primarily by three of the Big 4 firms – Deloitte, PWC and KPMG. Nor has any accountant or auditor working at these banks or relevant audit firms been fined or debarred as a result of the crash. Of the three firms, KPMG is the largest auditor in the finance sector, providing audit and other services to 30% of all major firms in London. Soon after the crash, the head of the FRC proclaimed that the auditors had a 'good' crisis.

There have been widespread allegations about the capture of the FRC by the Big 4, and it has made few material challenges or given fines of any significance to the Big 4 since its creation in 2006, according to the FRC website. In fact, there are several KPMG alumni who occupy senior positions in the FRC (Salmon 2013). The FRC used excuses like 'insufficient information to trigger an investigation', or 'we cannot start until the parliamentary enquiry has finished', or 'let's wait until the PRA finishes its investigation'. All this delayed the beginning of the investigation to 2016, when only a preliminary enquiry into whether or not there was a case to investigate was announced (Haddrill 2016).

Paul Moore (2012) wrote a strong letter of complaint to the Financial Reporting Council about the conduct of KPMG, requesting an investigation into their behaviour (see key extracts from this letter in Chapter 4). Yet no enforcement action was taken by the Financial Reporting Council.

Moore spent a considerable amount of personal time and effort urging the FRC to investigate KPMG but found the experience deeply frustrating and deliberately obfuscating. He felt that the FRC were protecting KPMG and was even suspicious that any documents or evidence he supplied to them would be leaked to KPMG by their regulator. This is what he said:

The FRC were doing everything in their power to avoid a public interest investigation into something that was very obvious. Their criticism that I did not give them enough evidence is absolute rubbish – they had plenty of evidence from my Treasury Select Committee representations to investigate KPMG (in 2009).

The FRC gave me a meeting with their legal advisor on 22/5/2012, a General Counsel for them. I went to this meeting with Mike Howarth. In that meeting we went over my concerns. I repeatedly asked him whether he had read my evidence to the Treasury Select Committee – he constantly said I cannot remember. I warned him that if he lied to me, I would report him to the Bar Council. I could not get him to do what was right. It was a waste of time. The FRC constantly tried to avoid the audit trail in our correspondence – they made it very hard for me to pursue my case. After the meeting I wrote to Stephen Haddrill, CEO of FRC, saying the meeting was completely unsatisfactory. What was absolutely clear was that the FRC were trying to avoid at all costs doing an investigation, and even if I had forced them to do so, the investigation would have been totally unfair and wrong. I asked the FRC in my correspondence whether they had private conversations with KPMG. They did not deny this, but refused to answer my questions. They were constantly kicking it into the long grass. I threatened to ask for a public enquiry into the FRC in my email to Stephen Haddrill.

At a meeting in September 2012 regarding an investigation into the collapse of HBOS, the Financial Conduct Authority specifically excluded an investigation of KPMG, and Mr Griffith-Jones (former head of KPMG and chairman of the FCA) was present. The FCA said it would 'take account of input from the auditors but not review their work nor seek to opine on relevant accounting standards and their application' (Aldrick 2013). Even during the PRA investigation into HBOS, when a number of key preliminary findings about the auditors were circulated to the FRC, they avoided launching an investigation into KPMG, to the surprise of the investigators (PRA 2015c). MP Jim Cousins (Treasury Committee 2010) quizzed the FRC chief executive Stephen Haddrill extensively about their 'protection' of the Big 4 and incompetence in implementing and maintaining audit quality. For example, Cousins asked rather pointedly (Treasury Committee 2010):

Is it not the situation that the fees the big four accountancy firms are getting from banks are absolutely enormous and that you are limited in what you can do as regulators because you have to protect them? We have a classic cartel.

Most of the answers were vague and defensive. The parliamentarian Andrew Tyrie MP stands out as a person determined to question the regulators in their failure to enforce, on a consistent basis, for many years after the crash. The next section explains his role in exposing HBOS enforcement failures.

Andrew Tyrie MP – Political Challenger

One key thread in the whole investigation and enforcement stage of the HBOS failure is Andrew Tyrie MP. He has been chair of the Treasury Select Committee for eight years, starting just after the banking crash, at a time which required significant scrutiny, reflection and reform. Since the crash, the number of banking scandals actually increased, regulators failed (the FSA was replaced by the FCA) and a new Banking Act was passed, but he persevered with the challenges. The Treasury Select Committee is a group of Members of Parliament with some experience or knowledge about financial services whose role it is to monitor key activities of the Treasury, one of the most influential civil service departments in the UK. In the case of HBOS, it was Tyrie who first brought Paul Moore to whistleblow under parliamentary protection, and later chaired a major enquiry into the HBOS failure which is now hailed as one of the highest quality investigations into a UK bank failure (Tyrie et al. 2013a). He did not stop there and recommended further enquiries into the regulatory and audit failures at HBOS, by the Prudential Regulatory Authority, the Financial Conduct Authority and the Financial Reporting Council. In fact, he persevered with the Financial Reporting Council, forcing them to investigate KPMG even though it was strictly supervised by the Department of Business, Innovation and Skills and not the Treasury. Throughout the aftermath of the financial crisis, and the growing negligence of banks, Tyrie did not lose his nerve or stamina in making senior people and institutions in enforcement accountable.

With Parliamentary Committees and investigations, powers and resources are often very limited – one of their key powers is public exposure and interrogation, as all the events are televised and documented. It can be very difficult to get to the truth due to the lack of resources. In the case of the HBOS investigation, he managed to convince government to fund an expert legal team to research and forensically question the HBOS leaders and stakeholders about their roles and actions in the management, auditing and supervision of the bank. David Quest QC was hired to perform this task, which he conducted very ably, and the resulting report (Tyrie et al. 2013a) revealed a catalogue of management and supervision failures in great detail, supported by a number of primary documents including Board minutes, confidential correspondence and regulatory reports, which would not normally be seen by the public. He then commissioned a subsequent and detailed independent examination of the role of the FSA in this debacle, and how much they knew beforehand and why they failed to act in a timely manner (PRA 2015a, 2015b, 2015c).

Collectively, these reports exposed a hubristic leadership, a failure of the Board in its governance and challenge, and a failure of the FSA in its supervision and enforcement. Sadly, the findings came too late for penalising the key leaders who led the downfall of HBOS, as their time limits for investigation had already expired under FSA rules. Tyrie admitted that the political establishment prevailing at the time was also responsible for fuelling the crisis (Tyrie et al. 2013c), something that would infuriate many of his peers and bring risk to his personal career and progression. However, there has not been a separate enquiry into the role of senior politicians in preventing effective regulation and governance of the financial sector.

A group of us were very concerned about the failure to investigate KPMG over the HBOS affair. The team included Brian Little, Professor Prem Sikka, Paul Moore, Ian Fraser (banking blogger and author of the bestselling book on RBS collapse *Shredded*), Tony Shearer (former CEO of Singer & Friedlander and partner at Coopers & Lybrand) and myself. We wrote a letter to the TSC (Little et al. 2015), backed by my own research on the HBOS audit failure (Shah 2015a) and Prem Sikka's extensive research on audit regulatory failures (Mitchell and Sikka 2011; Sikka 2009), and raised our serious concerns about both KPMG and the FRC. We claimed that the FRC is not fit to regulate accounting and should be replaced. We also actively worked with various media, writing a number of articles (Shah and Sikka 2015; Shah 2015c; Shah 2016a, 2016b) to raise our concerns, and even managed to get a major article in the *Financial Times* about our campaign (Agnew 2016). Our letter was considered by the TSC, and it influenced their decision to persevere with the FRC to investigate KPMG (Tornero 2016). The experience of running this campaign taught us that challenge is possible with limited resources and a diverse team, but it cannot be achieved simply by writing academic papers. Engaging with business executives, media and senior managers can really help shape a campaign and get it heard. In the process, we learnt about the processes of challenge, institutional inertia and resistance, and how systemic regulatory institutions can be questioned in the public eye by a few determined people. We also learnt that academics are not the sole possessors of truth and wisdom, and are often weak in institutional knowledge.

Initially the FRC responded to Tyrie with announcing a preliminary examination of the possibility of an enquiry, and it was very limited in scope (Tornero 2016). Tyrie immediately wrote back (Tyrie 2016) saying he was not satisfied with the process and approach, asking them to widen the scope, and also to hire independent experts to oversee their enquiry and report on it. This level of push has been long overdue, given that auditors were virtually unscathed from the financial crisis, but Tyrie is determined to use his influence and parliamentary authority to open the can of worms.

We now discuss what all this means for our knowledge of regulation and enforcement of systemic institutions.

Conclusion and Implications for Regulatory Enforcement

In spite of all the laws, regulations and regulatory institutions, people do matter when it comes to enforcement. Whether they are leaders inside regulatory bodies, parliamentarians, or leaders of Big 4 accounting firms or leaders of systemic banks, the actions and courage of a few people can make a difference to the outcome. Usually this influence and power has been abused by senior bankers, auditors and regulators. In failing to act in a timely fashion, auditors have broken their own professional codes but rarely get reprimanded or even investigated for professional misconduct in the case of systemic failure.

From the above, we see that as large, bureaucratic institutions, regulatory bodies such as the FSA and KPMG find it very difficult to 'care' when it comes to serious enforcement of systemically important banks. Form often dominates substance, and active challenging of large and powerful financial institutions requires leaders to have conscience and courage to mobilise support internally. Despite having considerable resources and power to challenge, they somehow fail to do so in time, even when armed with good information. It is also not clear what the risks of non-challenge are to an institution. The FSA has morphed into the FCA using the same building, address and most of the same staff. Similarly, KPMG and the FRC are still surviving, and managing to deflect any external investigation into the audit failure at HBOS.

The evidence presented here raises questions about the behaviour of senior regulators and auditors, opening possibilities for further research:

- Does 'other people's money' mean 'other people's worry' when it comes to prudential enforcement? Does the existence of large and inter-locking regulators mean that no one is personally responsible for systemic failure? If so, we have a fundamental flaw in our international financial system which is insoluble.
- There is personal risk when any individual decides to challenge a systemic bank, whether or not they are regulators. Does the situation change when a group decides to act in concert, whether as a Board or a team of regulators? The newly created Financial Policy Committee tasked to supervise prudential risks has been set up as a group, so can perhaps overcome this weakness.
- How much do we know about the psychology of challenge when things go wrong? For example, if a Board member or supervisor expresses concern, that could possibly increase their own workload, and break their normal routine of approving decisions and letting things continue as they are. More research is needed to understand why people fail to challenge in a timely way.
- When both KPMG and the FSA leadership never interviewed the Board of HBOS prior to the crisis, is it because they did not want to know about any skeletons in the cupboard? Is there an active strategy of 'don't ask, don't tell' among senior regulators? If so, how can we stop or prevent this for systemic institutions? Should there be a personal penalty for enforcement failure?
- We must research in detail how 'revolving doors', both at junior and senior levels, undermine effective enforcement. To what extent is their hiring by the regulatees deliberate or even a bribe? Are future job

prospects or cushy advisory contracts used actively or tacitly to silence influential regulators? Should there be bans or limits on this kind of recruitment, especially by the same firm supervised by a manager?

- Does change and complexity in the regulatory architecture introduce new risks of enforcement failure, instead of preventing system failure? What are these risks? Can they ever be foreseen and prevented? Who supervises prudential supervisors?

- The psychology, values and mind-set of senior regulators is key to effective regulation and enforcement. Should there be a belief and courage test in their recruitment, and should this be monitored on a continuous basis? The same should apply to audit partners in the Big 4, and if the same partner is involved in both audit and consultancy work (even for different clients), how do these undermine their psychology and courage in challenging audit clients? Not only is there conflict of interest at the level of the firm, there is conflict of interest at the level of the individual partner.

- After the crash, the chief executive of the newly created FCA, Martin Wheatley, was tough on errant banks and enforcement, but forced to resign by the Chancellor due to extensive lobbying by the banks (Elliot, 2015). When regulators personally care and decide to get tough, there can be political interference, even after a major banking crisis and fraudulent culture. The 'Finance Curse' of a major finance sector in one country is simply overwhelming (Shaxson and Christensen 2013). Does this mean that in a country housing a large financial sector, lurching from one financial crisis to another is simply inevitable and uncontrollable?

- Does the fact that all the key players in the HBOS fiasco were white men, coming from a similar cultural background, influence the governance and regulatory debacle of HBOS? How come no one took a firm line on Board diversity prior to the crash?

- To what extent are auditors and regulators prudent, risk averse and happy to do a 'job' and hide behind institutions? How can we prevent regulatory institutions from becoming too comfortable and comforting?

- Given the systemic nature of banking, there should be a special whistle-blowing protection regime as part of macro-prudential regulation. A pro-active attempt at inviting whistleblowers can also help.

- There should be a pro-active attempt to identify key banking people networks and influence, and break them, if macro-prudential regulation is intended to be effective.

- Regulators afraid to challenge, or found to use deliberate delay tactics and obfuscation, should be removed from their posts promptly. Should there be clear consequences for failing in timely enforcement actions?

- When KPMG accepted the highly conflicted task of investigating the dismissal of Paul Moore, was there someone in the firm worried about the criticism this would generate for the firm if there was a future investigation? What is the quality of internal conflicts of interest monitoring and policing of these firms? Do large Big 4 regulatory firms have any regulatory conscience whatsoever? If so, by whom and in what way is this monitored and enforced? Or are Big 4 firms too complex and too big to manage and control?

- The Big 4 audit firms, with their range of commercial services and interests, plus the advisory services provided to regulators, increase the likelihood of conflicts of interest and reduce the exercise of challenge to large and systemic banks who are major sources of revenue, directly and indirectly. Their size and multiple services and conflicts of interest increase prudential risks. If regulators are serious about preventing system failure and capture, this has to be tackled directly.

The final chapter examines the lessons and implications of the findings of this research. Reflecting back on Chapter 1, where flaws in finance theory and literature are identified in relation to culture and politics, we find that much more research is needed to expose this political reality in finance. HBOS was a very political organisation but tried to hide this and present a face of efficient management. It was at the epicentre of British banking, and its earthquake brought the system down. It was not competitive and efficient as theory had predicted, nor was it self-regulated by the markets. Deep problems were covered up until they mushroomed out of control. As a society, the lessons from this crisis must be learnt, especially for our knowledge and teaching in banking and finance. Serious and urgent changes are required to discourage such fraud, hubris and recklessness in future. We identify potential reforms to finance theory and teaching arising from this disastrous experience.

6 Findings and Implications for Finance Teaching and Research

The failure of HBOS and the losses generated were spectacular. Whilst we understand natural disasters like earthquakes, storms and floods, it is difficult to comprehend that an organisation created by humanity can have such a devastating social, cultural and economic impact. Even its history and heritage failed to stop the blowout. The reasons for this failure have been researched at length, both in this book and elsewhere. Although there has been significant blame poured on the leadership, management, accounting, auditing and regulation of HBOS, what is often forgotten or denied is the intellectual bankruptcy and corruption which created HBOS and also broke it in a very short time. Science without ethics, partial knowledge, disciplinary boundaries and the ideology of finance and accounting have all been exposed in this study. In this chapter, we will try to learn the intellectual lessons from the failure of HBOS, discussing how our theories and teaching curricula need to be revised to shape a more caring financial future.

Detailed and comprehensive interpretive case studies in finance are out of 'fashion' – sadly, even in research there are fashions which may surprise readers. However, such cases force the theoretical ideas to engage with the evidence which may not fit easily into neat boxes – as it can do in research papers. Given the breadth and depth of the HBOS failure, the intellectual lessons needed to be learnt. The data is quite revealing about the conflicts of interest and interdependencies between various professionals operating within and outside HBOS. Even regulators and politicians got away scot free, without any personal penalty. Grey areas of professional judgement and opinion can often be subverted, as in the UK there are very few successful prosecutions against firms and professionals for negligence or fraud. Just as HBOS was very powerful in banking, so was KPMG very powerful and still is hugely influential in the world of accounting and auditing. Whilst one went bust, nothing has happened to the other. In all cases, none of the professionals involved have been prosecuted or imprisoned in spite of the huge scale of the failure and losses. The one person who has stood out in this crisis, whistleblower Paul Moore, paid for his timely challenge with his health and career, even though he was doing so with integrity and professionalism. The outcomes of bad finance seem truly perverse, and things have to change if we are to build a better world. The deep culture of irresponsible power and influence is not sustainable by any stretch of the imagination.

The case reveals the flaws of disciplinary boundaries and the worship of ideologies of finance – 'disciplonatory'. Just as the industry of finance has become hugely powerful and influential in the era of financialisation, so has the discipline and its precepts and ideology. We know from human history and experience that power without accountability is always dangerous, and those who hold power must have profound public, social and environmental values to create a sustainable world. Words like 'care', 'concern' and 'compassion' must be central to the vocabulary of business and finance although they are presently missing. Professions of finance such as banking, accounting, actuarial science, auditing and law must embrace their public and ethical duty boldly. They need to be fearless to challenge and question power and authority and avoid becoming a servant to the master of greed and corruption. Otherwise their status and worth will evaporate over time. Studies in the fields of accounting, auditing and consultancy have shown that there is an increasing bias towards commercialisation and away from ethics and public interest (Mitchell and Sikka 2011; Sikka 2008; West 2003; Zeff 2003; Hanlon 1994). There is also a profound cultural bias in the science, culture and ethics of contemporary finance, though this is barely acknowledged and virtually ignored in the textbooks. It is mostly white men who developed the subject, declared its theories and scientific value and imposed them on the world and continue to police the science. Much more research needs to be done to unravel the 'unconscious' cultural bias in finance teaching and theory.

In the case of HBOS, we learnt how very few people inside the organisation had a whole view about the bank, its performance and challenges – the chairman, CEO and finance director. Given the size and complexity of the organisation, this is very surprising but perhaps not uncommon. The auditors and regulators at a senior level are legally required to take a whole view of the organisation and its travails, but somehow chose not to challenge decisively and firmly. If in education, we have continued to divide business into various subjects and disciplines, should we be surprised that very few people have the skill and ability to think and analyse holistically? The larger and more complex an organisation, the more difficult it is to analyse and evaluate as a whole entity. Even the financial statements do not aggregate the performance and risks well – there is a lot of subjectivity, and key aspects can get lost in the detail of the accounts. Non-executive Board directors have a legal responsibility to supervise, and therefore ought to go beyond learning the parts to see the wider whole. This means that education needs to be reformed to ensure that the inter-connections and weaving between disciplines happens constantly.

One of the greatest legacies of British rule in the colonial era is the philosophy of 'divide and rule'. In this case, we saw the HBOS relationship applying this in many different ways:

- Very few leaders had sight of the big picture of risk and culture in the organisation.
- Agendas and committees were divided and barriers placed against open Board discussions throughout the life of HBOS.
- Crosby was obsessed by ruling firmly and undermining challenge, and the chairman helped him achieve this. The appearance of an independent chairman was a fiction.
- Risks were divided and not consolidated, with no clear Group risk appetite and monitoring.
- Auditors were never invited to appear in front of the whole Board or questioned by them collectively as a Board.
- Corporate responsibility, culture and ethics were never discussed or debated as a whole issue for the Board in spite of their critical importance in the banking industry.

It is therefore possible that the deep specialisms and divisions of the finance academy – like between corporate finance, banking, accounting, auditing, private and public sector, risk measurement and management, culture and ethics, regulation and compliance – all serve to help finance leaders to divide and rule the expert practitioners of finance.

Whilst this may not be a deliberate conspiracy, it serves very well the interests of power who do not wish to be challenged or undermined. This means that the subject of finance and its ideology is in fact deeply political and helps the consolidation of power and exploitation. In crafting its expertise as a science, it also reduces the scope and possibilities of intellectual challenge, and the influence such challenges can have. It is no surprise therefore that even after the crash, the frauds committed by the industry continue, and the social paralysis of punishment and enforcement also persists. At heart is a deep intellectual hegemony captured by the so-called scientists which seems impenetrable to challenge by wider society who are often the victims of high finance. The complex maths, techniques, language and algorithms can be used to fence off any fundamental critique. Future research needs to examine this intellectual power and how it can be ruptured, challenged and mitigated. It is possible that because the discipline is so uncritical of the finance industry, and in fact supportive of its arbitrage and frauds, that it has survived and flourished in business schools which are often dependent on huge corporate endowments. Its ideology influenced regulatory failure and corporate malfeasance on an industrial scale. The politics of finance theory and 'scientific' ideology need to be studied and investigated further for their role in processes of financialisation. Just as we are now examining the behaviour and culture of bankers, similar studies need to be conducted on the behaviour, conflicts of interest and culture of expert finance scholars and academics.

When a subject like business or finance is divided into specialist disciplines, there needs to be an understanding of context and the wider impact on society and the environment. What seems apparent is that the specialisation of knowledge has had the opposite effect, distancing experts from the wider knowledge base and context, and developing their own language and code. Over time, this incapacitates even the potential for holistic thinking, as the silos are deep in the minds of the leaders and professionals. For example, in the case of HBOS, we have no sense in reading the interviews and reports that any leader had a concern for the systemic implications of the failure of such a big bank. They were simply not concerned about this overwhelming responsibility which came with their status and rewards. Specialisation and expertise can create an arrogance which reduces or removes conscience and instead fuels more and more hubris. Regulations and rules cannot require or enforce a 'conscience' among leaders, but that does not mean it is unimportant. Perhaps psychological testing of leaders' thinking may help unravel different levels of conscience and empathy.

Much of contemporary high finance has become technocratic, mechanised and abstract. As a result, people or environments affected by the models and decisions are often very distant from the trader or analyst. The industry has adapted the cold and whimsical character of money. The practice of their work often requires bankers to be distant and cold, so then why should we be surprised when they are later found to be reckless, greedy and insensitive? Future research should expose the cultural and emotional experiences of high finance and the implications this may have for its regulation and control. We saw this hubris in the case of HBOS. Perhaps given its declared ambitions, and the huge market backing it got from funds and investors, the blame should also go squarely on these distant investors keen to make a high return at any cultural, ethical, social or environmental cost. Where they are managing public funds like pension funds and investment trusts, should society also not make the managers equally accountable for such failures?

Business complexity and risk are evident throughout the investigations into HBOS. There were a range of products and services, international branches and subsidiaries and large numbers of managers at different levels of the organisation. There was an overwhelming reliance on secondary data and evidence, rather than a Board engagement directly with customers and their businesses. There was a significant reliance on processes and rhetoric like the 'three lines of defence' in the area of risk management which turned out to be neither lines nor defences. It is obvious that any service-based organisation that is growing very fast must create a prudent culture and give primacy to this. However, creating and retaining a good culture is never easy, and systems and processes cannot replace trust, integrity and professionalism. Growth through acquisitions and performance through targets is much easier than growth which is organic and based on supporting people and culture, and building ventures from the ground up where learning permeates the business. The FSA were right to warn about pace and cultural integration from the very start, but these warnings fell on deaf ears.

In stark contrast to received wisdom in finance, the financial markets warmly accepted the HBOS management bribery through dividends and share buy-backs. As a corporate act, bribery is illegal, but such forms of shareholder and market bribery have never been prosecuted. The dividends were signals of fictitious profits covering up the fact of high risk and poor controls and monitoring. This was disguising a wider malaise of greed and aggression inside the company, and excessive short-term risk-taking which later destroyed the bank. This had the effect of lifting management remuneration, including that of the non-executive chairman, whose rewards were tied to earnings and share price performance. Instead of asking questions as to why the founding CEO left soon after the creation of the merged bank, the markets accepted the transition to a young CEO without any significant banking experience. Somehow, the markets failed abjectly in stopping this hubris in time. Investors got sucked in by the fiction of rising share prices and got drawn into the bubble.

Ethics and culture need to be at the centre of finance education, and not virtually ignored or marginalised as they are today. Their study and engagement must go beyond abstract philosophy and engage with the student as a person, with values and beliefs which cannot be denied or supressed. If this was done twenty years ago, the kinds of leaders which HBOS had would probably never have risen to such positions of influence and hubris. Finance texts and theories are silent about leadership, but in this case we saw that a few leaders destroyed an historic institution in a very short time. This cannot continue. Leadership has to be an important component of any financial curriculum, and students must learn about the dangers of hubris and the realities of politics and power. HBOS leaders seemed blasé about law and regulation, with form overriding substance and spirit. In fact, they seemed strongly anti-regulation. We can no longer assume that respect for the rule of law and the spirit of regulation is a given among finance managers and leaders. It seems this will now need to be taught in the business schools and in the professions of law, finance and auditing. Innovative methods need to be developed to do this at a formative stage in young people's education. The state is not a separate entity whose taxes and regulations need to be avoided and undermined, but a key part of a sound economy and society, which business students must learn to respect and value.

When we closely examine the evidence on HBOS and the regular rhetoric from the Board and internal documents, the feeling one gets is that the leaders really did not understand the meaning of the word 'culture' and its significant importance to a banking organisation. Somehow, they expected everyone to be selfish (as they were selfish) and use financial incentives to get them to work together for enhancing overall performance. Themes like trust, relationships, values are much deeper than a written code or statement – they are primarily about belief and behaviour, and key to a sound financial system. If leaders do not understand it, how are they going to implement a 'good and prudent' culture and mind-set? Also, what does a 'diverse' and inclusive culture, where staff come from a range of cultures and beliefs, mean in practice? (Shah 2007a). The latest scandal at Wells Fargo Bank shows once again how distant the leaders were from understanding and creating a good culture – leaders preferred to blame when things went wrong rather than look in the mirror. With hindsight we know they failed miserably, but given the spate of continuing banking scandals all over the world, and the huge anger about banking culture expressed in the parliamentary enquiries (Tyrie et al. 2013c), there needs to be serious reform in the education and training of finance professionals. Culture and ethics need to be central to finance education instead of peripheral. It is possible that management were culturally naïve because of this lack of focus in the training and education of finance professionals. Education and research have played a critical role in detaching money and finance from its roots and over-laying it with false ideologies, fictitious theories and plain fraud. This fallacy is no longer sustainable. Somehow the fiction of money has permeated the everyday culture of banking and finance – lies and deceit have become com-monplace. Nobody really knows or cares what the truth is anymore.

In many ways, managing large and complex organisations is very difficult especially if the focus is on maintaining culture. Numbers and financial systems can give an impression of control and monitoring, but often people and values are excluded from the figures as culture is difficult to count. At HBOS, man-agement used numbers to monitor and control, thereby destroying culture and even challenge. Like financial audits, should we not be requiring independent cultural audits of large and systemic banks, given the huge importance of this? We know the banks would resist this, but it must be in the public interest to do so. And as we have seen time and again, with finance, the public interest must come first, as it is the public which gives banks the licence to operate. There are many criticisms of bank size and reach – culture is another reason why banks should be kept small and manageable.

Could all this bad behaviour have resulted from the primary utilitarian focus on wealth and profit maximisation preached by contemporary economics and finance? Were risk managers and internal auditors marginalised and ignored because they were seen as a hindrance to profits and growth? There is a more fundamental crisis created in an era of financialisation – the numbers are more important than people. Thus not only is finance education unwittingly excluding culture, but it is doing so deliberately as it wants to enhance focus on profits and performance. Culture, politics and ethics are seen as 'soft and vague' sciences in contrast to the hard-nosed precision of prices, profits and markets. The mind-set of finance practitioners seems increasingly hard-wired in a calcu-lative way, and at HBOS, the CEOs and chairman seemed incapable of appreciating culture and values, let alone living by them.

Sadly, just like government, public finance and taxation, regulation and its study are also relegated in the business school, where focus is more on value creation and teaching the formulae of success. If it is studied, like taxation, regulation is seen as a cost or burden on business, as opposed to a value and benefit. The language of economics turns a public good into a corporate bad. There is little discussion of the dynamics of regulation and the importance of respect for rules and the law. We know how valuable a banking licence is, and how responsible the role of a banker has to be in society. Being endowed with the opportunity to run a very large bank should inspire a heightened sense of duty and concern for effective and transparent and accountable management.

Again in the case of HBOS, this was very far from the truth, and regulation and regulatory processes were deliberately captured to undermine their effect. The morality of respect for rules and the law was replaced by a culture of arbitrage and exploitation of customers, both retail and commercial. In a similar way, auditors, both internal and external, were kept at bay, rather than being encouraged to question and challenge. There is no evidence to show that the NEDs asked the auditors to identify serious business problems that they should be made aware of. Instead, they sought comfort from auditors.

Professionals were constantly relied upon to provide 'expert comfort' to both the HBOS Board and the regulators. The reality was more about blame-shifting and spreading – the wider the number of hands in the pie, the lesser the risk to any one person. A reckless culture leads to reckless reliance on experts and big brands for comfort and assurance. The 'experts' tended to come from Big 4 accounting firms who provide a range of consultancy and audit services, and, in the case of HBOS, mainly from two firms – KPMG and PWC. Spin was applied in the way reports were worded and crafted, especially the executive summaries – for example, even when there were serious internal control problems, the report summary said overall the system was fit for purpose. Professional judgement and endorsement was politicised, delegated and managed, again with finance. The impression is that having a big bank as a client is like having a feeding trough, where the work and fees keep on rolling, and an audit or consulting firm should dare not challenge or critique the executive even where there are serious doubts. Once again, it's the power which determines the judgement, rather than the expert knowledge and findings. How can professionals as a group and as individuals maintain their independence and integrity when working in such highly conflicted and compromising roles?

The very idea of comfort in and through finance seems difficult to understand for the millions of people all over the world who have little food, water or shelter, and for whom everyday living is a struggle. All they seek is a basic wage and healthy living conditions. In the case of HBOS, we saw leaders occupying a world far removed from any sensibility of their privilege, and even when non-executives were paid tens and even hundreds of thousands for attending a few meetings a year, what they were constantly doing was seeking comfort, revenue and status. The problem transpired to be an excess of comfort, where such a profound issue as risk was neither understood nor well-managed, but this was not a concern for the Board. Finance research needs to look at the role of comfort in undermining culture and leadership.

When the chairman of the Risk Committee admitted that he did not understand why he was in that role, given his inexperience, the question we must ask is why did he accept the position in the first place? To challenge the executive at a meeting would be to invite discomfort. In fact, the opportunity for challenge was undermined by the shaping of agendas and prior agreement on controversial issues to avoid the NED Board coming together as a group to challenge the executive. The chairman constantly gave comfort to the CEO, who became so comfortable, that the ship ran aground. The deputy chairman loved being on the Board so much that he would do it again, even with the knowledge that the business sank. Finance leadership should be made to feel highly responsible, accountable and challenging, but somehow the reality is the opposite.

There is a factory of research papers on corporate governance, but rarely do they acknowledge the psychology in the boardroom, and how this can be manipulated to ensure minimal governance. They do not even elaborate or theorise on what they understand by the terms 'corporate' and 'governance', launching straight into empirical analysis. We saw clearly in the case of HBOS that although the chairman was supposed to be independent from the CEO, he was far from it. Even the salaries of NEDs can be very lucrative for retired executives who seek a part-time senior role with no executive responsibility and plenty of status for doing very little. It makes us wonder whether these cushy roles, statuses and salaries are a form of bribery for silence and a lack of challenge. The chair of the Audit Committee at HBOS earned in excess of a hundred thousand pounds for reducing challenge from the external auditors! The chairman earned nearly £700,000 for ensuring smooth Board ritual and minimising challenge. Perhaps accounting and finance researchers also are seeking comfort in their careers, accepting the rules of the game and playing by it, rather than challenging its core assumptions, lies and half-truths. Like the Board of HBOS, they too have become desensitised to the external world of inequality, fraud and corruption. In my view, a primary role of academics is to help protect public interest, but their lives have become ruled by form over substance. Perhaps they have allowed this to happen subconsciously.

Challenge in any organisation has serious consequences, as we saw here in the case of whistleblower Paul Moore. A primary role of a Board of governors is to challenge the executive. The reality is that they get paid for attending meetings, and there is no extra reward for challenge. Even for non-executive Board directors, there are real consequences of challenge and advantages of preserving the status quo. Let us suppose that a director in HBOS felt that the CEO was incompetent and needed to be removed and replaced. How easy would it be to implement that? Who is responsible for enacting it? Who would be in charge of finding a good replacement? Who would be blamed if this person did not do a good job? If instead, the director keeps quiet and the bank later goes into trouble, what are the consequences for him/her as a non-executive, financial and otherwise? We saw in the case of HBOS that the answer was nothing. Nothing happened to them. Research on governance needs to address these very real psychological, legal and moral flaws in the systems and processes of Board conduct. To have a non-executive Board, even if it were genuinely independent, is not a panacea. As we saw in HBOS, Board members often seek the position as a source of comfort and personal enhancement, rather than a job to be done to the highest professionalism and integrity.

We urgently need a holistic approach to finance, which recognises and understands the wider role of finance in society, instead of uprooting money and value from its origins and social construction. This requires a real and radical overhaul of theory and methods of teaching and training professionals, including the cultivation of a sense of history and an appreciation of culture and diversity among students. If in HBOS very few people looked at the big picture, what were the other leaders thinking and doing on the Board? Were they not wanting to see the big picture, what the bank was really about, how it was affecting the lives of its customers, personal and corporate, and how it was influencing society and the environment? It seems the NEDs primarily performed their function by reading reports prepared by the staff, rather than commissioning their own surveys and visiting branches and talking to employees and other stakeholders. This is real governance. Auditors are supposed to check internal systems and controls but failed to find any problems. They should have warned strongly about the fast-paced growth and increasing complexity of the business. They must have seen the greed suppressing the risks. Modern science and education have become very materialistic, technocratic and partial, and as a result, students and professionals become trained in a narrow way of thinking and behaving. So many 'successful' entrepreneurs consider themselves self-made, when in reality many factors have helped them succeed and continue to do so. For finance to become holistic, teaching approaches must respect the culture and values of the students and interact with them at a personal level. The cultural diversity of the world, which is often reflected in the classrooms of many universities, needs to be genuinely reflected in the content of finance theory and education. The project of science was meant to be open-minded, curious and reflective – contemporary finance has become closed-minded, greedy and unreflective about its impact on society and the ecosystem. As business schools have grown and expanded, a factory of research needs an outlet to protect jobs and tenure, so the finance research project has become motivated by personal careers, employability and security, rather than by a genuine search for truth, wisdom and global advancement.

The history of finance is rarely if ever taught in business schools, which are primarily utilitarian – textbooks are devoid of history. If it were, students would see how bubbles and crashes are common (C. Ferguson 2012, Reinhard and Rogoff (2011)), how the industry has been riddled with greed and corruption and how the rational theories of contemporary finance are very far from lived experience. History would also help them to see the wider impacts of finance on society and the environment, and how politics and power have often been captured by financiers through revolving doors with government and regulators (Palan et al. 2010; Tax Justice Network 2015; Shaxson 2012; Germain 2010; Strange 1986). Problems with the very science of risk measurement (McGoun 1995) and even economics and finance (Kay 2011; 2015) would be exposed if there was a critical engagement with the past. Regulatory and banking failures can help students understand what mistakes to avoid if there is to be sustainable success. Above all, history would expose the huge and enduring importance of culture and ethics in finance and accounting.

We were also surprised by the general ignorance around risk among the HBOS Board, and the compromises made in its measurement and management. If the nature and importance of risk was not understood by management, professionals and regulators, then we have to accept that the technical teaching of risk helps professionals distance themselves from the experience and politics of risk. Apart from Paul Moore and a few other people, there was little evidence of serious concern about the likelihood of failure. The science of risk seems to be creating a dissonance from the reality of risk. Furthermore, the connections between business strategy and risk are obvious, but, surprisingly, the regulators made statements where they said that it is not their role to comment on business strategy. This is also inconsistent, because the FSA did question business strategy in the early years but relented in later years. Political influence seems to have forced the FSA to change its regulatory approach and interpretation. The fact that most people involved with HBOS got away without punishment may continue to insure professionals from risk experience, and this is wrong. We need to re-examine our theories and educational approaches very carefully to understand why risk and worry are being removed from experience for some people.

Systemic risk is very real in banking, and large banks are systemically important institutions. When we look at the leadership and management of HBOS, there is no evidence of a fear or moral concern for the wider implications of its failure. How common is this in other banks? Who really 'cares' about systemic risk inside a bank, or outside within the regulatory and political establishment? Who is made responsible and accountable to exercise this care and concern? If it is not a person, and this process of monitoring is institutionalised by processes and committees, what is its real effectiveness? Who wins and who loses when we ignore the politics of risk? Could this monitoring be helped by regular and public risk reporting by banks including metrics and summary measures of portfolio risk? These are important questions which need to be addressed by scholars and concerned human beings.

There is growing evidence of the transactionalisation of finance, where humans are distanced from the process of decision-making, borrowing and saving, and instead technologies and intermediaries take over, where no one cares about the outcome. Both Halifax Building Society and the Bank of Scotland had strong relationship cultures, but this was quickly removed by the HBOS merger and new leadership ambition. The speed with which this happened should be shocking for any finance teacher and scholar. Emotion and concern should be unleashed, and not a dispassionate few bad apples kind of story – academics should rightfully be concerned and seriously reflective about their intellectual role in creating the crisis (Arnold 2009; McSweeney 2009).

It is urgent that we teach students the limitations of techniques, technologies, models and markets in the study of financial risk and institutions. While they may serve a purpose, their context is vitally important to understand, otherwise there will be a fallacy of misplaced concreteness. Where the influence of technocracy is ignored, finance will continue to flood the weak and the marginalised, keeping them away from any access to finance, whilst enriching the few experts who have mastered the art of speculation and exploitation. We urgently need to rehumanise finance, and allow people to discuss their everyday experiences with the industry, its jargon and its professionals. Basic aspects of saving, lending, borrowing and investment are not that complex and inaccessible to ordinary people, if explained properly and without any deliberate complexity. The industry has connived in making basic finance complex, and used every opportunity to rip off its customers through jargon, complexity, dishonesty and even fraud. In the UK, the outstanding work of Martin Lewis, known as 'Money-Saving Expert' (www.moneysavingexpert.com), has made a huge difference to the public awareness of frauds and cons in banking and finance, and his website has millions of followers. And yes, he does not even have a Master's degree in finance – he has succeeded because of his ignorance of the theories. In the process, Martin has challenged the jargon and complexity of banking and made ordinary people aware of hidden charges and terms and conditions which penalise them in their savings and mortgages. The academy needs to learn from his work and see how this knowledge can be used to help society become more fair, transparent and ethical.

Accounting and auditing have been designed to give transparency and accountability to stakeholders. In the case of HBOS, there were plenty of warning signs, especially in relation to fast growth, management inexperience and the funding and liquidity gaps. Also in terms of risk-taking, there were plenty of rumours in the market about how aggressive it was towards both retail and commercial lending, including its bias towards commercial property. Whilst the accounts did not give bright red flags, and also the audit reports were clean each year, discerning investors should have spotted the problems unless they were also fund managers, investing other people's money and happy to be on a joy ride. The regular profits and dividend growth were clearly very misleading in hindsight, but there was no major market whistleblowing. The auditors would have known what was really going on if they did their work diligently but kept quiet.

Regulators were concerned, and given their knowledge and expertise of the sector and the industry, did raise several warnings. However, they were not able to stop the juggernaut in time, nor ensure the removal of the incompetent leaders who ran HBOS. They seemed very compromised in their actions. Directors of the FSA did not get involved in directly challenging HBOS and its management in a timely manner, something they were duty-bound and resourced to do. Whilst there was no direct evidence of political interference, there were plenty of signs such as James Crosby's involvement on the Board of the FSA which would have compromised their position. It seems very surprising that someone who had already expressed strong views about light-touch regulation rose to the ranks of the FSA becoming vice-chairman, when his own bank was seen as an 'accident waiting to happen'. Although set up to be independent, the FSA turned out to be nothing but. The way regulatory institutions are structured, led and financed has a big impact on the way regulation is executed. Having a framework of law and principles does not necessarily mean that these will be adhered to or implemented.

Black (2014) examines regulatory disasters from all over the world and finds six contributory causes – incentives, organisational dynamics and complexity, ambiguous regulatory strategies, misunderstanding of problems and solutions, communication problems and weak trust and accountability structures. The HBOS case showed that the leaders had the wrong financial incentives which encouraged regulatory arbitrage and capture, the FSA was bureaucratic and complex and not incentivised to enforce and prosecute, the regulatory emphasis on Basel II became a major distraction, staff turnover and revolving doors hampered regulation and there were poor accountability structures for leaders in the FSA. The result was a man-made financial and economic collapse.

Institutions of risk, audit and regulation have a major influence on practice – theories and concepts do not naturally lead to direct implementation and enforcement. We saw that in the case of the FSA, even when it had rules and processes to take action, it failed in implementation, monitoring and enforcement repeatedly. People and politics filter the way rules are implemented – the revolving doors between the industry, regulators, auditors and consultants are wide open and totally unregulated. Similarly, professionals with big brand institutional badges played an influential role in the interpretation of risk and its measurement, control and implementation. Even accountability and audit were highly compromised by the Big 4 culture, actions and reports. Sometimes, members of the same firm acted as inspectors or consultants, changing roles like chameleons change colour. Finance scholarship must engage with the realities of institutions and their leadership and management systems and practices. They have a very influential role on the practice of finance.

There is a large literature on whether or not principles or rules should be applied in financial regulation (see e.g. Black 2002; McBarnet and Whelan 1992) given the reality of regulatory arbitrage. In the case of HBOS, we saw that in very large organisations where systems and processes are critical, there was a reliance placed on them and the substance got forgotten. Risk is a critical area of bank governance, but the Board relied on processes rather than the actual substance of risk. Similarly, audit and regulation were seen as processes to be managed and controlled rather than a source of serious warnings to the non-executive directors for them to take strong challenging and timely actions to stop the juggernaut that was HBOS. When people spend a lot of time operating in a bureaucratic and process mode, they seem to easily lose sight of the big picture even at a leadership level. Individuals who want to challenge may feel paralysed, and need ways of creating a challenging coalition, which is often very difficult in undemocratic corporations. This has very serious consequences.

Like HBOS there are a number of very large and influential banks all over the world. There is evidence that many of them lurch from one crisis to another – they are juggernauts where a few people are at the feeding trough, and no one has the power to stop them. They are too big to fail, so there is a state protection which fuels the hubris and arrogance. They are undemocratic and unaccountable – as even the financial reporting and audit processes are captured by them. Given their size and market sensitivity, they are deeply political institutions, and even regulators fear to contain them. There should be a different finance theory for these organisations which emphasises their political constitution and actions, and moves away from the rhetoric of competition, efficiency and rational management and judgement. Often the state is being used to undermine society and keep the competition out so that these ogres can fatten themselves. Even shareholders are divided and therefore ruled, in spite of the rhetoric of shareholder ownership. The Boards of such organisations have significant influence and authority for little personal financial risk. We need to theorise the political role and impact of these giant institutions on the practice of finance and on global markets and financial instruments. This then needs to go into the curriculum of finance teaching, and will hopefully deter the brightest and best from going to work for them.

The case raises a number of very serious concerns about the morality of contemporary finance theory and practice. We saw in Chapter 1 how the theory virtually ignores ethics and morality and implies a value-neutrality when it is anything but. Its positivistic approach also is a sham, as any researcher would be influenced and biased by their own values in conducting and analysing their research. There were no instances throughout the life of HBOS when the Board sat down and discussed what the values of the organisation were and what they stood for, even though there was a lot of rhetoric about corporate responsibility and culture. This should not be surprising and is synchronous with a theory which also tries to refuse to engage with its ethical precepts and tenets. An honest declaration of values is fundamental to any financial services institution, especially one that has such a huge retail branch and customer network, and is legally bound to treat customers fairly. In the end billions had to be paid out by retail banks, including HBOS, in PPI mis-selling compensation after the crash. Morality and relationships were forgotten when high-risk borrowing and lending were done, which eventually led to such a devastating bankruptcy. Leaders ignored their own moral duties and responsibilities for the sake of their personal rewards, bonuses and comforts. It is imperative that finance teaching and research places morality at its very heart. As a society, it is critical that we police the ethics of such an influential industry whose licence is granted by the state, and whose abuse can and often does devastate economy and society. Such policing should go beyond fines and increase personal culpability and penalty, and act as a deterrent for others with selfish and greedy outlooks.

Finance has become a 'derivative subject', and, like derivatives, it has forgotten the importance of the original assets which created it, and jumped on the bandwagon of risk, speculation and greed. The discipline has detached itself from the grassroots and any connectivity to society and the environment. Disciplonatory has uprooted finance from its purpose, and scientific policing, hubris and institutionalisation has kept it there. The whole system of money is built on trust, responsibility, fairness and accountability – and these fundamentals must be taught to all students. This must be at the core of finance research and education, and there needs to be a concern for a more holistic, equitable and responsible finance, with the academy helping to shape and monitor it. The corporate bias in business schools needs to be tampered by education about the public sector and its importance in economic life, and the extent to which businesses depend on it for their well-being and profitability. Taxation is not a cost but a corporate social responsibility. And financial markets are not there for lazy surplus profits, but for the equitable allocation of goods and services.

Stripping the fundamentals of finance from research and education has serious consequences for society. HBOS was a big money engine which went bust. Is money a financial instrument that we have created, but something of which we have totally lost control? Is the genie out of the bottle and cannot be put back in, and is now controlling us? Research on financialisation certainly exposes this as a serious problem. Nature has limits to growth, but somehow money can grow exponentially and be collected in an unlimited way. Similarly, debt has no natural limit, and there is no inter-generational consideration in finance about the problems of excessive borrowing and valuation for future societies and generations. What do interest rates mean for society and nature? Whose political and personal interest is preserved and whose sacrificed when interest rates change? Fiat money is backed by trust and confidence and sound economic management. How do we as a society monitor these qualities? Students of finance need to be exposed to these fundamental questions. The more we ignore or deny them, the more we will find that our theories of accounting and finance rely on very shaky foundations, and are prone to fall like a house of cards, again and again.

At the beginning of the book, we raised the possibility of the neo-liberal ideology being morally fraudulent, and at the same time deeply influential on the corruption and crises we see today. It may be easy to identify people to blame, but was there something deeper which went wrong? Whilst the parliamentary investigations have unearthed many profound issues, by their very construction they have avoided examining the ideology which influenced the wider failure of HBOS. However, the evidence and analysis presented here does point to a profound ideological malaise which infected banks, professional firms and regulators at that time. Leadership was heavily financialised and performance focused, ignoring culture and values. There was no sense of public or environmental risk concern or accountability. Governance and regulation proved to be more rhetorical and less challenging or punitive. When quizzed about the causes of the HBOS failure, the responses of the leaders were of surprise and a blaming of external market forces. Their actions, though, had been selfish, greedy and hubristic – symptoms of extreme neo-liberalism. Similarly, regulators allowed themselves to be ideologically and politically captured in an arena which had huge civic impacts. Politicians were deeply enamoured by temporary and unequal banking and financial market success, predicting the 'end of boom and bust'. The lack of any serious resistance before and after the crisis from the finance academy may also be seen as a facet of this ideological capture and fraud. They too have become selfish, greedy and performance oriented. Reforms would require a serious multi-cultural re-examination of core theories and beliefs in finance. Nothing less will do.

Bibliography

Admati, A. and Hellwig, M. (2013) *The Bankers' New Clothes*, Princeton, NJ: Princeton University Press.

Agnew, H. (2016) 'Accounting experts seek independent probe into KPMG's audit of HBOS', *Financial Times*, 25th January.

Aldrick, P. (2013) 'New watchdog's chairman urged to resign over auditors' role in HBOS debacle', *The Telegraph*, 7th April.

Angelides, P., Thomas, B., Born, B., Holtz-Eakin, D., Georgiu, B., Murren, H., Graham, B., Thompson, J., Hennessey, K. and Wallison, P. (2011) 'The financial crisis enquiry report', New York: Financial Crisis Inquiry Commission.

Arnold, P. (2009) 'Global financial crisis: The challenge to accounting research', *Accounting, Organizations and Society*, 34(6/7), pp. 803–809.

Arnold, P. (2012) 'The political economy of financial harmonisation: The East Asian financial crisis and the rise of international accounting standards', *Accounting, Organizations and Society*, 37(6), pp. 361–381.

Audit Inspection Unit (2011) 'Annual Report 2010/11', Financial Reporting Council, 19th July.

Auditing Practices Board (1999) 'The audit of banks and building societies in the United Kingdom', *Practice Note 19*, London: Auditing Practice Board.

Avakian, S. and Roberts, J. (2012) 'Whistleblowers in organisations: Prophets at work?', *Journal of Business Ethics*, 110(1), pp. 71–84.

Bainbridge, G. (2012) 'Parliamentary Commission on banking standards – Written evidence from Guy Bainbridge, KPMG', *House of Commons*, 14th November.

Bakan, J. (2004) *The Corporation: The Pathological Pursuit of Profit and Power*, New York: Free Press.

Baker, A. (2013) 'The gradual transformation? The incremental dynamics of macroprudential regulation', *Regulation & Governance*, 7(4), pp. 417–434.

Baker, A. (2014) 'The bankers' paradox: The political economy of macroprudential regulation', *Working paper*, Belfast, Northern Ireland: Queens University of Belfast.

Beck, U. (1992) *Risk Society: Towards a New Modernity*, London: Sage.

Bhimani, A. (2009) 'Risk management, corporate governance and management accounting: emerging interdependencies', Editorial, *Management Accounting Research*, 20(1), pp. 2–5.

Black, J. (2002) *Critical Reflections on Regulation*, London: London School of Economics – Centre for Analysis of Risk and Regulation.

Black, J. (2014) 'Learning from regulatory disasters', *Policy Quarterly*, 10(3), pp. 3–11.

Boatright, J. (1999) *Ethics in Finance*, Oxford: Blackwell.

Boyer, R. (2005) 'From shareholder value to CEO power: The paradox of the 1990's', *Competition and Change*, 9(1), pp. 7–47.

Brealey, R., Myers, S. and Allen, F. (2014) *Principles of Corporate Finance*, 11th edition, New York: McGraw-Hill.

Brown, G. (2006) 'Speech at Mansion House', *London*, 22nd June.

Brunsson, N. (2002) *The Organisation of Hypocrisy*, Copenhagen: Copenhagen Business School Press.

Burrows, G. and Black, C. (1998) 'Profit sharing in Australian Big 6 accounting firms: An exploratory study', *Accounting, Organizations and Society*, 23(5/6), pp. 517–530.

Carnegie, G. and Napier, C. (2010) 'Traditional accountants and business professionals – Portraying the accounting profession after Enron', *Accounting, Organizations and Society*, 35(3), pp. 360–376.

Chang, H. J. and Aldred, J. (2014) 'After the crash, we need a revolution in the way we teach economics', *Guardian*, 11th May.

Coggan, P. (2012) *Paper Promises – Money, Debt and the New World Order*, London: Penguin.

Cohan, W. (2011) *Money and Power – How Goldman Sachs Came to Rule the World*, New York: Penguin.

Cooper, D. and Robson, K. (2006) 'Accounting, professions and regulation: Locating sites of professionalism', *Accounting, Organizations and Society*, 31(4/5), pp. 415–444.

Cooper, D., Everett, J. and Neu, D. (2005) 'Financial scandals, accounting change and the role of accounting academics: A perspective from North America', *European Accounting Review*, 14(2), pp. 373–382.

Daly, H. and Cobb, J. (1994) *For the Common Good – Redirecting the Economy toward Community, Environment and a Sustainable Future*, Second edition, Boston: Beacon Press.

Das, S. (2011) *Extreme Money: Masters of the Universe and the Cult of Risk*, Financial Times Series, New York: FT Press.

Deegan, C. and Ward, A. (2013) *Financial Accounting and Reporting – An International Approach*, London: McGraw-Hill.

Dewing, I. and Russell, P. O. (2008) 'The individualisation of corporate governance: The approved persons' regime in UK financial services supervision', *Accounting, Auditing & Accountability Journal*, 21(7), pp. 978–1000.

Dewing, I. and Russell, P. O. (2014) 'Whistleblowing, governance and regulation before the financial crisis: The case of HBOS', *Journal of Business Ethics*, 134(1), pp. 155–169.

Douglas, M. and Wildavsky, A. (1982) *Risk and Culture*, Berkeley, CA: University of California Press.

Dunkley, E. (2015) 'UK draws line under banking bashing after scrapping assessment', *Financial Times*, 31st December.

Eales, B. (1994) *Financial Risk Management*, London: McGraw-Hill.

Eeckhoudt, L. and Gollier, C. (1995) *Risk – Evaluation, Management and Sharing*, Wheatsheaf, UK: Harvester.

Ekins, P., Hillman, M. and Hutchison, R. (1992) *Wealth Beyond Measure – An Atlas of New Economics*, London: Gaia Books.

Elliot, L. (2015) 'FCA chief's departure means its back to business as usual for the banks', *Guardian*, 17th July.

Engelen, E., Erturk, I., Froud, J., Johal, S., Leaver, A., Moran, M. and Williams, K. (2012) 'Misrule of experts? The financial crisis as elite debacle', *Economy and Society*, 41(3), pp. 360–382.

Erturk, I., Froud, J., Johal, S., Leaver, A. and Williams, K. (2007) 'Against agency: A positional critique', *Economy and Society*, 36(1), pp. 51–77.

Erturk, I., Froud, J., Johal, S., Leaver, A. and Williams, K. (2008) *Financialization at Work: Key Texts and Commentary*, Abingdon, UK: Routledge.

Ferguson, C. (Director). (2010) *Inside Job*, [Motion Picture], United States: Sony Pictures Classics.

Ferguson, C. (2012) *Inside Job: The Financiers Who Pulled Off the Heist of the Century*, London: One World.

Ferguson, N. (2012) *The Ascent of Money – A Financial History of the World*, New York: Penguin.

Feyerabend, P. (1975) *Against Method: Outline of an Anarchist Theory of Knowledge*, New York: New Left Books.

Financial Reporting Council (2013a) 'Statement following Parliamentary Committee of Banking Standards report into failure of HBOS', *FRC Press Release*, 10th April.

Financial Reporting Council (2013b) 'KPMG LLP and KPMG Audit Plc – Audit Quality Inspection', *FRC Public Report*, May.

Financial Reporting Council (2014) 'The FRC and its regulatory approach', *FRC London*, January.

Finel-Honigman, I. (2010) *A Cultural History of Finance*, London: Routledge.

Fleming, P. and Jones, M. (2012) *The End of Corporate Social Responsibility – Crisis and Critique*, London: Sage.

Folkman, P., Froud, J., Johal, S. and Williams, K. (2008) 'Intermediaries or Another Group of Agents?' In Erturk, I. et al. (eds.), *Financialization at Work*, pp. 150–162, Abingdon, UK: Routledge.

Frankfurter, G. and McGoun, E. (2002) *From Individualism to the Individual – Ideology and Inquiry in Financial Economics*, Farnham, UK: Ashgate Publishing.

Fraser, I. (2009) 'The recklessness of Cummings', *Ian Fraser Blog*, 13th July.

Fraser, I. (2012) 'The worst bank in the world? HBOS's calamitous seven year life', *Ian Fraser Blog*, 22nd June.

Fraser, I. (2015) *Shredded: Inside RBS – The Bank that Broke Britain*, Edinburgh, UK: Birlinn.

Froud, J., Johal, S., Leaver, A. and Williams, K. (2006) *Financialization and Strategy: Narrative and Numbers*, London: Routledge.

FSA (2012) 'Final Notice – Bank of Scotland Plc, Ref: 169628', *Financial Services Authority*, 9th March.

Gendron, Y. and Smith-LaCroix, J. (2015) 'The global financial crisis: Essay on the possibility of substantive change in the discipline of finance', *Critical Perspectives on Accounting*, 30, pp. 83–101.

Germain, R. (2010) *Global Politics and Financial Governance*, London: Palgrave Macmillan.

Goodhart, C. (2010) *The Future of Finance: The LSE Report*, London: The London School of Economics and Political Science.

Graeber, D. (2013) *Debt: The First 5000 Years*, New York: Meville House.

Haddrill, S. (2016) 'Letter to Andrew Tyrie re: KPMG investigation', Financial Reporting Council, 21st January.

Hamilton, P. (2004) 'Outline of Case – in the matter of Paul Moore', confidential memo to FSA and HBOS, 13th December.

Hancher, L. and Moran, M. (eds.) (1989) *Capitalism, Culture and Economic Regulation*, Oxford: Oxford University Press.

Hanlon, G. (1994) *The Commercialisation of Accountancy*, London: Macmillan Press.

Hare, R. D. (1996) *Without Conscience: The Disturbing World of the Psychopaths Among Us*, New York: The Guilford Press.

Harney, S. and Dunne, S. (2013) 'More than nothing? Accounting, business and management studies and the research audit', *Critical Perspectives on Accounting*, 24(4/5), pp. 338–349.

Hawken, P. (1994) *The Ecology of Commerce: A Declaration of Sustainability*, London: Phoenix.

Hechter, M. (2008) 'The rise and fall of normative control', *Accounting Organizations and Society*, 33(6), pp. 663–676.

Heffernan, M. (2011) *Wilful Blindness: Why We Ignore the Obvious at Our Peril*, New York: Bloomsbury.

Hendry, J. (2013) *Ethics and Finance: An Introduction*, Cambridge, UK: Cambridge University Press.

Hertz, N. (2001) *The Silent Takeover – Global Capitalism and The Death of Democracy*, London: William Heinemann.

Hillier, D., Ross, S., Westerfield, R., Jaffe, J. and Jordan, B. (2016) *Corporate Finance*, Third edition, London: McGraw-Hill.

Hobson, O. (1953) *A Hundred Years of the Halifax – The History of the Halifax Building Society, 1853–1953*, London: B.T. Batsford.

Hopkin, P. (2012) *Fundamentals of Risk Management: Understanding, Evaluating and Implementing Effective Risk Management*, London: Kogan Page.

Hopwood, A. (1998) 'Exploring the modern audit firm: An introduction', *Accounting, Organizations and Society*, 23(5/6), pp. 515–516.

Hopwood, A. (2007) 'Whither accounting research?', *The Accounting Review*, 82(5), pp. 1365–1374.

Hopwood, A. (2009) 'Exploring the interface between accounting and finance', *Accounting, Organizations and Society*, 34(5), pp. 549–550.

Houlder, V. (2013) 'Big 4 accountants wield "undue influence" over UK tax system', *Financial Times*, 26th April.

House of Lords (2011) 'Auditors: Market concentration and their role', Volumes I and II, *Select Committee on Economic Affairs*, House of Lords, UK.

Hull, J. (2012) *Risk Management and Financial Institutions*, Hoboken, NJ: John Wiley Publishing.

Hume, N. (2009) 'Sir James Crosby's full statement, FT Alphaville', *Financial Times*, 11th February.

Humphrey, C. (2008) 'Auditing research: A review across the disciplinary divide', *Accounting, Auditing & Accountability Journal*, 21(2), pp. 170–203.

Humphrey, C., Loft, A. and Woods, M. (2009) 'The global audit profession and the international financial architecture: understanding regulatory relationships at a time of financial crisis', *Accounting, Organizations and Society*, 34(6/7), pp. 810–825.

Hutton, W. (2010) *Them and Us*, London: Little Brown.

Jensen, M. and Meckling, W. (1976) 'Theory of the firm: Managerial behaviour, agency costs and ownership structure', *Journal of Financial Economics*, 3(4), pp. 305–360.

Jones, A. (2010) 'Details of secret bank talks revealed', *Financial Times*, 20th December.

Jones, A. (2011) 'Lord Lawson baffled by bank auditors', *Financial Times*, 4th January.

Jones, S. (2009a) 'FSA: s'ok, KPMG said HBOS was fine', *Financial Times*, 11th February.

Jones, S. (2009b) 'KPMG to FSA: Yours!', *Financial Times*, 11th February.

Kay, J. (2011) 'The map is not the territory – An essay on the state of economics', *Institute for New Economic Thinking*, 3rd October.

Kay, J. (2015) *Other People's Money – Masters of the Universe or Servants of the People?*, London: Profile Books.

Kets de Vries, M. (2012) 'The psychopath in the C suite: Redefining the SOB', Insead Working paper 119.

King, M. (2016) *The End of Alchemy: Money, Banking and the Future of the Global Economy*, London: Little, Brown.

Korten, D. C. (1995) *When Corporations Rule the World*, London: Earthscan.

KPMG (2005) 'HBOS plc – Review of issues set out in the Outline Case from Paul Moore', *KPMG Board Paper*, 28th April.

Lee, S. (2009) 'The rock of stability? The political economy of the Brown government', *Policy Studies*, 30(1), pp. 17–32.

Lewis, M. (2011) *The Big Short: Inside the Doomsday Machine*, New York: W.W. Norton & Company.

Lewis, M. (2012) *Boomerang: The Biggest Bust*, New York: Penguin Books.

Lewis, M. (2014) *Flash Boys: Cracking the Money Code*, New York: W.W. Norton & Company.

Lewis, M. (2016) 'Debt and mental illness are a marriage made in hell – This is how to cope', *Daily Telegraph*, 5th April.

Little, B., Fraser, I., Sikka, P., Shearer, T., Moore, P. and Shah, A. (2015) *Expert Group Request to Investigate KPMG over its failures over HBOS*, Email to Treasury Committee, 7th December.

Luyendijk, J. (2015) *Swimming with Sharks: My Journey into the World of Bankers*, London: Guardian/Faber & Faber.

Mackenzie, D. (2006) *An Engine, Not a Camera: How Financial Models Shape Markets*, Cambridge, MA, and London: MIT Press.

Marnet, O. (2010) 'Bias in the boardroom – Effects of bias on the quality of board decision making', Exeter University Working paper.

Martin, I. (2013) 'Nice Sir Mervyn King still allowed the ship to crash – Despite the plaudits, the governor of the Bank of England's economic theories were hopelessly misguided', *The Telegraph*, 25th June.

McBarnet, D. and Whelan, C. (1991) 'The elusive spirit of the law: formalism and the struggle for legal control', *The Modern Law Review*, 54(6), pp. 848–873.

McBarnet, D. and Whelan, C. (1992) 'International Corporate Finance and the Challenge of Creative Compliance'. In Fingleton, J. (ed.), *The Internationalisation of Capital Markets and the Regulatory Response*, pp. 129–142, London: Graham & Trotman.

McBarnet, D. and Whelan, C. (1999) *Creative Accounting and the Cross-eyed Javelin Thrower*, London: Wiley.

McClenaghan, M. (2012) 'Big four accountancy firms donate £1.9m in services to political parties since 2009', *Guardian*, 10th July.

McConnell, P. and Blacker, K. (2011) 'The role of systemic people risk in the global financial crisis', *The Journal of Operational Risk*, 6(3), pp. 65–123.

McCracken, S., Salterio, S. and Gibbins, M. (2008) 'Auditor-client management relationships and roles in negotiating financial reporting', *Accounting, Organizations and Society*, 33(4/5), pp. 362–383.

McDonald, L. and Robinson, P. (2009) *A Colossal Failure of Common Sense – The Incredible Inside Story of the Collapse of Lehman Brothers*, New York: Three Rivers Press.

McFall, J.et al. (2009a) 'Banking crisis: Reforming corporate governance and the city', Ninth Report of Session 2008–2009, House of Commons Treasury Committee.

McFall, J.et al. (2009b) 'Banking crisis: Regulation and supervision', Fourteenth Report of Session 2008–2009, House of Commons Treasury Committee.

McGoun, E. (1995) 'The history of risk "measurement"', *Critical Perspectives on Accounting*, 6(6), pp. 511–532.

McGoun, E. (1997) 'Hyperreal finance', *Critical Perspectives on Accounting*, 8(1/2), pp. 97–122.

McKenna, F. (2011) 'The Button Down Mafia: How the public accounting firms run a racket on investors and thrive while their clients fail', *Re: The Auditors*, 9th February.

McManus, J. (2014) '"Chinese walls" not the best solution for KPMG', *The Irish Times*, 3rd March.

McSweeney, B. (2009) 'The roles of financial asset market failure denial and the economic crisis: Reflections on accounting and financial theories and practices', *Accounting, Organizations and Society*, 34(6/7), pp. 835–848.

Medland, D. (2013) 'Whistleblowing almost killed me – Paul Moore interview', *Financial Times*, 5th June.

Mikes, A. (2011) 'From counting risk to making risk count: Boundary work in risk management', *Accounting, Organizations and Society*, 36(4), pp. 226–245.

Miller, P., Kurunmaki, L. and O'Leary, T. (2008) 'Accounting, hybrids and the management of risk', *Accounting, Organizations and Society*, 33(7/8), pp. 942–967.

Millo, Y. and MacKenzie, D. (2009) 'The usefulness of inaccurate models: Towards an understanding of the emergence of financial risk management', *Accounting, Organizations and Society*, 34(5), pp. 638–653.

Mitchell, A. and Sikka, P. (2011) *The Pin-Stripe Mafia: How Accountancy Firms Destroy Societies*, London: Association for Accountancy & Business Affairs.

Modigliani, F. and Miller, M. (1958) 'The cost of capital, corporation finance and the theory of investment', *The American Economic Review*, 48(3), pp. 261–297.

Monbiot, G. (2000) *The Corporate Takeover of Britain*, London: Palgrave Macmillan.

Moore, M. (2001) *Stupid White Men*, New York: ReganBooks.

Moore, P. (2012) 'Letter from Paul Moore to David Andrews', Financial Reporting Council, 10th January.

Moore, P. (2015) *Crash, Bank, Wallop – The Memoirs of the HBOS Whistleblower*, Great Britain: New Wilberforce Media.

Moran, M. (1991) *The Politics of the Financial Services Revolution – The USA, UK and Japan*, Basingstoke, UK: Palgrave Macmillan.

Murphy, R. (2013) 'HMRC and the Big 4: The process of capture of our regulatory authority has reached danger point', Tax Research Blog, 26th April.

Murphy, R. (2015) *The Joy of Tax*, London: Transworld Publishers.

Pagano, M. (2009) 'Brown's nemesis – Will Paul Moore prove to be PM's downfall?', *The Independent*, 15th February.

Palan, R., Murphy, R. and Chavagneux, C. (2010) *Tax Havens: How Globalisation Really Works*, New York: Cornell University Press.

Parker, L. (2008) 'Interpreting interpretive accounting research', *Critical Perspectives on Accounting*, 19(6), pp. 909–914.

Parker, L. and Guthrie, J. (2014) 'Addressing directions in interdisciplinary accounting research', *Accounting, Auditing & Accountability Journal*, 27(8), pp. 1218–1226.

PCES (2014) *Economics, Education and Unlearning, Post-Crash Economics Society*, Manchester, UK: University of Manchester.

Perman, R. (2012) *Hubris: How HBOS wrecked the best bank in Britain*, Edinburgh: Birlinn.

Power, M. (2005a) 'The invention of operational risk', *Review of International Political Economy*, 12(4), pp. 577–599.

Power, M. (2005b) 'Organisational Responses to Risk: The Rise of the Chief Risk Officer'. In Hutter, B. and Power, M. (eds.), *Organizational Encounters with Risk*, pp. 132–148, Cambridge, UK: Cambridge University Press.

Power, M. (2007) *Organised Uncertainty – Designing a World of Risk Management*, Oxford: Oxford University Press.

Power, M. (2009) 'The risk management of nothing', *Accounting, Organizations and Society*, 34(6/7), pp. 849–855.

Power, M., Ashby, S. and Palermo, T. (2013) 'Risk culture in financial organisations – A research report', London: London School of Economics.

PRA (2015a) 'The failure of HBOS plc: A report by the Financial Conduct Authority and the Prudential Regulatory Authority, UK', Published by PRA and FCA, November.

PRA (2015b) 'Report into the FSA's enforcement actions following the failure of HBOS', Andrew Green QC, Published by PRA and FCA, November.

PRA (2015c) 'Oral Evidence – Independent review of the report into the failure of HBOS', House of Commons, Treasury Committee, HC654.

Price Waterhouse Coopers (2004) 'HBOS plc: Skilled Persons Report under Section 166 of the Financial Services and Markets Act (2000)', *PriceWaterhouseCoopers*.

Rajan, R. (2005) 'Has Financial Development made the world Riskier?' Proceedings – Economic Policy Symposium, Jackson Hole, Federal Reserve Bank of Kansas City, Issue August, pp. 313–369.

Rajan, R. and Zingales, L. (2003) *Saving Capitalism from the Capitalists*, New York: Crown Business.

Rawstone, T. and Salmon, J. (2012) 'Fiddling while his bank burned: His disastrous reign at HBOS cost taxpayers £20bn but the REAL scandal is how arrogant Blair crony has escaped blame for so long', *Mail Online*, 8th December.

Reinhard, C. and Rogoff, K. (2011) *This Time Is Different – Eight Centuries of Financial Folly*, Princeton, NJ: Princeton University Press.

Roggi, O. and Altman, E. (eds.) (2013) *Managing and Measuring Risk – Emerging Global Standards and Regulation After the Financial Crisis*, World Scientific Series in Finance, Vol. 5, New York and London: World Scientific Publishing Company.

Ross, S., Westerfield, R. and Jordan, B. (2012) *Fundamentals of Corporate Finance*, Ninth edition, New York: McGraw-Hill International Edition.

Salmon, J. (2013) 'Criticism as SEVEN watchdog members set to investigate KPMG are revealed as current and former employees', *This is Money*, 19th April.

Santoro, M. and Strauss, R. (2013) *Wall Street Values: Business Ethics and the Global Financial Crisis*, New York: Cambridge University Press.

Sassen, S. (2001) *The Global City – New York, London, Tokyo*, Princeton, NJ: Princeton University Press.

Sassen, S. (2012) *Cities in a World Economy*, Fourth edition, Thousand Oaks, CA: Pine Forge Press.

Saunders, A. and Cornett, M. (2014) *Financial Institutions Management – A Risk Management Approach*, Eighth edition, New York: McGraw-Hill.

Shah, A. (1995) 'Accounting policy choice: The case of financial instruments – Creative accounting by UK companies', *European Accounting Review*, 4(2), pp. 397–399.

Shah, A. (1996a) 'Creative compliance in financial reporting', *Accounting, Organizations and Society*, 21(1), pp. 23–39.

Shah, A. (1996b) 'The dynamics of international bank regulation', *Journal of Financial Regulation and Compliance*, 4(1), pp. 371–385.

Shah, A. (1996c) 'International bank regulation – Objectives and outcomes', *Journal of International Banking and Financial Law*, 11(6), pp. 255–258.

Shah, A. (1996d) 'The credit rating of banks', *Journal of International Banking and Financial Law*, 11(8), pp. 361–365.

Shah, A. (1996e) 'Why capital adequacy regulation for banks?', *Journal of Financial Regulation and Compliance*, 4(3), pp. 278–291.

Shah, A. (1996f) 'Corporate governance and business ethics', *Business Ethics: A European Review*, 5(4), pp. 225–233.

Shah, A. (1996g) 'Regulating derivatives: Operator error or system failure', *Journal of Financial Regulation and Compliance*, 4(1), pp. 17–35.

Shah, A. (1997a) 'Analysing systemic risk in banking and financial markets', *Journal of Financial Regulation and Compliance*, 5(1), pp. 37–48.

Shah, A. (1997b) 'Regulatory arbitrage through financial innovation', *Accounting, Auditing & Accountability Journal*, 10(1), pp. 85–104.

Shah, A. (1997c) 'The social dimensions of financial risk', *Journal of Financial Regulation and Compliance*, 5(3), pp. 195–207.

Shah, A. (2007a) *Celebrating Diversity: How to Enjoy, Respect and Benefit from Great Coloured Britain*, Suffolk, UK: Kevin Mayhew Publishers.

Shah, A. (2007b) 'Jain business ethics', *Accountancy, Business and the Public Interest*, 6(2), pp. 115–130.

Shah, A. (2012) 'Diversity: Boardroom diversity – The opportunity', London: Mazaars LLP.

Shah, A. (2014) 'Financial literacy is shockingly low and the Academy must do more', *The Conversation*, 9th September.

Shah, A. (2015a) 'The chemistry of audit failure – A case study of KPMG', *Suffolk University Working paper*.

Shah, A. (2015b) 'Systemic Regulatory Arbitrage – A case study of KPMG', Suffolk University Working paper.

Shah, A. (2015c) 'SBS analysis: HBOS collapse', *Suffolk Business School Blog*, 17th November.

Shah, A. (2015d) 'The political economy of regulatory risk management – A case study of HBOS', Suffolk University Working paper.

Shah, A. (2016a) 'The FRC's evasiveness over HBOS tells us its unfit for purpose', *Ian Fraser Blog*, 30th March.

Shah, A. (2016b) 'Are KPMG really masters of the universe?', *Tax Research Blog*, 15th March.

Shah, A. (2016c) 'Q. What did universities learn from the financial crash? A. Nothing', *Guardian*, 2nd February.

Shah, A. and Baker, R. (2015) 'Defining financial risk', paper presented at the BAFA annual conference, University of Manchester, Manchester, March 23–25.

Shah, A. and Sikka, P. (2015) 'HBOS report does little to tackle systemic problems', *The Conversation*, 20th November.

Shah, A. and Rankin, A. (2017) *Jainism and Ethical Finance*, London: Routledge, forthcoming.

Sharman, C. (2012) 'The Sharman inquiry: Going concern and liquidity risks: Lessons for companies and auditors', Financial Reporting Council, June.

Sharp, T. (2013) 'HSBC investor concerns show bank failure still haunts KPMG', *The Herald*, 25th May.

Shaw, E. (2012) 'New Labour's Faustian pact?', *British Politics*, 7(3), pp. 224–249.

Shaxson, N. (2007) *Poisoned Wells: The Dirty Politics of African Oil*, New York: Palgrave Macmillan.

Shaxson, N. (2012) *Treasure Islands – Tax Havens and the Men Who Stole the World*, London: Vintage Books.

Shaxson, N. and Christensen, J. (2013) 'The Finance Curse: Britain and the World Economy', Tax Justice Network.

Shefrin, H. (2000) *Beyond Greed and Fear: Understanding Behavioural Finance and the Psychology of Investing*, Cambridge, MA: Harvard Business School Press.

Shiller, R. J. (2012) *Finance and the Good Society*, Princeton, NJ: Princeton University Press.

Sikka, P. (2008) 'Enterprise culture and accountancy firms: new masters of the universe', *Accounting, Auditing & Accountability Journal*, 21(2), pp. 268–295.

Sikka, P. (2009) 'Financial crisis and the silence of the auditors', *Accounting, Organizations and Society*, 34(6/7), pp. 868–873.

Sikka, P. and Wilmott, H. (1995) 'The power of 'independence': Defending and extending the jurisdiction of accounting in the United Kingdom', *Accounting, Organizations and Society*, 20(6), pp. 547–581.

Sikka, P., Willmott, H. and Puxty, T. (1995) 'The mountains are still there – Accounting academics and the bearings of intellectuals', *Accounting, Auditing & Accountability Journal*, 8(3), pp. 113–140.

Sikka, P., Filling, S. and Liew, P. (2009) 'The audit crunch: Reforming auditing', *Managerial Auditing Journal*, 24(2), pp. 135–155.

Simmel, G. (1978) *The Philosophy of Money*, London: Routledge.

Skapinker, M. (2014) 'Auditors escape attempts to tame them', *Financial Times*, 19th February.

Stein, M. (2011) 'A culture of mania – a psychoanalytic view of the incubation of the 2008 credit crisis', *Organisation*, 18(2), pp. 173–186.

Strange, S. (1986) *Casino Capitalism*, Oxford: Basil Blackwell.

Subcommittee on Investigations (2011) *Wall Street and the Financial Crisis: Anatomy of a Financial Collapse*, Washington, DC: United States Senate Permanent Committee on Investigations.

Sunderland, R. (2013) 'KPMG's role in both HBOS and Co-op meltdowns means installing its former boss as a senior regulator is absurd', *Daily Mail*, 21st November.

Syal, R., Bowers, S., Wintour, P. and Jones, S. (2013) 'Margaret Hodge urges accountancy code of practice over role in tax laws', *Guardian*, 26th April.

Taibbi, M. (2009) 'The great American bubble machine', *Rolling Stone*, 9th July.

Taibbi, M. (2014) 'The vampire squid strikes again – The mega banks' most devious scam yet', *Rolling Stone*, 12th February.

Tax Justice Network (2015) *The Greatest Invention – Tax and the Campaign for a Just Society*, London: Commonwealth Publishing.

Tett, G. (2010) *Fool's Gold – How Unrestrained Greed Corrupted a Dream, Shattered Global Markets and Unleashed a Catastrophe*, London: Abacus.

Tett, G. (2015) *The Silo Effect: The Peril of Expertise and the Promise of Breaking Down Barriers*, New York: Simon & Schuster.

Thaler, R. H. (2013) *Misbehaving – The Making of Behavioural Economics*, New York: Norton & Co.

Tomasic, R. (2011) 'The financial crisis and the haphazard pursuit of financial crime', *Journal of Financial Crime*, 18(1), pp. 7–31.

Tornero, C. M. (2016) 'Timeline: FRC preliminary inquiries of KPMG's audit of HBOS', *The Accountant*, 25th February.

Tosi, H., Werner, S., Katz, J. and Gomez-Mejia, L. (2008) 'Testing the Pay–Performance Relation'. In Erturk, I. et al. (eds.), *Financialization at Work*, pp. 120–133, Oxon, UK: Routledge.

Treasury Committee (2009) 'Banking crisis: Regulation and supervision', HC767, House of Commons.

Treasury Committee (2010) 'Audit and accountancy – Oral and written evidence', HC365, House of Commons.

Treasury Committee (2013) 'Appointment of John Griffith-Jones as chair designate of Financial Conduct Authority', HC 721, House of Commons.

Turner (2009) 'The Turner review – A regulatory response to the global banking crisis', Financial Services Authority, March.

Tweedie, N. (2013) 'The Labour Party's unholy alliance with the co-operative bank', *The Telegraph*, 22nd November.

Tyrie, A. (2016) 'Letter to Stephen Haddrill CEO of FRC', Financial Reporting Council, 3rd February.

Tyrie, A. et al. (2013a), 'An accident waiting to happen: The failure of HBOS, Parliamentary Commission on Banking Standards', Fourth Report of Session 2012–2013, House of Commons.

Tyrie, A. et al. (2013b) 'Parliamentary commission on banking standards', HC 175-III, House of Commons.

Tyrie, A. et al. (2013c) 'Changing banking for good', HC 175-II, House of Commons.

Tyrie, A. et al. (2015) 'Oral evidence: Independent review of the report into the failure of HBOS', HC 654, House of Commons Treasury Committee.

Tyrie, A. et al. (2016) 'Review of the reports into the failure of HBOS', HC 582, House of Commons.

van der Zwan, N. (2014) 'Making sense of financialization', *Socio-Economic Review*, 12(1), pp. 99–129.

Vasagar, J. and Evans, R. (2002) 'KPMG conflicts of interest revealed', *Guardian*, 1st July.

Vollmer, H., Mennicken, A. and Preda, A. (2009) 'Tracking the numbers: Across accounting, finance, organisations and markets', *Accounting, Organizations and Society*, 34(5), pp. 619–637.

Watson, M. (2013) 'From regulatory capture to regulatory space?', Oxford: The Foundation for Law, Justice and Society.

Way, C. (2005) 'Political insecurity and the diffusion of financial market regulation', *The Annals of the American Academy of Political and Social Science*, 598(1), pp. 125–144.

Webb, R. (2014) 'Bank bonuses just encourage greedy or dishonest staff', *The Conversation*, 26th August.

West, B. (2003) *Professionalism and Accounting Rules*, Oxford: Routledge.

Whyte, D. and Wiegratz, J. (eds.) (2016) *Neoliberalism and the Moral Economy of Fraud*, London: Routledge.

Xu, L. and Zia, B. (2012) 'Financial literacy around the world: An overview of the evidence with practical suggestions for the way forward', Policy Research Working Papers, World Bank.

Zeff, S. (2003) 'How the U.S. accounting profession got where it is today: Part 2', *Accounting Horizons*, 17(4), pp. 267–286.

Index